BEGINNER'S
Georgian

WITH ONLINE AUDIO

BEGINNER'S
Georgian

WITH ONLINE AUDIO

Dodona Kiziria

HIPPOCRENE BOOKS, INC.
New York

Audio files available at www.hippocrenebooks.com

Online audio edition, 2021

Text Copyright © 2008 Dodona Kiziria
Audio Copyright © 2008 Hippocrene Books

For information, address:

HIPPOCRENE BOOKS, INC.
171 Madison Avenue
New York, NY 10016
www.hippocrenebooks.com

Cataloging-in-Publication data available from the Library of Congress

ISBN 978-0-7818-1419-5
Previous edition ISBN: 978-0-7818-1230-6

Printed in the United States of America.

For my brother, Benito Kiziria who has been a source of the most generous help and encouragement for as long as I can remember.

ჩემს ძმას, ბენიტო კიზირიას მისი უშურველი დახმარებისა და თანადგომისათვის მთელი ჩემი ცხოვრების მანძილზე.

ACKNOWLEDGEMENTS

I want to express my heartfelt gratitude to my indefatigable editors, Lynn Visson, Mary Tahan, and Michael Carroll whose help went far beyond the call of duty, and whose comments were invaluable for my work on this textbook.

Many thanks to Lia Mekhashishvili, Vaso Rukhadze, and Niko Berdzenishvili who lent their voices and performing talent to bring to life all the dialogues in this book. I would also like to thank Yaron Aldema who expertly conducted our little "quartet" at World Music Connections/AM Studios in New York City.

I am much indebted to my cousin Nunu Urotadze, who read every single version of the manuscript and whose eagle eyes never missed even a minor transgression against Georgian grammar or spelling. My niece Inna Kiziriya and my cousin Giuli Abashidze have provided unflagging spiritual support in all my endeavors.

Special thanks to Professor Howard Aronson who many years ago inspired me to teach Georgian and started it all.

CONTENTS

Audio files available for download at:
http://www.hippocrenebooks.com/beginners-online-audio.html

INTRODUCTION

Geography and Climate

The Republic of Georgia, as the country is known today, is situated in the South Caucasus, to the east of the Black Sea which forms the country's western boundary. It is bordered by Russia to the north, Azerbaijan to the east, and Turkey and Armenia to the south. The capital, Tbilisi, in the fifth century became the center of political power of central and eastern Georgia (the regions of Kartli and Kakheti).

Georgia is mostly a mountainous country, with the Great Caucasian Mountain Range stretching along its northern border and the Lesser Caucasus Mountains delineating its southern provinces. The Kolkhida lowlands spread along the Black Sea, and in the east, rich arable valleys along the River Alazani nourish Georgia's famous vineyards.

The western regions enjoy a mild, subtropical climate, while the central and eastern parts of the country have colder winters and hotter summers. From time immemorial the climate of the entire country has been particularly well suited to the cultivation of various types of grapes, and Georgian wines compete with the best wines of Europe. In fact, it is believed that Georgian valleys and lowlands are the birthplace of viniculture.

Population

According to the 2002 census, the population of Georgia is just over four million, with 80 percent of the people Georgian, 6.5 percent Azeri, 6 percent Armenian, 1.5 percent Russian, and just over 3 percent of various other ethnicities: Abkhazian, Ossetian, Chechen, Kurd, Turk, etc. A sizable Jewish community dates back to the fifth century BC.

1

The majority of Georgians are Orthodox Christians, although during the last decade American missionaries of various Christian dominations have been making inroads among them. Muslims make up about 10 percent of the population; some of them are Georgians living mostly in the southwestern region of Achara. They are the descendants of those forced to convert to Islam during the eleventh-century invasion of the Seljuk Turks. There is a small percentage of Catholics, while the Armenians, though Orthodox Christians like the Georgians, are of the Armenian-Gregorian confession.

Until the collapse of the Soviet Union, there was almost no emigration from Georgia. During the past decade, however, because of economic hardships and other social and political problems plaguing the country, Georgian émigré communities have been growing in various countries of Europe and America. The largest of them are in France, Germany, England, and the United States. A large area in the northeastern part of Turkey once was an important cultural center of the Georgian kingdom, and as a result about a million and a half people of Georgian and Laz descent live in Turkey.

The Georgian Language

The Georgian language (*kartuli ena*) is the official language of the Republic of Georgia. It is spoken by about four million people living in the country and by ever-growing communities of Georgian émigrés across Europe, the Middle East, and the United States.

Though the majority of linguists consider Georgian to be a non-Indo-European language, there are those who argue that it has a genetic link to the Indo-European family of languages from which it digressed significantly due to its geographic isolation. Some scholars thought it might be possible to prove a link between Georgian and Basque, another non-Indo-European language of unknown origin. This fascinating but controversial—and by now mostly rejected—hypothesis still has a few diehard believers both inside and outside of Georgia.

Georgian, or *kartuli*, and three other languages related to it: Mengrelian (*megruli*), Laz (*lazuri*), and Svan (*svanuri*) form a group known as the Kartvelian languages of the South Caucasus. Georgian and European linguists believe that these languages branched off from their common ancestral proto-Kartvelian language in the second millennium BC. Today, about half a million people living in the region of Mengrelia (*samegrelo*) and other parts of Georgia speak Mengrelian. The majority of the some thirty thousand Laz speakers live mostly in Turkey. Svan, spoken by the inhabitants of a mountainous northwestern region, is probably the most archaic of the four Kartvelian languages. According to the 1979 Soviet census, about twenty-five thousand people spoke Svan, but today that number has dwindled to less than fifteen thousand. Both Mengrelians and Svans living in Georgia are bilingual, speaking their native language as well as Georgian (*kartuli*). Georgians proper, however, do not understand either Svan or Mengrelian unless they have been exposed to them for a significant period of time.

The first Georgian alphabet, *asomtavruli*, probably modeled on Greek and Phoenician letters, was created sometime in the early fourth century when the Christian faith began to spread first in Kartli in central Georgia, and then to other regions. Conversion to Christianity required the intense study of scriptures, and Georgian clerics dedicated themselves zealously to this task, often traveling to Greece, Palestine, and even Egypt in order to immerse themselves in teachings of the new-found faith. The early Georgian *asomtavruli* texts were chiseled on the floors of churches inside and outside of Georgia. The oldest of them found in Palestine is dated at about 430 AD. Another one, inscribed around year 493 AD, is in the church of Bolnisi in central Georgia. Used until the ninth century, *asomtavruli* underwent gradual changes, and over the following two centuries the resulting alphabet was transformed into *mxedruli*, a more rounded, "curly" shaped alphabet. The word *mxedruli*, derived from *mxedari* (a horseman), indicates the spread of literacy beyond strictly clerical circles. This is the alphabet that has been used in Georgia since the eleventh century to the present.

The gradual development of the Georgian language can be traced through a great number of literary works produced throughout the fifteen centuries since the creation of its first alphabet. Apart from translations of scriptural writings, the earliest Georgian literary works were hagiographies, that is, lives of Christian saints and martyrs. The oldest among them, *The Martyrdom of Shushaniki*, was written in the second half of the fifth century. A great variety of other ecclesiastic and secular genres comprise an impressive body of Georgian medieval literature, which reached its height in the eleventh to twelfth centuries.

The Georgian language displays surprising stability and consistency in its grammatical system. Today, eighth-grade students can read with relative ease eleventh-century texts, and almost any Georgian, young or old, can quote stanzas from the twelfth-century narrative poem *The Knight in the Tiger's Skin*, a part of high-school curriculums.

Up to the nineteenth century, Georgians learned how to read and write in churches and monasteries, some of which developed into important cultural centers. Institutions of formal education, schools for elementary literacy, gymnasiums and religious seminaries, open mostly to the nobility and members of the emerging middle class, appeared in the early nineteenth century after Georgia became a part of the Russian empire. In accordance with the Imperial government's aggressive policy of Russification, the language used in these institutions was exclusively Russian. Since the mid-nineteenth century Georgian intellectuals intensified their efforts to restore their native tongue to its proper place in the country's cultural life. Gradually, they managed to obtain permission from Russian censors to publish newspapers and magazines in Georgian. Many other prominent Georgian intellectuals of the period contributed to the resurrection and development of Georgian culture, and to the establishment of an educational system in their native language. A writer and educator, Jacob Gogebashvili (1840–1912) holds a very special place among them. In 1876 he published *Deda ena* (Mother Tongue), a primer for first graders of elementary school. Still today, *Deda ena* remains the basic model for primers for Georgian first graders.

On January 26, 1918, a day of seminal importance for Georgia, Tbilisi University, the first and only university in the entire South Caucasus at that time, was inaugurated. It was open to men and woman of any ethnicity and of any religious beliefs, and courses were taught both in Georgian and Russian. A group of Georgian scholars who had been educated in Russian and European universities had worked for years to overcome numerous financial and political difficulties to achieve this goal.

After a brief period of independence from 1918 to 1921, Georgia was incorporated into the Soviet Union. Whatever the shortcomings of the highly centralized, state-run Soviet educational system, Georgians benefited from the government's campaign of universal literacy and free education. Trying to counteract the Russification policy of imperial Russia, the Soviet government encouraged native-language education in all of its republics to ensure the speedy elimination of the illiteracy of over 70 percent of its population. In numerous educational institutions located in areas densely populated by various ethnicities, parents could choose to send their children to Georgian, Russian, Armenian, or Azeri schools. In the late 1930's, learning Russian also became obligatory in elementary and high schools. Although the majority of courses in the university and various colleges (pedagogical, technical, medical, etc) were taught in Georgian, each of these institutions also had several Russian-language departments. Georgians and non-Georgians wishing to study fields not available at Georgian universities could enroll in universities in Russia or other republics of the Soviet Union by passing the entrance exams. The 1979 census showed that Georgia was at the top of the list, with the greatest number of people with college and university degrees.

The political unrest in Georgia after the collapse of the Soviet Union caused a serious setback to the country's educational system. In the past four to five years, however, significant improvements have taken place as the education system decentralized and underwent changes in its curriculum and structure. Many young Georgians are taking advantage of new opportunities that allow them to study abroad. Pressures of globalization and of the job market have required the younger generation of Georgians to acquire fluency in foreign languages, especially English, and in a number of schools all courses are now taught in English, German, or French. However, the vibrant intellectual and cultural life of the country testify to the fact that *kartuli ena* continues to be of primary importance for Georgians.

Brief Survey of the History of Georgia

Georgians call their country *Sakartvelo*, which literally means *a place for Georgians*. Historians have speculated that the name *Georgia*, used mainly in the West, comes from the Greek word *georgios* (a farmer), and that it probably refers to the population of the western part of contemporary Georgia, known to the Greeks of the Hellenistic period as the Kingdom of Colchis.

As archeological findings demonstrate, *the place for Georgians* has one of the world's oldest and richest histories; the first well-developed human settlements already existed in this region some five thousand years ago. A recent discovery of human fossils in the village of Dmanisi in central Georgia pushed that estimate much further back. The well preserved skulls, dated as being between 1.8 to 1.17 million years old, made international news, and are now believed to be the earliest humans outside Africa.

Two early Georgian kingdoms known to the ancient Romans and Greeks were Colchis and Iberia, Western and Eastern Georgia respectively. The Greeks had colonies along the shores of the Black Sea, and the Greek and Aramaic languages were widely used throughout the territory of ancient Colchis. Two Greek myths are associated with this part of the Caucasus. The first is that of Jason and the Argonauts, who stole the Golden Fleece from Aeetes, king of Colchis with the help of the king's daughter, Media. The other is the myth of Prometheus, chained to a Caucasian mountain for bringing fire to mankind. Georgians in fact have their own version of the Prometheus myth, whose willful hero, Amirani, was also chained to the highest mountain of the Caucasus for his disobedience to God; some historians believe that the Greeks borrowed the plot from the Colchians.

At various times from the second century BC to the third century AD, Romans, Persians, and later the Byzantine empire competed with one another for control of Colchis and Iberia. Many protracted battles resulted in the breaking up of the territory into several smaller principalities, of which Kartli, with the capital city of Mtskheta, in today's central Georgia, enjoyed relative independence. It was the ruler of Kartli, king Mirian, who first adopted Christianity at the beginning of the fourth century and made it the dominant religion of his kingdom. The official date of the conversion is the year 337 AD, and thus Georgia was one of the first countries to convert to Christianity. St. Nino, a woman from Cappadocia who was ordained to the priesthood in Jerusalem, preached Christianity to the Georgians and is one of the most revered saints of the Georgian Orthodox Church. Legend has it that Nino made a cross to baptize the king and his family from vine branches and bound them together with her own hair. Vine branches are gnarled and twisted, and for this reason, the classic Georgian cross has its horizontal beam slightly bent downward in a hint at its original shape.

The adoption of Christianity gave a boost to the development of the Georgian alphabet, and consequently to the emergence of written literature. By the fifth century, virtually the entire New Testament had been translated into Georgian, and church services were conducted in the native language of the local population. In addition, Georgian clergymen wrote many remarkable original religious works—hymns, prayers, homilies, *vitas* of martyrs for the Christian faith, and historical chronicles.

A great Georgian poet of the twentieth century, Galaktion Tabidze, called Georgia a battlefield between two seas. At various times, the country was invaded and laid waste by Persians, Arabs, Turks, and smaller Muslim tribes from the North Caucasus. Georgia occupied an advantageous position at the crossroads between Europe and Asia. It was also a part of the Silk Road from East to West, and neighboring rulers were eager to impose their control over the territory. The invasion of the Seljuk Turks in the second half of the eleventh century was particularly horrifying; towns and villages were looted and destroyed, churches gutted and set on fire, thousands murdered or taken into slavery. According to Georgian chroniclers, dead bodies clogged the rivers. There are places in contemporary Georgia whose names hearken back to the period of those invasions: *Nakalakari* (a place where a town used to be), *Nasoflari* (a place where a village used to be), and many others testify to the devastation brought upon the country by the invaders.

Nevertheless, Georgian principalities managed to maintain political unity and relative independence for five more centuries. From the end of the eleventh to the beginning of the thirteenth century Georgia experienced a period of cultural revival, a flourishing economy, and the expansion of its political might under the leadership of two remarkable rulers. King David IV (1089–1125) liberated Georgia from the Turks, united the eastern and western regions of the country, and expanded the boundaries of his kingdom far into the North and South Caucasus. A great statesman, he promoted religious tolerance towards all ethnicities living in his kingdom, and was an extraordinarily talented military leader who personally supervised and won many battles against overwhelming odds. A philosopher and poet of remarkable passion and sensitivity, his outstanding success in rebuilding the country earned him the title of King David the Builder.

Another highly venerated ruler of Georgia was David's great-granddaughter, Tamar (1184–1213). As a sign of particular respect and admiration, Georgians call her not Queen but King Tamar. Numerous poems, songs, and folk legends dedicated to her praise her beauty and wisdom. The period of her reign was a veritable golden age of Georgian culture as Tamar strengthened and maintained the political gains inherited from her glorious ancestor and continued the reconstruction of the country. Many new churches were built, old ones were restored and repaired, and arts and literature flourished. It was during her reign that the most revered Georgian poet Shota Rustaveli wrote his monumental narrative poem, *The Knight in the Tiger's Skin*, still considered the most outstanding example of Georgian poetic genius. In the introductory stanzas of the poem, the poet declares that his creation is dedicated to King Tamar. The poem has been translated into several European languages as well as Arabic.

Tamar's death marked the beginning of the gradual decline of Georgian statehood. The most devastating blow was delivered at the end of the thirteenth century by the Mongol invasion, which in its brutality surpassed that of the Seljuk Turks; for a long time Georgia was unable to recover from this disaster. Although in the following centuries the country experienced a few brief interludes of relative peace and prosperity, it was split into small politically and economically weak principalities that were intermittently invaded and looted by their powerful neighbors, Turkey and Persia.

In the seventeenth century, there were two separate Georgian kingdoms, West Georgia with the capital at Kutaisi, and East Georgia with the capital in Tbilisi. The last valiant king of East Georgia, Erekle II, successfully fought many difficult battles against the Turks, Persians, and numerous marauding North Caucasus tribes who invaded and looted villages, capturing hostages and demanding a heavy price for their release. After many years of war and facing the threat of yet another Persian invasion, Erekle appealed to the Russian Empress Catherine the Great to take Georgia under Russia's protection, swearing allegiance to her and promising to defend Russia's interests in the Caucasus.

In July 1783 a treaty was signed between Georgia and Russia in the fortress of Georgievsk in the North Caucasus, in which the ruler of the *Kartli* and *Kakheti* (eastern Georgia), Erekle II, recognized the Russian emperor as their sole sovereign. For its part, Russia, while guaranteeing Georgia's internal sovereignty and territorial integrity, was to come to Georgia's aid against its enemies. The agreement was soon to be tested.

In 1795 when overwhelming Persian forces invaded eastern Georgia, the Russian troops stationed in the North Caucasus did not hasten to help the Georgians. The seventy-five-year-old Erekle fought desperately, but lost his last battle—the only one in which he was defeated. Tbilisi was razed to the ground and thousands of people were slaughtered. After Erekle's death a few years later, in 1801 by a decree of Emperor Alexander I of Russia, the kingdom of Kartl-Kakheti was incorporated into the Russian empire. The crown prince, heir to the Georgian throne, David Batonishvili, was taken to St. Petersburg as an "honored guest" never to return to his homeland. In 1810 west Georgia, the kingdom of Imereti, was also annexed by Russian forces. For the next two hundred years Georgia remained a colony of the Russian empire.

Throughout the nineteenth century, though secure from the threat of their traditional enemies, Georgians had to endure Russia's political domination. The policy of Russification, the brutal suppression of several revolts against heavy taxes, and the humiliating subordination of the Georgian Church to Russia's Holy Synod triggered a powerful national movement in the second half of the nineteenth century. Georgian intellectuals, poets, writers, and public figures all contributed to the awakening of a national spirit in the country.

An outstanding personality of the time and the descendent of an ancient aristocratic family, Ilia Chavchavadze (1837–1907) was a brilliant poet and novelist as well as a political activist. He founded several public, cultural, and educational organizations, and edited the most progressive contemporary Georgian language journal, *Iveria* (first issue appeared in 1877). Ilia Chavchavadze's main political and social goal was the revival of Georgia's statehood, Georgian culture, language, and literature. He was bitterly opposed to the political Marxist movement and worked for a revolutionary path to freedom in Georgia. In 1907, Chavchavadze was assassinated by his political opponents. Years later, the Georgian Church canonized him as St. Ilia the Truthful.

The October revolution of 1917 in Russia brought Vladimir Lenin and his Bolshevik party to power. While the government in Moscow was busy fighting the civil war, Georgia experienced a brief period of independence under the leadership of Georgian Marxists. Noe Zhordania, a member of the Marxist (Georgian Social Democratic) party, was chosen to be the head of the government, and on May 26, 1918, the country celebrated its liberation from the Russian empire. Though they were loyal allies of the Bolsheviks, Zhordania's government strove to maintain the political independence of the country and its national goals. Such a policy was not well received by the Bolsheviks in Moscow. In February 1921, the Eleventh Red Army units entered Georgia, removed the Zhordania government and established Bolshevik power. From then on until the end of the 1980s Georgia was one of the Soviet republics. Joseph Stalin, the Georgian dictator of the Soviet empire since the early 1920s till his death in 1953, did not spare his homeland. Along with thousands of ordinary citizens, many outstanding Georgian scholars, poets, artists, writers, and political figures fell victim to political purges.

During World War II Georgians fought side by side with the Russians and other peoples of the Soviet Union against Nazi Germany; 350,000 citizens of Georgia died, and thousands more were wounded.

During the 1980s, the last decade of the Soviet era, the national liberation movement regained momentum in Georgia. On April 9, 1989, Soviet troops dispersed a peaceful pro-independence demonstration. Twenty people were killed and poison gas was used to discourage further such protests, but this event led to a wave of more demonstrations, strikes, and public disobedience. Ignoring the pressure and military threats from Moscow, an open, multiparty and democratic election was held in October 1990. The political coalition *Round Table* won the election by an overwhelming majority, and a long-time Georgian political dissident, Zviad Gamsakhurdia, became the first president of Georgia. In a referendum organized by Gamsakhurdia on March 31, 1991, Georgia declared its independence from the Soviet Union.

A passionate patriot, Gamsakhurdia was too inexperienced and lacked flexibility in dealing with his Georgian political opponents. He antagonized many of his former colleagues and soon found himself quite literally under fire. Unhappy at the prospect of losing an important piece of strategic "property," the Soviet government in Moscow aided the opposition by providing troops and military hardware, and simultaneously stirred up separatist movements in the regions of Abkhazia and South Ossetia. On January 6, 1992, Gamsakhurdia was forced to flee to Chechnya. He was killed or committed suicide on December 24, 1993, while trying unsuccessfully to return to power in Georgia.

After almost two years of devastating civil war, in the spring of 1992 Eduard Shevardnadze, the former Soviet Minister of Foreign Affairs, returned to his native Georgia as the champion of Gamsakhurdia's opponents. Following his successful negotiations with the West and his role in hastening the end of the Soviet Union, Shevardnadze was seen (especially by the U.S.) as a person who could restore order to war-ravaged Georgia and move the country towards democracy and economic prosperity. These hopes, however, were soon dashed as Georgia was inundated by a wave of corruption far more brazen and rampant than that of the Soviet era. Numerous political, economic, and social problems disrupted the people's lives, and more than 300,000 refugees fleeing from the war raging in the separatist regions of Abkhazia and South Ossetia exacerbated the country's economic hardships. Over a million people, among them 900,000 ethnic Georgians, left the country in search of jobs.

In the year 2003, public discontent peaked when it became clear that Shevardnadze did not intend to give up power at the end of the second term of his presidency. A thirty-six-year-old lawyer, Mikheil Saakashvili, who for a short period of time had served as Georgia's Minister of Justice, headed a powerful political coalition demanding Shevardnadze's resignation. On November 23, 2003, a mass demonstration in support of Saakashvili was held in front of the central government building. The demonstrators held up red roses as a sign of their peaceful position; Shevardnadze was forced to resign. The movement that led to this event became known as the "Rose Revolution," and on January 4, 2004, Saakashvili won the presidential election with 96 percent of the vote.

With significant financial and political support from the United States and the European Union, Saakashvili succeeded in significantly reducing corruption and in creating a more favorable atmosphere for the country's economic development and improved social services. The long-suffering population of Georgia still has a long way to go, however, to achieve genuine political stability and economic prosperity.

Even this perfunctory overview of Georgia's history attests to the courage and endurance of its people who, against all odds, kept their faith, culture, and language alive. In spite of the violence and devastation their country endured, Georgians remain the world's most hospitable people, and no one who has visited Georgia will ever forget the warmth and kindness showered on guests by their hosts. Georgian cuisine is legendary and Georgian wines would delight the most discriminating tastes; the elaborate tradition of Georgian *supra* (ritual of toasts at a festive table) is unforgettable. The beauty of the Georgian countryside is breathtaking and the magnificent medieval cathedrals, monasteries and churches are truly awe-inspiring.

Georgians have excelled in many areas of art, literature, cinema, and theater. Georgian dancers have dazzled audiences on every continent. The Russian émigré composer Igor Stravinsky called the art of Georgian folk singing the eighth marvel of the world. Robert Sturua, who has staged internationally acclaimed performances of Shakespeare's works, is considered one of the greatest theater directors of modern times. Paata Burchuladze has conquered all the major opera houses around the globe with his magnificent bass voice. The composer Gia Kancheli is highly respected by fans of modern music on both sides of the Atlantic. The stunning ballet dancer Nino Ananiashvili has graced the best theatrical stages of the world, and George Balanchine (whose real name was Balanchivadze), the celebrated founding father of modern ballet choreography, was also Georgian. His father, Meliton Balanchivadze was one of the founders of modern Georgian opera. Many Americans are familiar with the fragrance *Prince Matchabelli,* created by Prince Georges Matchabeli, a descendant of one of the ancient aristocratic Georgian families who fled Georgia after the Bolshevik takeover. The crown-shaped top of his original perfume bottles was a miniature replica of the Matchabeli family crown.

Georgian history has known many outstanding military leaders whose skill and courage were admired even by their enemies. Soviet Army officers during World War II included many highly decorated Georgians, and the four-star American general John Malchase Shalikashvili, who served as Chairman of the Joint Chiefs of Staff in the late 1990s, is also of Georgian descent. His father, Dimitri Shalikash-vili, an officer in the independent Georgian army under Zhordania's government had to emigrate following the events of 1921. In the spring of 1992 on the invitation of President Shevardnadze, General Shalikashvili traveled to Georgia and visited his ancestral house in Kakheti, where a century ago King Erekle II had fought against the Persians.

Learning the Georgian language is the first step towards a better understanding and appreciation of the rich and unique culture and history of this country.

How to Study Georgian

1. This book offers an interactive approach to the Georgian language. To achieve fluency in your listening comprehension it is therefore essential to listen to the audio each time you study a lesson.

2. Your first priority is to learn the Georgian alphabet and recognize the sounds the letters represent. The three chapters which precede Lesson 1—on the Georgian alphabet, borrowed words, numbers, days of the week, etc.—are designed for that purpose. Do not get discouraged if your pronunciation is not perfect. It will improve gradually. Georgians will be able to understand you even if you speak with a noticeable accent. **It's more important to make sure that your grammar is correct.**

3. Begin reading the first dialogue in Lesson 1 only after you can easily recognize all the letters and can read with relative ease. Read the English text first so that you understand the topic of the dialogue. Then familiarize yourself with the vocabulary and try to memorize some of the key words.

4. In the audio, each dialogue is read twice, first at normal speed and then at slow speed with intervals long enough for you to pronounce short segments of the dialogue. You should study the dialogues in two steps. Step one: listen to the recording of the text at normal speed while simultaneously reading along in the Georgian text. Step two: read aloud short segments of the text during the intervals provided on the audio. Repeat steps one and two as many times as necessary to memorize the dialogue. To check how well you have learned the text, imagine that you are an interpreter: cover the Georgian text with a sheet of paper, look at the English text and repeat each sentence in Georgian. Only after you can do such "interpreting" should you move to the grammar and exer-cise sections. Study each lesson as described in this paragraph.

5. Insofar as possible, do the exercises without referring back to the dialogue or the vocabulary. 15

6. Do not get frustrated if you don't understand the grammatical logic of the sentences right away. Only a few grammar rules are explained in each lesson, progressing from simpler to more difficult items. After completing the first two or three dialogues, however, it would be very helpful to read Appendix I and II to get a general idea about the Georgian nominal and verbal system. The various endings of verbs and nouns will thus become less mysterious. You do not have to memorize any of the rules explained in these chapters; you will learn these rules gradually lesson after lesson.

7. In Appendix III, patterns of verb conjugations are provided. When you feel more confident and would like to compose sentences using verbs in various tenses, you can refer to this chapter to find the correct forms for each tense.

8. If you are not familiar with grammatical terms, refer to Appendix IV which offers user-friendly explanations of the terms used in this textbook.

9. If you learn all the lessons diligently, you will know as much Georgian as a second-year college student who has taken three or four semesters of the language. This will be quite an achievement! The grammar material provided in the textbook will be useful for further study of Georgian if you decide to improve your knowledge of the language.

10. Georgian is a challenging language, but it is also one of the most fascinating languages of the world. Learning it is the first step to better understanding Georgia's ancient cultural traditions, its exquisite art and literature, its past, and its present.

Abbreviations

acc.	accusative case
adj.	adjective
adv.	adverb
aor.	aorist tense
asp.	aspirated
com.	comparative
conj.	conjunction
cons.	consonant
d.o.	direct object
dat.	dative case
dem.	demonstrative
erg.	ergative case
fut.	future tense
gen.	genitive case
imp.	imperative mood
imperf.	imperfect tense
ind. obj.	indirect object
instr.	instrumental case
int.	interrogative
n.	noun
nom.	nominative case
num.	numeral
opt.	optative tense
pl.	plural
pol.	polite, informal form
post.	postposition
pres.	present tense
pron.	pronoun
rel.	relative
s.o.	someone
s.th.	something
sing.	singular

subj.	subject
sup.	superlative
unasp.	unaspirated
verbal n.	verbal noun

THE GEORGIAN ALPHABET

The Georgian alphabet consists of 33 letters—5 vowels (numbers 1, 5, 9, 14, and 20 in the list below) and 28 consonants. The phonetic transcription used in this book was adopted by the Georgian Academy of Science in 2002.

	Letters	Name of Letter	Transliteration
1.	ა	an	a
2.	ბ	ban	b
3.	გ	gan	g
4.	დ	don	d
5.	ე	en	e
6.	ვ	vin	v
7.	ზ	zen	z
8.	თ	tan	t
9.	ი	in	i
10.	კ	k'an	k'
11.	ლ	las	l
12.	მ	man	m
13.	ნ	nar	n
14.	ო	on	o
15.	პ	p'ar	p'
16.	ჟ	zhan	zh
17.	რ	rae	r
18.	ს	san	s
19.	ტ	t'ar	t'
20.	უ	un	u
21.	ფ	par	p
22.	ქ	kan	k
23.	ღ	ghan	gh
24.	ყ	q'ar	q'
25.	შ	shin	sh
26.	ჩ	chin	ch
27.	ც	tsan	ts
28.	ძ	dzil	dz

19

29.	წ	ts'il	ts'
30.	ჭ	ch'ar	ch'
31.	ხ	xan	x
32.	ჯ	jan	j
33.	ჰ	hae	h

- Each letter denotes a single sound; the letter combinations in the list above (numbers 16, 23, 25, 26, 27, 28, 29, and 30) are used to approximate the corresponding English sounds. These combinations are used in transliterating Georgian words into English.

- Each letter of a word is pronounced; there are no mute letters similar to the English final -e.

- There are no capital letters.

- The stress (very light!) is always on the first syllable.

- Like English, Georgian is read and written from left to right.

- There are no articles in Georgian, neither definite (the) or indefinite (a).

- Georgian nouns do not have gender markers.

How to Pronounce Georgian Sounds

While learning the alphabet, listen to the audio and try to imitate Georgian sounds as closely as possible. Do not get frustrated if you think your pronunciation is less than perfect! You will gradually get it right. It is important, however, to recognize the different sounds in order to improve your oral comprehension and writing skills.

The following explanations do not follow the standard order of the Georgian alphabet; instead, letters are introduced in the order of the degree of difficulty for English speakers of the sounds they represent, from simpler to more complex. The sounds of the letters correspond to the letters in bold in the English words.

Taking a few days to learn the letters and sounds will indeed be time well spent. After finishing this chapter you should be able to read without the help of English transliteration.

Vowels

The five Georgian vowels are clear, open sounds devoid of half tones.

Vowel	Pronunciation	Georgian words
ა (an)	father, cup	მამა [mama] father
ი (in)	beat, seen	თითი [titi] finger
ე (en)	get, bet	ენა [ena] tongue
ო (on)	dog, smog	ორმო [ormo] ditch
უ (un)	moon, soon	უთო [uto] iron

Consonants: Part One

These consonants usually present the least difficulty, as they are almost equivalent in pronunciation to a number of English consonants.

After listening to the audio recording and reading each line of Georgian words several times, cover the English transliteration and read the words without looking at them. When you can read the Georgian words with ease, proceed to the next letter.

Consonant	As in	Georgian words	
თ (tan)	**t** as in b**u**t, **ou**t *While pronouncing this sound, move the tip of your tongue lower than you would while speaking English. Press the tip of the tongue against your teeth.*	თათი [tati] paw	თითი [titi] finger
დ (don)	**d** as in **d**og, **d**own *Tip of the tongue is in the same position as while pronouncing* თ.	დიდი [didi] big	დედა [deda] mother

მ (man)	m as in me, mom	მამა [mama] father	მუმია [mumia] mummy
ვ (vin)	v as in very, visa	ვადა [vada] deadline	თავი [tavi] head
ს (san)	s as in guess, stress	სასა [sasa] palate	სესია [sesia] session
ზ (zen)	z as in zoo, bazooka	ზაზა [zaza] man's name	ვიზა [viza] visa
ლ (las)	l as in look, light *Tip of the tongue should be against your upper teeth, not above them.*	ლალი [lali] girl's name	ლოლუა [lolua] icicle
გ (gan)	g as in glib, grim	გუგული [guguli] cuckoo	გეგმა [gegma] plan
ბ (ban)	b as in book, bullet	ბებია [bebia] grandfather	ბაბუა [babua] grandmother
ნ (nar)	n as in noon, none	ნანა [nana] girl's name	ნუნუ [nunu] girl's name
პ (par)	p as in pellet, pencil	პაპა [papa] porridge	პესვი [pesvi] root
კ (kan)	k as in cook, book	კალი [kali] woman	კალაკი [kalaki] city
შ (<u>sh</u>in)	<u>sh</u> as in <u>sh</u>e, <u>sh</u>oe	შუშა [<u>sh</u>u<u>sh</u>a] glass	შეშა [<u>sh</u>e<u>sh</u>a] firewood

ჩ (chin)	**ch** as in **ch**oose, **ch**aste	ქუჩა [ku**ch**a] street	ჩამიჩი [**ch**ami**ch**i] raisins
რ (rae)	**r** as in **cr**ater, b**r**illiant *Try to roll your **r**,* *as the Georgians do!*	რომელი [**r**omeli] which	როგორი [**r**ogo**r**i] what kind
ჰ (hae)	**h** as in **h**ave, **h**oe	ჰავა [**h**ava] climate	ჰაერი **h**aeri] air
ჯ (jan)	**j** as in **j**udge, **j**uice	ჯუჯა [**j**u**j**a] dwarf	ჯეჯილი [**j**e**j**ili] wheat field
ჟ (zhan)	**zh** as in vi**s**ion, a**z**ure	ჟანგი [**zh**angi] rust	ჟუჟუნა [**zh**u**zh**una] girl's name
ძ (dzil)	**dz** as in ku**dz**u	ძაძა [**dz**a**dz**a] black outfit	ძიძა [**dz**i**dz**a] wet nurse

 ## Consonants: Part Two

Certain Georgian consonants may sound very similar to each other, but they are pronounced differently. Learn the five sets of similar consonant pairs shown below.

Each consonant pair represents two similar sounds; one is *aspirated* and the other is not. An *aspirated* sound produces a slight waft of air coming out of your mouth. An *unaspirated* sound does not. The first consonant in each pair presented below is an aspirated sound, the second is its unaspirated equivalent. Two short lists of words follow each pair of consonants; the list on the left-hand side contains examples of aspirated sounds (თ *t*, ქ *k*, etc.), the list on the right-hand side has the unaspirated equivalents (ტ *t'*, კ *k'*, etc.).

Listen to the audio of the following sets of paired consonants and pronounce each word with your palm in front of your mouth to make sure you are pronouncing it correctly. (Note that

Georgian non-fricative sounds are sharper than the English, much as in Russian, Spanish, or Italian.)

	Cons.	As in	Examples	
Asp.	თ (tan)	**t** as in bu**t**	თათი [tati] paw	თითი [titi] finger
Unasp.	ტ (t'ar)	**t'** as in **t**ake	ატამი [at'ami] peach	ტატამი [t'at'ami] athletic floor mat

თ t	ტ t'
თუთა [tuta] mulberry	ტუტა [t'ut'a] ashes
თუთუნი [tutuni] tobacco	ტიტინი [t'it'ini] baby talk

	Cons.	As in	Examples	
Asp.	ქ (kan)	**k** as in coo**k**	ქალი [kali] woman	ქალაქი [kalaki] city
Unasp.	კ (k'an)	**k'** as in **c**ake	კოკა [k'ok'a] pitcher	კალამი [k'alami] pen

ქ k	კ k'
ქაქანი [kakani] blubber	კაკაბი [k'ak'abi] partridge
ქურქი [kurki] fur coat	კურკა [k'urk'a] (cherry) stone

	Cons.	As in	Examples	
Asp.	ჩ (chin)	<u>ch</u> as in <u>ch</u>oose	ქუჩა [ku<u>ch</u>a] street	ჩამიჩი [<u>ch</u>ami<u>ch</u>i] raisins
Unasp.	ჭ (ch'ar)	sharply voiced <u>ch</u>, *(No equivalent in English)*	ბიჭი [bi<u>ch</u>'i] boy	ჭრიჭინა [<u>ch</u>'ri<u>ch</u>'ina] cricket

ჩ <u>ch</u>	ჭ <u>ch</u>'
ჩაჩი [<u>chach</u>i] nightcap	ჭაჭა [<u>ch</u>'a<u>ch</u>'a] Georgian vodka
ჩენჩი [<u>chench</u>i] chaff	ჭინჭი [<u>ch</u>'in<u>ch</u>'i] duster

Cons.	As in	Examples	
Asp.	ფ (par)	p as in pellet	ფაფა [papa] porridge	ფესვი [pesvi] root
Unasp.	პ (p'ar)	p' as in pepper	პეპე [p'ep'e] man's name	საპონი [sap'oni] soap

ფ p	პ p'
ფაფა [*papa*] papa	პაპა [*p'ap'a*] grandfather
ფური [*puri*] ox	პური [*p'uri*] bread

Cons.	As in	Examples	
Asp.	ც (tsan)	ts as in pizza, its	ცეცე [tsetse] tsetse (fly)	ცოლი [tsoli] wife
Unasp.	წ (ts'il)	denotes voiced ც.	წები [ts'ebo] glue	წუთი [ts'uti] minute

ც ts	წ ts'
ციმციმი [tsimtsimi] twinkle	წამწამი [ts'amts'ami] eyelash
ცუნცული [tsuntsuli] tiptoeing	წუმწუმა [ts'umts'uma] matches

Consonants: Part Three

These consonants may be the most challenging to pronounce.

Cons.	As in	Georgian words	
ღ (ghan)	denotes a sound similar to French *r*. *Try to pronounce* *r using the middle of* *your tongue.*	ღუღუნი [ghughuni] warble	ღომი [ghomi] grits
ხ (xan)	like **ch** in Ba**ch** and Lo**ch**-Ness	ხახა [xaxa] throat	ხერხი [xerxi] saw

ყ (q'ar)   *Try to raise the middle*   ყავა   ყაყაჩო
              part of the tongue to   [q'ava]   [q'aq'acho]
              the roof of your mouth   coffee   poppy
              and pronounce **k**.

                                      ბაყაყი   წყალი
                                      [baq'aq'i]   [ts'q'ali]
                                      frog   water

ყ [q'] is the most challenging sound of the Georgian language, but with a little perseverance it can be mastered. If your pronunciation does not sound quite like that on the audio right away, don't worry! Georgians will understand you.

BORROWED WORDS AND PERSONAL NAMES IN GEORGIAN

If you feel comfortable with the Georgian alphabet, you can skip this section and go directly to Lesson 1. This chapter, however, provides useful information about the Georgian language and culture, and also allows you to check up on your ability to recognize Georgian letters and pronounce them correctly.

 Borrowed Words

Over the centuries, Georgian has absorbed many foreign words and names, adapting them to its own grammatical structure.

> All borrowed words and personal names that end in a consonant have thus acquired the nominative case ending -ი. The nominative case is the basic form for nouns in Georgian. (See Appendix I for more on case endings.)

Below is a list of a few easily recognizable words borrowed from European languages over the past two centuries. Read them slowly and try to understand their meaning without looking at the English translation.

Nouns	Pronunciation	Translation
ტურისტი	[t'urist'i]	tourist
კომპიუტერი	[k'omp'iut'eri]	computer
პრეზიდენტი	[p'rezident'i]	president

27

Place Names	Pronunciation	Translation
ლონდონი	[londoni]	London
იაპონია	[iap'onia]	Japan
ამერიკა	[amerik'a]	America

Personal Names	Pronunciation	Translation
ჯონი	[joni]	John
ტაისონი	[t'aisoni]	Tyson
ლინდა	[linda]	Linda

When addressing a person, the -ი ending is dropped:

Personal Names	Pronunciation	Translation
ჯონ!	[jon]	John!
ტაისონ!	[t'aison]	Tyson!

All other vowels remain unchanged:

Personal Names	Pronunciation	Translation
პამელა!	[p'amela]	Pamela!
ლინდა!	[linda]	Linda!

Georgian Names

 ## Last names

Georgians have a very strong sense of their ancestral origin. Although
they consider themselves as ethnically Georgian, they often specify
the regions of their family roots even though they may have never
lived in those regions: კახეთი [k'axeti] in East Georgia, იმერეთი
[imereti] or გურია [guria] in West Georgia.

The older generation of Georgians could identify most last names
as specific to a given village or town, but even non-Georgians can
roughly identify a person's geographic ancestry by his or her last

name. Thus, the last names of East Georgians end most frequently with -შვილი [shvili] *child*, and in West Georgia the majority of the endings are -ძე [-dze] *son*. In Central Georgia both endings are possible. Mingrelian names end in -ია, [-ia], -ვა [-va], and -ა [-a], while names of upper Svaneti natives often end with -იანი [-iani].

It is significant that the meaning of the Georgian word for *last name*, გვარი [gvari], implies *family clan* or even *tribe*. It points to the region where a family name originated.

1. **Last names in East and Central Georgia**

თედიაშვილი   გურამიშვილი
[Tediashvili]   [Guramishvili]

2. **Last names in Central and Western Georgia**

აბაშიძე   მელაძე
[Abashidze]   [Meladze]

3. **Mingrelian last names**

გამსახურდია   უბილავა
[Gamsaxurdia]   [Ubilava]

4. **Upper Svaneti last names**

ხერგიანი   ფარჯიანი
[Xergiani]   [Parjiani]

 First names

Below is a list of a few first names. In parentheses are the abbreviated *diminutive* forms or nicknames similar to Bill for William or Jonny for Jonathan. They are used only in informal situations. The ending -კო [-k'o] can be added to almost any name, male or female, to form a diminutive.

Male	Female
არჩილი (აჩიკო) Ar<u>ch</u>ili (Achik'o)	თამარი (თამრიკო) Tamari (Tamrik'o)
გიორგი (გოგი) Giorgi (Gogi)	ქეთევანი (ქეთი) Ketevani (Keti)
დავითი (დათიკო) Daviti (Datik'o)	ელენე (ელიკო) Elene (Elik'o)

How to address people

Both in formal and informal situations, Georgians address each other by their first names. Addressing someone by his or her last name sounds rude or bossy.

When addressing a person with whom one is not on familiar terms, the following words must be used:

ბატონო	[bat'ono]	equivalent of Mr. or Sir
ქალბატონო	[kalbat'ono]	equivalent of Ms.

Some, but not all of the first names following these words may lose their final -ი [-i].

Unfortunately, there are no clear rules indicating which names lose the end vowel. Don't worry about making a mistake; you'll gradually pick up the right forms.

A. Some names losing the final -ი [i]

ბატონო დავით [bat'ono Davit]	Mr. David
ქალბატონო თამარ [kalbat'ono Tamar]	Ms. Tamar
ბატონო ნიკოლოზ [bat'ono Nik'oloz]	Mr. Nikoloz
ქალბატონო რუსუდან [kalbat'ono Rusudan]	Ms. Rusudan

B. Some names retaining the final -ი [i]

ბატონო ირაკლი [bat'ono Irak'li]	Mr. Irakli
ქალბატონო ლალი [kalbat'ono Lali]	Ms. Lali
ბატონო გიორგი [bat'ono Giorgi]	Mr. Giorgi
ქალბატონო ეთერი [kalbat'ono Eteri]	Ms. Eteri

USEFUL WORDS & EXPRESSIONS

This chapter introduces some useful words and expressions with which you can practice reading and the pronunciation of Georgian sounds.

 ## Numbers

As is the case with most languages, the hardest thing is to memorize the numbers from 1 to 10. Many words and especially abstract nouns are derived from numbers. Memorizing them will thus help you to recognize these words and eventually enlarge your vocabulary.

1	ერთი	[erti]	6	ექვსი	[ekvsi]
2	ორი	[ori]	7	შვიდი	[shvidi]
3	სამი	[sami]	8	რვა	[rva]
4	ოთხი	[otxi]	9	ცხრა	[tsxra]
5	ხუთი	[xuti]	10	ათი	[ati]

 ## How to tell time

რომელი საათია?	[romeli saatia]	What time is it?
ოთხი საათია.	[otxi saatia]	It's four o'clock.
შვიდი საათია.	[shvidi saatia]	It's seven o'clock.
ცხრა საათია.	[tsxra saatia]	It's nine o'clock.

 ## Days of the week

The key word in learning the days of the week is შაბათი [shabati] derived from Sabbath or Saturday. Monday is two days removed

33

from Saturday; Tuesday is three days removed from Saturday and so on. Thus we have the following names:

ორშაბათი	Monday	ორ(ი) + შაბათი	
[orshabati]		[or(i)+shabati]	
სამშაბათი	Tuesday	სამ(ი) + შაბათი	
[samshabati]		[sam(i)+shabati]	
ოთხშაბათი	Wednesday	ოთხ(ი) + შაბათი	
[otxshabati]		[otx(i)+shabati]	
ხუთშაბათი	Thursday	ხუთ(ი) + შაბათი	
[xutshabati]		[xut(i)+shabati]	
პარასკევი	Friday		
[p'arask'evi]			
შაბათი	Saturday		
[shabati]			
კვირა	Sunday		
[k'vira]			

 Parts of the day

დილა	morning	დილას	in the morning
[dila]		[dilas]	
დღე	day	დღეს	today
[dghe]		[dghes]	
საღამო	evening	საღამოს	in the evening, tonight
[saghamo]		[saghamos]	
ღამე	night	ამაღამ	(late) tonight
[ghame]		[amagham]	
ხვალ	tomorrow	ზეგ	the day after tomorrow
[xval]		[zeg]	

Names of the months

There are two sets of names for the months of a year, ancient and modern. The modern, derived from Latin names, were gradually adopted around the sixteenth century, and are in use today. However, you may come across the ancient names in poetry or in religious texts.

იანვარი	[ianvari]	January
თებერვალი	[tebervali]	February
მარტი	[mart'i]	March
აპრილი	[ap'rili]	April
მაისი	[maisi]	May
ივნისი	[ivnisi]	June
ივლისი	[ivlisi]	July
აგვისტო	[agvist'o]	August
სექტემბერი	[sektemberi]	September
ოქტომბერი	[oktomberi]	October
ნოემბერი	[noemberi]	November
დეკემბერი	[dek'emberi]	December

Dates

Referring to days of the month, Georgians use only cardinal numbers (two, five, ten, etc.).

სამი მარტი	[sami mart'i]	the third of March
ოთხი აპრილი	[otxi ap'rili]	the fourth of April
ხუთი მაისი	[xuti maisi]	the fifth of May

The first day of any month is an exception to this rule; in this case the ordinal number პირველი [p'irveli] *first* is used:

პირველი იანვარი	[p'irveli ianvari]	the first of January
პირველი ივნისი	[p'irveli ivnisi]	the first of June

დღეს ორი ივლისია. [dghes ori ivlisia]   Today is the second
                                            of July.
ხვალ ათი აგვისტოა. [xval ati agvist'oa]   Tomorrow is the tenth
                                            of August.

 Family members

In Georgian, the word *relatives* (ნათესავები) covers a wide circle
of people related to each other by blood or by marriage. Below is a
short list of immediate family members.

დედა	[deda]	mother
მამა	[mama]	father
ცოლი	[tsoli]	wife
ქმარი	[kmari]	husband
მეუღლე	[meughle]	spouse
შვილი	[shvili]	child
ვაჟი	[vazhi]	son
ქალიშვილი	[kalishvili]	daughter
და	[da]	sister
ძმა	[dzma]	brother

 Tongue twisters

Here are a few Georgian tongue twisters. Read them aloud several times and learn them by heart. Like tongue twisters in any language, they may not offer wisdom but are excellent for practicing
pronunciation.

კაპიკი გაკაპიკკებულა.
[k'ap'ik'i gak'ap'ik'ebula.]
Kopeck became a kopeck.

ჭრიჭინა ჭრიჭინებს.
[ch'rich'ina ch'rich'inebs.]
The cricket is chirping.

ბაყაყი წყალში ყიყინებs.
[baq'aq'i ts'q'alshi q'iq'inebs.]
A frog is croaking in the water.

Lesson 1
გაკვეთილი პირველი

Meeting in the street
შეხვედრა ქუჩაში

🎧 **შეხვედრა ქუჩაში**
[shexvedra kuchashi]

თამაზ შონია ქართველი სტუდენტია, ქევინ მილერი
ამერიკელი. თამაზი და ქევინი ხვდებიან ერთმანეთს ქუჩაში.
[tamaz shonia kartveli st'udent'ia, kevin mileri amerik'eli.
tamazi da kevini xvdebian ertmanets kuchashi.]

თამაზი: გამარჯობათ. თქვენ აქ ცხოვრობთ?
tamazi: [gamarjobat. tkven ak tsxovrobt?]

ქევინი: დიახ, აქ ბინას ვქირაობ.
kevini: [diax, ak binas vkiraob.]

თამაზი: ძალიან სასიამოვნოა. მეც აქ ახლო ვცხოვრობ.
ჩემი სახელია თამაზი. თქვენი?
tamazi: [dzalian sasiamovnoa. mets ak axlo vtsxovrob. chemi
saxelia tamazi. tkevni?]

ქევინი: ჩემი სახელია ქევინი.
kevini: [chemi saxelia kevini.]

თამაზი: თქვენ ამერიკელი ხართ თუ ინგლისელი?
tamazi: [tkven amerik'eli xart tu ingliseli?]

ქევინი: ამერიკელი. თქვენ ქართველი?
kevini: [amerik'eli. tkven kartveli?]

თამაზი: დიახ, ქართველი. რა კარგად ლაპარაკობთ
ქართულად!
tamazi: [diax, kartveli. ra k'argad lap'arak'obt kartulad!]

ქევინი: გმადლობთ.
kevini: [gmadlobt.]

თამაზი: დიდი ხანია თბილისში ცხოვრობთ?
tamazi: [didi xania tbilisshi tsxovrobt?]

ქევინი: უკვე სამი თვეა.
kevini: [uk've sami tvea.]

თამაზი: აქ სწავლობთ თუ მუშაობთ?
tamazi: [ak sts'avlobt tu mushaobt?]

ქევინი: ვსწავლობ და ვმუშაობ. ინგლისურს ვასწავლი
სკოლაში.
kevini: [vsts'avlob da vmushaob. inglisurs vasts'avli sk'olashi.]

Meeting in the street

Tamazi Shonia is a Georgian student, Kevin Miller is American.
Tamazi and Kevin meet each other in the street.

Tamazi: Hello. Do you live here?

Kevin: Yes, I am renting an apartment here.

Tamazi: Pleased to meet you. I also live near here. My name is
Tamazi. Yours?

Kevin: Pleased to meet you. My name is Kevin.

Tamazi: Are you American or British?

Kevin: American. You (are) Georgian?

Tamazi: Yes, Georgian. How well you speak Georgian!

Kevin: Thank you.

Tamazi: Have you been living for long in Tbilisi?

Kevin: It's already been three months.

Tamazi: Are you working or studying here?

Kevin: I am studying and working, teaching English in a school.

თამაზი: მართლა? რა საინტერესოა!
tamazi: [martla? ra saint'eresoa!]

ქევინი: თქვენ მუშაობთ თუ სტუდენტი ხართ?
kevini: [tkven mushaobt tu st'udent'i xart?]

თამაზი: სტუდენტი ვარ.
tamazi: [st'udent'i var.]

ქევინი: თქვენ ლაპარაკობთ ინგლისურად?
kevini: [tkven lap'arak'obt inglisurad?]

თამაზი: ვლაპარაკობ, მაგრამ ცუდად.
tamazi: [vlap'arak'ob, magram tsudad.]

ქევინი: ძალიან სასიამოვნოა თქვენი გაცნობა.
kevini: [dzalian sasiamovnoa tkveni gatsnoba.]

თამაზი: მეც მოხარული ვარ, რომ გაგიცანით.
tamazi: [mets moxaruli var, rom gagitsanit.]

ქევინი: ნახვამდის.
kevini: [naxvamdis.]

თამაზი: ნახვამდის. კარგად იყავით.
tamazi: [naxvamdis. k'argad iq'avit.]

Tamazi: Really? How interesting!

Kevin: Do you work or are you a student?

Tamazi: I am a student.

Kevin: Do you speak English?

Tamazi: I do, but poorly.

Kevin: Very nice to meet you.

Tamazi: I'm also glad to have met you.

Kevin: Goodbye.

Tamazi: Goodbye. Take care.

Vocabulary

Georgian	Transcription	Meaning
შეხვედრა	[shexvedra]	meeting
ქუჩაში	[kuchashi]	in the street
ცხოვრობს *pres.*	[tsxovrobs]	(he) lives
სწავლობს *pres.*	[sts'avlobs]	(he) studies
ენა	[ena]	language
ენას *dat./acc.*	[enas]	
ხვდებიან *pres.*	[xvdebian]	(they) meet
ერთმანეთი	[ertmaneti]	each other
გამარჯობა(თ)	[gamarjobat]	hello *(ending -თ [t] is required for pol.)*
თქვენ *pl./pol.*	[tkven]	you *(pl.)*
აქ	[ak]	here
ცხოვრობ(თ) *pres.*	[tsxovrobt]	(you) live, are living
დიახ *pol.*	[diax]	yes
ბინა	[bina]	apartment, residence
ბინას *dat./acc.*	[binas]	
ვქირაობ *pres.*	[vkiraob]	(I) rent, am renting
ძალიან	[dzalian]	very
სასიამოვნო	[sasiamovno]	pleasant, nice
მეც	[mets]	I too
ახლო	[axlo]	near, nearby
ჩემი	[chemi]	my
სახელი	[saxeli]	name
თქვენი *pl./pol.*	[tkveni]	your
ამერიკელი	[amerik'eli]	American *(person)*
თუ	[tu]	or
ინგლისელი	[ingliseli]	British *(person)*
რა	[ra]	what, how
ლაპარაკობ(თ) *pres.*	[lap'arak'obt]	(you) speak
ქართულად	[kartulad]	in Georgian *(language)*
გმადლობ(თ) *pol.*	[gmadlobt]	thank you
დიდი	[didi]	big, large, great *(here: long)*
ხანი	[xani]	period, spell of time

უკვე	[uk've]	already
სამი	[sami]	three
თვე	[tve]	month
სწავლობ(თ) *pres.*	[sts'avlobt]	(you) study, are studying
მუშაობთ *pres.*	[mushaobt]	(you) work, are working
ინგლისური	[inglisuri]	English
ინგლისურს *dat./acc*	[inglisurs]	
ვასწავლი *pres.*	[vasts'avli]	(I) teach, am teaching
სკოლაში	[sk'olashi]	in a school
მართლა	[martla]	really, indeed
საინტერესო	[saint'ereso]	interesting
სტუდენტი	[st'udent'i]	student
ვარ	[var]	I am
ინგლისურად *adv.*	[inglisurad]	in English
მაგრამ	[magram]	but
ცუდად	[tsudad]	badly, poorly
თქვენი	[tkveni]	your
გაცნობა	[gatsnoba]	meeting, getting acquainted
მოხარული	[moxaruli]	glad
რომ *conj.*	[rom]	that
გაგიცანი(თ) *aor.*	[gagitsanit]	I have met you, I got acquainted with you
ნახვამდის	[naxvamdis]	goodbye (*lit.*: till the next meeting)
კარგად	[k'argad]	well
იყავით *past./imp.*	[iq'avit]	(you) be (*lit.*: you were)

 ## Idiomatic Expressions and Culture Notes

- თქვენ [tkven] and თქვენი [tkveni] are plural forms of *you* and *your*. As in most European languages, this is also used as a polite form for addressing a person. You should always use the polite form when addressing your superiors, someone significantly older than you, or someone you are meeting for the first time.

- ძალიან სასიამოვნოა [dzalian sasiamovnoa] literally means *it's very pleasant* or *it's very nice.*

- In spoken Georgian the initial letter -გ [-g] in გმადლობთ [gmad-lobt] *thank you* is usually dropped, and the word is pronounced as მადლობთ [madlobt].

- სამი თვეა [sami tvea] means *it has been three months.*

- The word სკოლა [sk'ola] *school* in Georgian *always* refers to the pre-college level, including the grades from elementary to high school, but is *never* used in reference to institutions of higher education, a college or university.

- კარგად იყავი [k'argad iq'avi] *be well* or more formal კარგად იყავით [k'argad iq'avit] *be well* is the usual formula added to or used instead of goodbye.

Grammar

I. Verbs

In Georgian, just like in English, a sentence usually has a *verb*, the word that denotes an action (*hit, think, run*) or state of being (*am, is, are*). However, Georgian verbs do not work quite the same way as their English counterparts. (In this and the following lessons, please refer to Appendix IV if any grammatical terms are unfamiliar to you.)

- One of the biggest differences between Georgian and English verbs is that **Georgian verbs do not have an infinitive**, i.e. a neutral form like English *to live, to speak, to work*, etc. You should therefore memorize **the active forms** that will be gradually introduced in this and in the following lessons.

- English verbs have a marker only in the third person singular (*he, David, my sister, your dog,* etc.). For example, *I think*, but *he think-s; we do*, but *John do-es*. Georgian verbs have specific markers whether they refer to the first, second, or third persons. In the following, notice that the prefix ვ- [v-] added to the verb marks the first person singular form *I*, while the verb marker for second person plural *you* is the letter -თ [-t] added to the end of the verb.

მე ვ-ცხოვრობ I live   თქვენ ცხოვრობ-თ you *(pl.)* live
[me] [v-tsxovrob]   [tkven] [tsxovrob-t]

• Unlike English, in Georgian sentences **personal pronouns** (*I, you, he, we, etc.*) **that function as the subject** (one who acts or is acted upon) **of the verb can be omitted**. The person markers of the verbs clearly identify the subject; and therefore, the personal pronouns are frequently, but not always, dropped:

Verbs without personal pronouns

ვ-ლაპარაკობ	(I) speak	ლაპარაკობ-თ	(you) speak
[v-lap'arak'ob]		[lap'arak'ob-t]	
ვ-მუშაობ	(I) work	მუშაობ-თ	(you) work
[v-mushaob]		[mushaob-t]	
ვ-ასწავლი	(I) teach	ასწავლი-თ	(you) teach
[v-asts'avli]		[asts'avli-t]	

In this lesson most of the verbs are in the *present tense*, i.e. they denote actions that are conducted habitually (*I **live** in this house.*) or are in progress right now (*I **am watching** the Olympic games.*).

II. The suffix -ც [-ts] *too*

The suffix -ც [-ts] can be added to almost any word except a verb and translates as *too*:

მე [me]   მეც [mets]
I   I **too**

თქვენ [tkven]   თქვენც [tkvents]
you   you **too**

სტუდენტი [st'udent'i]   სტუდენტიც [st'udent'its]
student   a student **too**

ამერიკელი [amerik'eli]
American

ამერიკელიც [amerik'eli**ts**]
an American **too**

ქართველი [kartveli]
Georgian

ქართველიც [qartveli**ts**]
a Georgian **too**

III. Simple sentences formed with enclitic -ა [a]

You can compose simple sentences adding the ending -ა [a], called **enclitic** -ა [a], to the final word in a short statement. You should remember, however, that enclitic -ა [a] stands for *is* and can be used **only** in sentences where the subject is the **third person singular**.

Correct	*Incorrect
ქევინი ამერიკელია.	*მე ამერიკელია.
[kevini amerik'elia]	[me amerik'elia]
Kevin (he) **is** *American.*	*I is American.*
თამაზი სტუდენტია	*თქვენ სტუდენტია.
[Tamazi st'udent'ia]	[tkven st'udent'ia.]
Tamazi (he) **is** *a student.*	*You is a student.*
ლალი ქართველია.	*თამაზი და ლალი ქართველია.
[lali kartvelia.]	[me kartvelia.]
Lali (she) **is** *Georgian.*	*Tamasi and Lali is Georgian.*

In the examples below, enclitic -ა [a] is attached to adjectives (words that modify nouns), adding the meaning *it is*:

Adj.	Adj. with Enclitic -a	Adj.	Adj. with Enclitic -a
კარგი	კარგია.	სასიამოვნო	სასიამოვნოა.
[k'argi]	[k'argia]	[sasiamovno]	[sasiamovnoa]
good	*It's good.*	*pleasant*	*It's pleasant (nice).*
ცუდი	ცუდია.	საინტერესო	საინტერესოა.
[tsudi]	[tsudia]	[saint'ereso]	[saint'eresoa]
bad	*It's bad.*	*interesting*	*It's interesting.*

- The word რა [ra] means *what*, but if you place it before an adjective with enclitic -ა [a] at the end, it means *how* and usually expresses an exclamation.

Adj.	რა [ra]+ Adj.	Translation
კარგი [k'argi]	რა კარგია! [ra k'argia]	How good (wonderful)!
ცუდი [tsudi]	რა ცუდია! [ra tsudia]	How bad (unpleasant)!
სასიამოვნო [sasiamovno]	რა სასიამოვნოა! [ra sasiamovnoa]	How pleasant (nice)!
საინტერესო [saint'ereso]	რა საინტერესოა! [ra saint'eresoa]	How interesting!

- Adverbs (words that modify verbs) can be formed from adjectives by dropping the final -ი [i] and by adding -ად [ad]. If the adjective ends with a vowel other than -ი [i], simply add -დ [d] to the adjective without dropping the final vowel.

Adj.	Adverbs	Adj.	Adverbs
კარგი [k'argi] *good*	კარგ-ად [k'arg-**ad**] *well*	მოკლე [mok'le] *short*	მოკლე-დ [mok'le-**d**] *shortly*
ცუდ-ი [tsudi] *bad, poor*	ცუდ-ად [tsud-**ad**] *badly, poorly*	სასიამოვნო [sasiamovno] *pleasant, nice*	სასიამოვნო-დ [sasiamovno-**d**] *pleasantly, nicely*

- In Georgian there are two sets of adjectives denoting national and/or ethnic origin, one referring to person(s), the other to everything else. The former have the ending -ელი [-eli] or in some irregular cases -ი [-i]; the latter have the ending -ული [-uli] if the word contains the letter რ [r] or -ური [-uri] if the word does not have it.

	Adjectives	
	Persons	**Non-persons**
Georgian	ქართველი	ქართული
	[kartveli]	[kart-uli]
American	ამერიკელი	ამერიკული
	[amerik'eli]	[amerik'-uli]
British/English	ინგლისელი	ინგლისური
	[ingliseli]	[inglis-uri]
German	გერმანელი	გერმანული
	[germaneli]	[german-uli]
French	ფრანგი	ფრანგული
	[prang-i]	[prang-uli]
Russian	რუსი	რუსული
	[rus-i]	[rus-uli]

The following are a few examples of adjectival phrases with ethnic/national adjectives. Note how the adjectives change their endings depending on whether the nouns they modify are persons or non-persons:

ქართველი პოეტი
[kartveli p'oet'i]
Georgian poet

ამერიკული ჯაზი
[amerik'uli jazi]
American jazz

ქართული ენა
[kartuli ena]
Georgian language

გერმანელი მეგობარი
[germaneli megobari]
German friend

ამერიკელი ბიზნესმენი
[amerik'eli biznesmeni]
American businessman

გერმანული ლიტერატურა
[germanuli lit'erat'ura]
German literature

- When referring to a language, the ending -ად -[ad] denotes the English *in*. (Note that the ending -ი [-i] is dropped before -ად -[ad] is added).

ქართულ-ი   ქართულ-ად [kartul-ad]   **in** Georgian
ინგლისურ-ი   ინგლისურ-ად [inglisur-ad]   **in** Englsih

ფრანგულ-ი	ფრანგულ-ად [prangul-ad]	**in** French
გერმანულ-ი	გერმანულ-ად [germanul-ad]	**in** German
რუსულ-ი	რუსულ-ად [rusul-ad]	**in** Russian

IV. Question word order

Word order in questions is the same as in direct statements. However, when asking a question, the intonation rises slightly at the end of the sentence.

მართლა? ↑	მართლა.
[martla]	[martla]
Really?	*Really.*

დიდი ხანია? ↑	დიდი ხანია.
[didi xania]	[didi xania]
Has it been long?	

სამი თვეა? ↑	დიახ, სამი თვეა.
[sami tvea]	[diax, sami tvea]
Has it been three months?	*Yes, three months.*

Exercises

I. Using the adjectives below, write the phrases *how beautiful*, *how exciting*, etc.

1. ლამაზი beautiful   _____

2. ცუდი bad   _____

3. სასიახარულო exciting   _____

4. დიდი big, large   _____

5. უცნაური strange   _____

6. პატარა small, little   _____

II. Choose the correct form of adjectives for use with the following nouns.

1. გერმანული, გერმანელი   German   _____
   ბანკი bank
2. ქართული, ქართველი   Georgian   _____
   ღვინო wine
3. რუსი, რუსული   Russian   _____
   სტუდენტი student
4. ფრანგი, ფრანგული   French   _____
   დიპლომატი diplomat
5. ამერიკული, ამერიკელი   American   _____
   გაზეთი newspaper

III. Change the adjectives into adverbs and translate them.

1. ესპანური (Spanish) _____   _____

2. პოლონური (Polish) _____   _____

3. არაბული (Arabic) _____   _____

4. იტალიური (Italian) _____   _____

IV. Translate the sentences below into Georgian.

A.

I speak Spanish well.   _____

Do you speak Italian?   _____

I speak Arabic and Polish.   _____

B.

I am an American student. My name is John (ჯონი). I live and work in Tbilisi. I am renting an apartment here. I speak Georgian, but poorly.

_____

_____

V. Fill in the blank spaces below with the words you learned in this lesson.

1. თამაზი: გამარჯობათ. თქვენ აქ _____?

2. ქევინი: დიახ, აქ _____ ვქირაობ.

3. თამაზი: თქვენ _____ ხართ თუ _____?

4. ქევინი: მე _____ ვარ.

5. თამაზი: რა კარგად _____ ქართულად!

Lesson 2

გაკვეთილი მეორე

On the phone

ტელეფონით საუბარი

ტელეფონით საუბარი

თამაზი და ქევინი უკვე კარგი მეგობრები არიან. ქევინი
თამაზის ბინაში რეკავს.

ქევინი:	**ალო!**
ლალი:	გისმენთ.
ქევინი:	ბოდიში, თამაზი სახლშია?
ლალი:	თომასი? **სხვაგან მოხვდით.**
ქევინი:	ეს შონიას ბინაა?
ლალი:	დიახ, შონიას ბინაა.
ქევინი:	თამაზი სახლშია?
ლალი:	ვინ კითხულობს?
ქევინი:	მე მისი მეგობარი ვარ, ქევინი.
ლალი:	აა, ძალიან სასიამოვნოა. მე ლალი ვარ, თამაზის და.
ქევინი:	გამარჯობათ, ლალი. თამაზის **სიხოვეთ, თუ შეიძლება?**
ლალი:	ახლავე დავუძახებ.
თამაზი:	ქევინ, გამარჯობა. როგორა ხარ?
ქევინი:	კარგად. შენ?
თამაზი:	მეც კარგად. **რაშია საქმე?**
ქევინი:	ეხლა რას აკეთებ? დაკავებული ხარ?
თამაზი:	არა, **ახალ ამბებს** ვუყურებ ტელევიზორში.
ქევინი:	**მოდი, კინოში წავიდეთ.**
თამაზი:	ძალიან კარგი. "**რუსთაველში**" წავიდეთ.
ქევინი:	იქ **რა გადის?**
თამაზი:	ძველი ქართული ფილმი, "დათა თუთაშხია."
ქევინი:	რაზეა ეს ფილმი?
თამაზი:	ქართველ რობინ ჰუდზე.
ქევინი:	მართლა? ძალიან კარგი. წავიდეთ.
თამაზი:	ერთ საათში მზად იყავი.
ქევინი:	მზად ვიქნები.

On the phone

Tamazi and Kevin are already good friends. Kevin calls Tamazi's apartment.

Kevin: Hello!
Lali: Speaking.
Kevin: Excuse me, is Tamazi at home?
Lali: Thomasi? (You have) a wrong number.
Kevin: Is this the Shonia residence?
Lali: Yes, it is the Shonia residence.
Kevin: Is Tamazi at home?
Lali: Who is asking?
Kevin: I am his friend, Kevin.
Lali: Aa, how nice! I am Lali, Tamazi's sister.
Kevin: Hello, Lali. Is Tamazi at home?

Lali: I'll call him right away.
Tamazi: Kevin, hello. How are you?
Kevin: I'm fine. And you?
Tamazi: Me, too. What's up?
Kevin: What are you doing now? Are you busy?
Tamazi: No, I am watching the news on television.
Kevin: Let's go to a movie (theater).
Tamazi: Very good. Let's go to *Rustaveli*.
Kevin: What are they showing there?
Tamazi: An old Georgian movie, *Data Tutashxia*.
Kevin: What is this movie about?
Tamazi: About a Georgian Robin Hood.
Kevin: Really? Very well, let's go.
Tamazi: Be ready in an hour.
Kevin: I'll be ready.

 **Vocabulary**

მეგობრები *pl.*	[megobrebi]	friends
მეგობარი *sing.*	[megobari]	friend
რეკავს *pres.*	[rek'avs]	(he) calls, is calling, telephoning
ბოდიში	[bodi<u>sh</u>i]	excuse me, sorry
სახლი	[saxli]	house, home
სახლში	[saxl<u>sh</u>i]	at home
ეს	[es]	this
შონია	[<u>sh</u>onia]	personal last name
ვინ	[vin]	who
კითხულობს *pres.*	[k'itxulobs]	*here:* asks, is asking
მე	[me]	I
მისი	[misi]	his/her
და	[da]	*here:* sister *(also conj. meaning* and*)*
ახლავე	[axlave]	right away
დავუძახებ *fut.*	[davu<u>dz</u>axeb]	I will call (him)
როგორ	[rogor]	how
ხარ *sing.*	[xar]	(you) are
საქმე	[sakme]	matter, business (to be done)
ეხლა	[exla]	now
რა	[ra]	what
რას *dat./acc.*	[ras]	
აკეთებ *pres.*	[ak'eteb]	(you) do, are doing
დაკავებული	[dak'avebuli]	busy
არა	[ara]	no
ახალი	[axali]	new
ამბები	[ambebi]	events, news
მოდი	[modi]	come, let's
კინო	[k'ino]	movie, movie theater
ძველი	[<u>dz</u>veli]	old
ფილმი	[pilmi]	film, movie
დათა თუთაშხია	[data tuta<u>sh</u>xia]	first and last name *(male)*

რაზეა	[razea]	what is (it) about
ერთი	[erti]	one
საათი	[saati]	an hour
ერთ საათში	[ert saat<u>sh</u>i]	in an hour
მზად	[mzad]	ready
იყავი *aor./imp.*	[iq'avi]	be; order, request
ვიქნები *fut.*	[viknebi]	(I) will be

Idiomatic Expressions and Culture Notes

- ალო is used only when answering the phone. It should not be used when greeting a person either over the phone or when meeting someone face to face.

- გისმენთ means literally: *I am listening.* This is a standard formula when answering a phone call.

- სხვაგან მოხვდით means literally: *you turned up in a different place.* It is the standard formula one hears if a person dials a wrong number.

- სთხოვეთ or თხოვეთ is a polite request to call someone to the phone.

- თუ შეიძლება means literally: *if it is possible*, and may be translated as *please.* You should use this expression when asking for a favor, big or small. The precise equivalent of *please* in Georgian is გეთაყვა, but it sounds too quaint and is seldom used.

- რაშია საქმე means literally: *in what* (რა-ში-ა) *is the matter?* Depending on context and intonation, the expression may have a variety of meanings: *What's up?*, *What's going on?*, *What is happening?*

- ახალი ამბები means *news (on radio or TV; lit.: new events)*

- მოდი წავიდეთ means *let's go*. (See the grammar section on this expression in Lesson 11, p. 185.) კინოში წავიდეთ with or without მოდი means *let's go* (*to see*) *a movie*.

- რუსთაველი is the name of the largest movie theater in Tbilisi. It is situated on the main street, Rustaveli Avenue. Both the street and the theater are named after the twelfth-century Georgian poet Shota Rustaveli.

- რა გადის means *what is on, what are they showing?* This question can also be asked about any theatrical or opera performance.

Grammar

I. Negative statements

In order to make a negative statement in Georgian (*I do not know, I do not speak, etc*), you should place the negative particle არ (*not*) before the verb. In such sentences, the negation არ and the following verb become inseparable units. This means that *no words may be placed between the negative particle and the verb that follows it.*

Affirmative	Negative
მე აქ ვცხოვრობ. I live here.	მე აქ **არ** ვცხოვრობ. I **do not live** here.
მე ვლაპარაკობ ინგლისურად. I speak English.	მე **არ** ვლაპარაკობ ინგლისურად. I **do not speak** English.
თქვენ ლაპარაკობთ არაბულად. You speak Arabic.	თქვენ **არ** ლაპარაკობთ არაბულად. You **do not speak** Arabic.

II. Singular forms of the verb *to be* and their negation

The ending -ა is added to the negative particle არ when it is placed before any **monosyllabic verb**, such as ვარ *I am* and ხარ *you* *are.* This ending is called **euphonic -ა**. It should not be confused with **enclitic -ა**. Enclitic -ა is synonymous with the verb არის *is*, while **euphonic -ა** simply facilitates pronunciation.

ხარ *you are**

Affirmative		Negative	
მე გარ	I am	მე არა გარ	I am not
შენ ხარ	you are	შენ არა ხარ	you are not
ის არის	he/she/it is	ის არ არის	he/she/it is not

Since there is **no infinitive in Georgian (neutral forms such as *to be, to go, to run, etc.*), verbs throughout this book will be presented in one of their active forms—in this case, **ხარ** *you are*, the 2nd person singular present-tense form.

Afirmative sentence	Negative sentence
მე ვარ ტურისტი. I am a tourist.	მე არა ვარ ტურისტი. I am **not** a tourist.
შენ ხარ სტუდენტი. You are a student.	შენ არა ხარ სტუდენტი. You are **not** a student.
ის არის იტალიელი. He/she is Italian.	ის არ არის ინგლისელი. He/she is **not** Italian.

The Georgian verb *be* in the third person singular form არის *is* is frequently replaced by **enclitic -ა**. In negative sentences, however, only the full form of the verb must be used and **enclitic -ა** is dropped.

Afirmative sentence	Negative sentence
ქევინი ამერიკელია. Kevin **is** American.	ქევინი არ არის ამერიკელი. Kevin **is not** American.
ეს თქვენი ბინაა. This **is** your apartment.	ეს არ არის თქვენი ბინა. This **is not** your apartment.
ეს ქართული გაზეთია. This **is** a Georgian newspaper.	ეს არ არის ქართული გაზეთი. This **is not** a Georgian newspaper.

III. Postpositions

In the Georgian language, there are no prepositions such as *in, on, out, for, at,* etc. Instead, Georgian has *postpositions,* i.e. suffixes that are added directly to nouns. Each postposition is used with nouns in a specific *case.*

Case is the grammatical function of a noun or pronoun. Modern English has shed most of its case *forms.* Only three cases remain: nominative (*he, who*); accusative or objective (*him, whom*); and genitive or possessive (*his, whose*). Georgian, however, does have an active case system in which nouns, pronouns, and adjectives *change forms,* i.e. they *decline* in seven cases: *nominative, ergative, dative/ accusative, genitive, instrumental, adverbial,* and *vocative.* (See Appendix I for more on the Georgian case system.)

In Georgian, postpositions added to nouns in various cases function like English prepositions.

- The postposition **-ში** corresponds to English *in, at,* or *to.* It is added to nouns in the *dative/accusative case.* At this point the following rule of thumb will be sufficient: nouns with an **-ი** ending in their basic (*nominative case*) form drop the final vowel and **-ში** is added to the stem of the noun. All other endings remain unchanged.

nom.	სახლ-ი	სკოლა	სარკე	კინო	რუ
	house	school	mirror	movie	creek

dat.	სახლში	სკოლაში	სარკეში	კინოში	რუში
	at home	**at** school	**in** a mirror	**in** a movie	**in** a creek

- If the subject of a sentence is 3rd person singular, **enclitic -ა** *is* can be added to a noun with the postposition **-ში** *at, in.* In the sentences below the subjects are underlined.

დედა სახლშია.	Mother **is** at home.
ლალი კინოშია.	Lali **is** at the movies.
არჩილი ბანკშია.	Archili **is** in the bank.
ჩემი ძმა სკოლაშია.	My brother is at (a middle) school.

IV. ა *This is . . .* and *Here is . . .*

The word **ა** *this is* is very often used in Georgian, mostly when you are pointing at something or someone. Depending on the context, it may be translated into English as: *this is, here is, here you are*, etc. It is usually placed in the beginning of the sentence: *the verb is should always be omitted if a sentence starts with* **ა**.

ა წიგნი.	**This** [is] a book.
ა შენი წიგნი.	**Here** [is] your book.
ა იქ არის ჩემი სკოლა.	Over **there** [is] my school.
ა თამაზი!	**Here** [comes] Tamazi!

Exercises

I. Negate the following declarative sentences.

A.

1. მე აქ ვცხოვრობ.   _____
   I live here.

2. თქვენ სკოლაში მუშაობთ.   _____
   You work in a school.

3. ქევინი გაზეთს კითხულობს.   _____
   Kevin is reading a newspaper

B.

1. მე ქართველი სტუდენტი ვარ. _____
   I am a Georgian student.

2. შენ დაკავებული ხარ?   _____
   Are you busy?

3. ლალი აქ არის.   _____
   Lali is here.

C.

1. დღეს ბანკი ღიაა.
   The bank is open today.
   _____

2. კვირას სკოლა დაკეტილია.
   On Sunday the school is closed.
   _____

3. თამაზი სახლშია.
   Tamazi is at home.
   _____

II. In the sentences below, replace the full form of არის _he/she/it_ **is with** _enclitic_ **-ა.**

1. ეს თამაზის სახლი არის.
   _____

2. ქევინი კარგი სტუდენტი არის.
   _____

3. ლალი დაკავებული არის.
   _____

III. Add postposition -ში _in, at, to_ **to the nouns listed below.**

1. საათი_____
2. ქუჩა _____
3. გაზეთი _____

4. ჩიკაგო _____
5. ბანკი _____
6. პერუ _____

IV. Fill in the blank spaces below with the words you learned in this lesson.

1. თამაზი: გამარჯობა, ქევინ. როგორა _____?

2. ქევინი: _____. შენ?

3. თამაზი: _____ კარგად. მოდი, _____
   წავიდეთ.

4. ქევინი: რომელ _____? რა _____?

5. თამაზი: _____ ქართული _____.

6. ქევინი: მართლა? _____.

7. თამაზი: ერთ საათში _____ _____.

8. ქევინი: ძალიან კარგი. მზად _____.

Lesson 3
გაკვეთილი მესამე

Visiting Tamazi
სტუმრად თამაზისთან

სტუმრად თამაზისთან

ქევინი თამაზისთან მიდის სტუმრად.

ქევინი:	გამარჯობა, თამაზ! შეიძლება?
თამაზი:	ქევინ! შემოდი. აი, ეს ჩემი დაა, ლალი.
ქევინი:	ჩვენ უკვე **ვიცნობთ ერთმანეთს**, მაგრამ მხოლოდ ტელეფონით.
ლალი:	დიახ, ვიცნობთ. **მობრძანდით.**
ქევინი:	რა დიდი და ლამაზი ბინაა!
ლალი:	დიახ, საკმაოდ დიდია. ეს სასტუმრო ოთახია, ეს ჩემი მშობლების საწოლი ოთახი. ეს თამაზის ოთახია, ეს კი ჩემი. იქ სასადილო და სამზარეულოა. ეს საპირფარეშო და აბაზანა.
თამაზი:	ქევინ, რას დალევ, ჩაის თუ ყავას?
ქევინი:	ყავას სიამოვნებით დავლევ.
ლალი:	როგორი ყავა გიყვართ, მაგარი თუ სუსტი?
ქევინი:	საშუალო.
ლალი:	რძით?
ქევინი:	დიახ, თუ შეიძლება.
ლალი:	შაქრით?
ქევინი:	არა, უშაქროდ.
თამაზი:	აი, გასინჯე. ეს ლალის **ხაჭაპურია.**
ქევინი:	რა გემრიელია! ეს მართლა თქვენ გააკეთეთ?
ლალი:	რასაკვირველია მე გავაკეთე. **სხვათა შორის,** ქევინ, მოდი, **შენობით ვილაპარაკოთ.** ჩვენ უკვე მეგობრები ვართ, არა?
ქევინი:	ნამდვილად ვართ, ლალი. შენი ხაჭაპური ძალიან გემრიელია.
ლალი:	თუ გემრიელია, **კიდევ გადაიღე.**
ქევინი:	სიამოვნებით გადავიღებ.

Visiting Tamazi

This morning Kevin comes to visit Tamazi. He rings the bell. Tamazi opens the door.

Kevin: Hello, Tamaz! May I?

Tamazi: Kevin! Come in. This is my sister, Lali.

Kevin: We've met, but only on the phone.

Lali: Yes, we've met. Please, come in.

Kevin: What a large and beautiful apartment!

Lali: Yes, it is rather large. This is a guestroom; this is my parents' bedroom. This is Tamazi's room, and this is mine. There is a kitchen and a dining room. These are a toilet and a bathroom.

Tamazi: Kevin, what would you like to drink, tea or coffee?

Kevin: I would be glad to have some coffee.

Lali: How do you like your coffee, strong or weak?

Kevin: Medium.

Lali: With milk?

Kevin: Yes, please.

Lali: With sugar?

Kevin: No, without sugar.

Tamazi: Here, try. This is Lali's *khachapuri*.

Kevin: How delicious! Lali, did you really make this?

Lali: Of course I made it. By the way, Kevin, let's use the informal *you*. We are already friends, aren't we?

Kevin: Indeed we are, Lali. Your *khachapuri* is most delicious.

Lali: If it's delicious, have (some) more.

Kevin: I'll have more with great pleasure.

Vocabulary

სტუმრად *adv.*	[st'umrad]	visiting
სტუმარი	[st'umari]	visitor, guest
თამაზისთან	[tamazistan]	Tamazi's place, Tamazi's apartment
შემოდი *aor./imp.*	[shemodi]	come in
აი	[ai]	here, here is
ვიცნობთ *pres.*	[vitsnobt]	(we) are acquainted, (we) know
ერთმანეთი	[ertmaneti]	each other
ერთმანეთის *dat./acc.*	[ertmanets]	
მხოლოდ	[mxolod]	only
საკმაოდ	[sak'maod]	rather
ოთახი	[otaxi]	room
სასტუმრო ოთახი	[sast'umro otaxi]	guest room
მშობლები	[mshoblebi]	parents
მშობლების *gen.*	[mshoblebis]	
საწოლი	[sats'oli]	bed
კი	[k'i]	and, while, one the other hand
სასადილო	[sasadilo]	dining room
სამზარეულო	[samzareulo]	kitchen
საპირფარეშო	[sap'irparesho]	toilet
აბაზანა	[abazana]	bathroom
დალევ *fut.*	[dalev]	(you) will/would drink
ჩაი	[chai]	tea
ჩაის *dat./acc.*	[chais]	
ყავა	[q'ava]	coffee
ყავას *dat./acc.*	[q'avas]	
სიამოვნებით	[siamovnebit]	with pleasure, my pleasure
დავლევ *fut.*	[davlev]	(I) will drink
როგორი	[rogori]	what kind

Georgian	Transcription	English
გიყვართ *pres.*	[giq'vart]	(you) like, love
მაგარი	[magari]	strong
სუსტი	[sust'i]	weak, feeble
საშუალო	[sashualo]	medium, middle
რძე	[rdze]	milk
რძით *instr.*	[rdzit]	with milk
შაქარი	[shakari]	sugar
შაქრით *instr.*	[shakrit]	with sugar
უშაქროდ	[ushakrod]	without sugar
გასინჯე *aor./imp.*	[gasinje]	taste (it), have a bite!
გემრიელი	[gemrieli]	delicious
გააკეთეთ *aor.*	[gaak'etet]	(you) made
რასაკვირველია	[rasak'virvelia]	of course
ვართ *pres.*	[vart]	we are
ნამდვილად	[namdvilad]	indeed
კიდევ	[k'idev]	more, again, one more time
გადაიღე *aor./imp.*	[gadaighe]	(you) take, have some (more)
გადავიღებ *fut.*	[gadavigheb]	(I) will have some

 ## Idiomatic Expressions and Culture Notes

- In Georgia, children used to live with their parents until they got married. As a rule, sons continued to live in their parents' house even after getting married. In time, it became their responsibility to take care of their elderly parents. After getting married, daughters would move to their husbands' apartment. The tradition still continues, although with the changing economic situation in the country, some young couples nowadays rent or buy their own apartment if they can afford it.

- **მიდის სტუმრად** means *goes for a visit, is visiting.*

- **შეიძლება?** literally means *is it possible?* However, when used as a question, it is the equivalent of *may I?* The expression is used whenever one asks permission to do something: enter the room, borrow a book, use a phone, etc.

- **აი** is a word often used when one points at something, naming an object or person. It is the exact equivalent of the French *voilà.*

- **ვიცნობთ ერთმანეთს** means *we know each other* or *we are aquainted with each other.* The question *do you know such-and-such person* will be, for example, **იცნობთ ლალის?** *Do you know Lali?,* and **იცნობთ ჯონს ბროუნს?** *Do you know John Brown?.*

- **მობრძანდით** is a very formal and polite form used when inviting someone in. Georgians have a rather strict code of formal speech, and it is prudent to use this form when speaking to someone older than you or higher in rank, as well as to a person you are meeting for the first time.

- **ხაჭაპური** *a cheese bread* is the pride of traditional Georgian cuisine.

- **სხვათა შორის** means *by the way.*

- **შენობით ვილაპარაკოთ** means *let's speak using* **შენ** (instead of the formal **თქვენ**).

- **კიდევ გადაიდე** means *take some more*; literally: *take over (and put on your plate).*

Grammar

I. Verbs in the present tense

Below is a chart of the present tense conjugation of the verb **აკეთებ** *you do, make.* You will find a detailed discussion on verb conjugations and charts in Appendix III at the end of the book. Look at the chart below and memorize the person markers in both singular and plural forms.

აკეთებ (you do, make)
Person	Singular		
1st	მე	ვ-აკეთებ	I do
2nd	შენ	აკეთებ	you do
3rd	ის	აკეთებ-ს	he/she does

Person	Plural		
1st	ჩვენ	ვ-აკეთებ-თ	we do
2nd	თქვენ	აკეთებ-თ	you do
3rd	ისინი	აკეთებ-ენ	they do

If we remove the verb stem, we can clearly see the person markers for the present tense:

Present Tense Person Markers
Person	Singular		
1st	მე	I	ვ-stem
2nd	შენ	you	stem
3rd	ის	he/she	stem-ს

Person	Plural		
1st	ვ-stem ჩვენ	we	ვ-stem-თ
2nd	თქვენ	you	stem-თ
3rd	ისინი	they	stem-ენ

Look at this chart and memorize all person markers. The majority of Georgian verbs have these markers in present tense. Verbs for the 2nd person singular pronoun შენ *you* have no marker. The rest of the forms have specific markers both in singular and plural.

II. The dative/accusative case

Of the seven cases of Georgian noun declensions, the dative/accusative case is one of the most frequently used. The marker of the case is the ending -ს added to the nouns. Only nouns with the nominative ending -ი drop the final vowel before adding the ending -ს.

Nom.

გაზეთ-ი	ენა	კიბე	უთო	ბუ
newspaper	language	stairs	iron	owl

Dat./Acc.

გაზეთ-ს	ენა-ს	კიბე-ს	უთო-ს	ბუ-ს
newspaper	language	stairs	iron	owl

If the noun is preceded by any type of *qualifier* (pronoun, adjective, numeral, etc.), the qualifier will remain unchanged unless it has an -ი ending. In that case the qualifier will drop the final vowel.

Nom.	Dat./Acc.	Translation
ინგლისურ-ი ენა	ინგლისურ ენას	English language
სამ-ი ბუ	სამ ბუს	three owls
მოკლე კიბე	მოკლე კიბეს	short stairs
პატარა უთო	პატარა უთოს	small iron

In the examples above, the adjective **ინგლისური** *English* and the numeral **სამი** *three* both lose their nominative ending -ი when the words they modify are put in the dative/accusative case (**ენას** *language* and **ბუს** *owls*, respectively).

- The dative/accusative case is used when the noun functions as *the direct or indirect object of the action expressed by the verb*. In the sentences below, the underlined nouns and their qualifiers function as direct objects.

ირაკლი გერმანულ გაზეთს კითხულობს.
Irakli reads <u>a German newspaper</u>.

კევინი ინგლისურ ენას ასწავლის.
Kevin is teaching <u>the English language</u>.

ნინიკო პატარა ბუს ხატავს.
Niniko is drawing <u>a little owl</u>.

გია მოკლე წერილს წერს.
Gia is writing <u>a short letter</u>.

III. Postposition -ზე *on, at, to,* and *about*

Another postposition used in this lesson is -ზე, which corresponds to the English *on, at, to,* and *about.* It is attached to nouns in the dative/accusative case, in a manner similar to -ში, that is, nouns with an -ო ending in their basic (or nominative case) form drop the final vowel and -ზე is added to the stem of the noun. All other endings remain unchanged. Note that the dative/accusative case ending -ს is also dropped.

nom.	აივან-ი	კაბა	ხე	თარო	პერუ
	balcony	dress	tree	shelf	Peru
dat./acc.	აივან-ს	კაბა-ს	ხე-ს	თარო-ს	პერუ-ს
dat./acc. + ზე	აივანზე	კაბაზე	ხეზე	თაროზე	პერუზე
	to/on a balcony	on a dress	on a tree	on a shelf	about Peru

ჩვენ ვლაპარაკობთ საქართველოზე.
We speak about Georgia.
აივანზე პატარა მაგიდაა.
There is a small table on the balcony.
ქევინი საინტერესო პროექტზე მუშაობს.
Kevin works on an interesting project.

- **Enclitic -ა** can be added to nouns with postposition -ზე.

შენი წიგნი მაგიდაზეა.	Your book is on the table.
ჩემი კატა ხეზეა.	My cat is on a tree.
მანანა კონცერტზეა.	Manana is at the concert.

Remember that the use of postpositions in Georgian does not always coincide with that of prepositions in English. You should try to memorize them a few expressions at a time.

IV. The dative-/accusative-case postposition -თან *with s.o., at s.o.'s place*

Another postposition that can be added to the dative/accusative case is -თან. In this lesson we will discuss the use of this postposition *with personal names*.

The personal names that lose their final -ი will drop the case ending -ს before -თან like the postpositions -მი and -გე. The names that do not lose their final -ი will have -თან added after the case ending -ს (see *Borrowed Words and Personal Names in Georgian* on page 27).

Nom.	Dat./Acc.	+ თან	Translation
მიხეილ-ი	მიხეილ-ს	მიხეილ-თან	at Michael's
თამაზი	თამაზი-ს	თამაზი-ს-თან	at Tamazi's
თინა	თინა-ს	თინა-ს-თან	at Tina's
ელენე	ელენე-ს	ელენე-ს-თან	at Helen's
ნუნუ	ნუნუ-ს	ნუნუ-ს-თან	at Nunu's

ქევინი თამაზისთან მიდის.
Kevin is going to Tamazi's place.

ჩვენ ახლა არჩილთან ვართ.
We are now at Archil's place (with Archil).

ლალი ქევინთან ქართულად ლაპარაკობს.
Lali speaks with Kevin in Georgian.

V. The negative particle არა and the *tail question*

არა at the end of a sentence corresponds to the English *tail question*:

თქვენი და სტუდენტია, არა?
Your sister is a student, **isn't she?**

ჩვენ მეგობრები ვართ, არა?
We are friends, **aren't we?**

ისინი ქართულად ლაპარაკობენ, არა?
They speak Georgian, **don't they?**

დღეს ხუთშაბათია, არა?
Today is Thursday, **isn't it?**

Exercises

I. Fill in the blanks, adding appropriate person markers to the verbs. Note that in the sentences below all the verbs in parentheses are in the "simplest" form, the 2nd person singular.

1. ჩემი მშობლები აქ _____
   (ცხოვრობ).
   My parents live here.

2. ქევინი ქართულ ენას _____
   (სწავლობ).
   Kevin is studying Georgian [language].

3. მე კარგ ხაჭაპურს _____
   (აკეთებ).
   I make good khachapuri.

4. შენ ფრანგულ გაზეთს _____
   (კითხულობ)?
   Are you reading a French newspaper?

5. ქართულად რა კარგად _____
   (ლაპარაკობ)!
   How well you speak Georgian!

6. თამაზი და ლალი აქ _____
   (მუშაობ).
   Tamazi and Lali work here.

II. Put the nouns below in the dative/accusative case, and add postpositions -მი and -ზე. Remember that these adjectives are added to nouns in the dative/accusative case, minus the case ending -ს.

	nom.	dat./acc.	-მი	-ზე
1.	ოთახი	_____	_____	_____
2.	კინო	_____	_____	_____
3.	კვირა	_____	_____	_____
4.	თვე	_____	_____	_____

III. Add the postposition -თან to the personal names below; names that lose the final -ი are highlighted.

1. თამარი _____
2. ვასო _____
3. **მურმანი** _____

4. ქეთინო _____
5. ლამა _____
6. ნათელა _____

IV. Translate the following sentences into Georgian:

1. You *(sing.)* are a student, aren't you?

_____

2. Lali is your sister, isn't she?

_____

3. This is your apartment, isn't it?

_____

4. You *(pol.)* live here, don't you?

_____

V. The verbs below are given in the 2nd person singular form. Conjugate them orally referring to the chart given in the Grammar section of this lesson.

ლაპარაკობ (speak)
ქირაობ (rent)
ცხოვრობ (live)
რეკავ (ring)
მუშაობ (work)
კითხულობ (ask, read)
სწავლობ (study)
იცნობ (are acquainted, know)
წერ (write)
თამაშობ (play)

Lesson 4

გაკვეთილი მეოთხე

Kiln bread

თონის პური

თონის პური

დილით ადრე ქევინი და ლალი ერთმანეთს ხვდებიან ქუჩაში.

ლალი: ქევინ! გამარჯობა! სად მიდიხარ?
ქევინი: მაღაზიაში. პური მინდა ვიყიდო.
ლალი: მეც **პურზე მივდივარ**. შენ როგორი პური
            გინდა, ჩვეულებრივი თუ **თონის პური**?
ქევინი: დღეს თონის პური მინდა ვიყიდო, მაგრამ არ
            ვიცი სად.
ლალი: თონე აქ ახლოს არის. აი, იმ ქუჩაზე.
ქევინი: **რა ღირს** თონის პური?
ლალი: ორმოცდაათი **თეთრი**.
ქევინი: ერთი კილო?
ლალი: არა, ერთი ლავაში. აი, თონე აქ არის, ამ
            სარდაფში.
ქევინი: რა საინტერესოა!
ლალი: (ეკითხება გამყიდველ ქალს): **ღეიდა**, პური
            გაქვთ?
გამყიდველი: გვაქვს.
ლალი: ცხელია?
გამიდველი: **კი**, ცხელია. რამდენი გინდა?
ლალი: ორი ლავაში.
გამყიდველი: ერთი **ლარი**.
ქევინი: ლალი, მოდი, **დღეს მე გადავიხდი**, კარგი?
ლალი: არა, არა! დღეს მე გადავიხდი. შენ ხვალ
            გადაიხადე.
ქევინი: კარგი, მაგრამ ხვალ უსათუოდ მე გადავიხდი.
ლალი: **კი, ბატონო**. ხვალ შენ გადაიხადე.
ქევინი: ლალი, თუ დრო გაქვს, მოდი, მე და შენ
            დღეს ბაზარშიც წავიდეთ. ჩემი მაცივარი სულ
            ცარიელია.
ლალი: წავიდეთ. დღეს მე თავისუფალი ვარ.

Kiln bread

Early in the morning Kevin and Lali meet each other in the street.

Lali:	Kevin, hello! Where are you going?
Kevin:	To the store. I want to buy bread.
Lali:	I'm also going to buy bread. What kind of bread do you want, regular or oven-baked?
Kevin:	Today I want to buy oven-baked bread but I don't know where (to do so).
Lali:	The kiln is close to here. There, on that street.
Kevin:	How much does oven-baked bread cost?
Lali:	50 tetri.
Kevin:	One kilogram?
Lali:	No, one *lavash*. Here is the kiln, in this cellar.
Kevin:	How interesting!
Lali:	(asking the saleswoman) Auntie, do you have bread?
saleswoman:	We do.
Lali:	Is it hot?
saleswoman:	Yes, it's hot. How many do you want?
Lali:	Two *lavashis*.
saleswoman:	One *lari*.
Kevin:	Lali, let me pay today, OK?
Lali:	No, no! I will pay today. You pay tomorrow.
Kevin:	OK, but tomorrow I will pay for sure.
Lali:	As you wish. You'll pay tomorrow.
Kevin:	Lali, if you have time, let's you and I also go together to the market. My refrigerator is completely empty.
Lali:	Let's go. I'm free today.

Vocabulary

თონე	[tone]	kiln or oven
თონის *gen.*	[tonis]	
თონის პური	[tonis p'uri]	*lit:* kiln bread
პური	[p'uri]	bread
სად	[sad]	where
მიდიხარ *pres.*	[midixar]	you are going
მაღაზია	[maghazia]	store
მინდა	[minda]	I want
ვიყიდო *opt.*	[viq'ido]	(should, want to) buy
როგორი	[rogori]	what kind
გინდა *pres.*	[ginda]	you want
ჩვეულებრივი	[chveulebrivi]	regular, ordinary
ახლოს	[axlos]	close by, near
ქუჩა	[kucha]	street
იმ ქუჩაზე	[im kuchaze]	on that street
ღირს *pres.*	[ghirs]	costs
ორმოცდაათი	[ormotsdaati]	fifty
კილო	[k'ilo]	kilogram
(*abbrev. of* კილოგრამი)	[k'ilogrami]	
ლავაში	[lavashi]	*lavash,* flat kiln bread
სარდაფი	[sardapi]	cellar
ამ სარდაფში	[am sardapshi]	in this cellar
ეკითხება *pres.*	[ek'itxeba]	is asking (*s.o.*)
გამყიდველი	[gamq'idveli]	salesperson
ქალი	[kali]	woman
დეida	[deida]	aunt, auntie
გაქვთ *pl./pres.*	[gakvt]	you have
გვაქვს *pres.*	[gvakvs]	we have
ცხელი	[tsxeli]	hot
კი	[k'i]	yes (*informal*)
რამდენი	[ramdeni]	how many
ორი	[ori]	two

გადავიხდი *fut.*	[gadavixdi]	I will pay
ხვალ	[xval]	tomorrow
გადაიხადე *aor./imp.*	[gadaixade]	you pay
უსათუოდ	[usatuod]	by all means, for sure, without fail
დრო	[dro]	time
გაქვს *sing./pres.*	[gakvs]	you have
ბაზარი	[bazari]	farmer's market
თავისუფალი	[tavisupali]	free

 Idiomatic Expressions and Culture Notes

- თონის პური *kiln bread*, commonly called *lavashi*, is very popular in Georgia as well as in most Middle Eastern countries. It may be of various shapes and thickness. In Tbilisi, kiln bread is of average thickness. In many places in the city you can buy a freshly baked *lavash* straight from the kiln.

- პურზე მივდივარ means *I am going for bread*. (lit.: *I am going on the bread*.)

- რა ღირს means *How much is it?*, *What does it cost?*

- თეთრი and ლარი are Georgian currencies. თეთრი refers to small change and literally means *white*, since early Georgian coins were made of silver. One *lari* equals one hundred *tetris*. After the collapse of the Soviet Union in 1991, these currencies replaced the Russian ruble. As with all currencies, the value of the *lari* fluctuates; initially, one dollar was equal to two *laris* and 20 *tetris*. As of the beginning of 2008, the rate of exchange was one dollar to 1 *lary*, 75 *tetri*. The exchange rate will, no doubt, keep on changing.

- დიდა, literally *aunt* or *auntie*, is a standard form of addressing a stranger, an older woman. The word ქალბატონო *Madam*, may also be used but it is more formal in tone, and implies deference to the person being addressed.

- კი followed with ბატონო (კი, ბატონო) is a fixed formula, and literally means *yes, sir* or *yes, master*. It is used when addressing either men or women. It expresses agreement, consent, and can also be translated as *of course*.

- დღეს მე გადავიხდი means *Today I will pay.* Georgians often insist that they pay the bill for their friends, be they local or foreign. Traditional honor requires it, and these chivalrous rules are followed even when one can barely afford to do so. It would be prudent not to abuse this kind of generosity, and also not to feel obliged to reciprocate.

Grammar

I. Verbs of motion in the present tense

prefix + დი + verb *be*

- The majority of verbs denoting motion have one common stem, **-დი-**.

- The prefixes indicate the direction of the movement.

- There are seven basic prefixes, roughly corresponding to the English *to, in, up, down, over, etc.* One of the most frequently used prefixes is **მი-**. Together with the stem **მი-დი-** it forms the basis of the verb *go*.

- At this point we will use only the prefix **მი-**. Others will be introduced gradually.

- In the chart below, the components of the verb are separated by a dash to make the structure clear. Usually they must be written as one word.

Present Tense of the Verb *go*
prefix მი + დი + verb *be*

	Singular		Plural
1st	მე	მი-ვ-დი-ვარ	ჩვენ	მი-ვ-დი-ვარ-თ
		I am going		we are going
2nd	შენ	მი---დი-ხარ	თქვენ	მი---დი-ხარ-თ
		you are going		you are going
3rd	ის	მი---დი-ს	ისინი	მი---დი-ან
		he/she/it is going		they are going

დღეს ისინი ოპერაში **მიდიან**.
Today **they are going** to the opera.

ხვალ ჩვენ ჩიკაგოში **მივდივართ**.
Tomorrow **we are going** to Chicago.

შენ სკოლაში არ **მიდიხარ**?
Aren't **you** *(sing.)* **going** to school?

კვირას სტუდენტები სად **მიდიან**?
Where **are** the students **going** on Sunday?

- In negative sentences the particle **არ** must be always placed before the verb:

მე **არ** მივდივარ.   I am **not** going.
შენ **არ** მიდიხარ.   You are **not** going.

Below is a list of some other verbs of motion that conjugate in the same manner as the verb *go*. Notice the different prefixes:

შე-ვ-დი-ვარ   I am going **in** (or **into**)
ა-ვ-დი-ვარ   I am going **up**
ჩა-ვ-დი-ვარ   I am going **down**, I am arriving **to**

II. Word order in affirmative and interrogative sentences

Affirmative sentence word order

The word order of Georgian sentences is rather flexible. You can rearrange words without fundamentally changing their meaning, although

some shift of emphasis may occur. At this point you don't need to
worry about this as long as the sentence is intelligible.

The following is an example of how word order may be changed;
in each version the boldfaced words are emphasized. The first
example (with the *) shows the most frequently used neutral form:

*თამაზი გაზეთს კითხულობს.
*Tamazi a newspaper is reading.

გაზეთს **თამაზი** კითხულობს.
A newspaper **Tamazi** is reading.

კითხულობს გაზეთს თამაზი.
Is reading a newspaper Tamazi.

თამაზი კითხულობს **გაზეთს**.
Tamazi is reading **a newspaper**.

Note, however, that a sentence may include groups of words that
form *inseparable units that should never be broken up*. Such units
are:

* A noun and all preceding qualifiers (adjectives, possessive pronouns, numerals) that specify, describe or identify it;

* The negative particle არ *not* and the verb that follows it.

* Other types of inseparable units will be introduced later.

In the sentences below the inseparable units are underlined.

*ნინო <u>დიდ ბინაში</u> <u>არ ცხოვრობს</u>.
*Nino <u>in a large apartment</u> <u>does not live</u>.

ნინო <u>არ ცხოვრობს</u> <u>დიდ ბინაში</u>.
Nino <u>does not live</u> <u>in a large apartment</u>.

<u>არ ცხოვრობს</u> ნინო <u>დიდ ბინაში</u>.
<u>Does not live</u> Nino <u>in a large apartment</u>.

<u>დიდ ბინაში</u> ნინო <u>არ ცხოვრობს</u>.
<u>In a large apartment</u> Nino <u>does not live</u>.

III. Interrogative sentence word order with pronouns საღ *where*, ვინ *who*, and ვისი *whose*

The majority of interrogative pronouns (*who, why, where, which,* etc.) also form inseparable units with verbs that follow them with or without negation არ. In the following example sentences, the inseparable units are underlined.

A. საღ *where*

<u>საღ მიღიან</u> ღღეს ქევინი ღა ლალი?
<u>Where are going</u> today Kevin and Lali?

ღღეს <u>საღ მიღიან</u> ქევინი ღა ლალი?
Today <u>where are going</u> Kevin and Lali?

ქევინი ღა ლალი ღღეს <u>საღ მიღიან?</u>
Kevin and Lali today <u>where are going?</u>

ქევინი ღა ლალი <u>საღ მიღიან</u> ღღეს?
Kevin and Lali <u>where are going</u> today?

B. ვინ *who*

<u>ვინ ლაპარაკობს</u> ქართულაღ?
<u>Who speaks</u> in Georgian?

ქართულაღ <u>ვინ ლაპარაკობს?</u>
In Georgian <u>who speaks?</u>

<u>ვინ არ ლაპარაკობს</u> ქართულაღ?
<u>Who does not speak</u> in Georgian?

ქართულაღ <u>ვინ არ ლაპარაკობს?</u>
In Georgian <u>who does not speak?</u>

<u>ვინ მუშაობს</u> კარგაღ?
<u>Who works</u> well?

კარგაღ <u>ვინ მუშაობს?</u>
Well <u>who works?</u>

<u>ვინ არ მუშაობს</u> კარგაღ?
<u>Who does not work</u> well?

კარგად ვინ არ მუშაობს?
Well who does not work?

C. The pronoun ვისი forms inseparable units only with the verb *to be* expressed with **enclitic -ა** (*is*) added to it: ვისი + ა.

ვისია ეს გაზეთი?
Whose newspaper is this? (Whose is this newspaper?)
ეს გაზეთი ვისია?
This newspaper whose is?

ვისია ეს კატა?
Whose cat is this? (Whose is this cat?)
ეს კატა ვისია?
This cat whose is?

IV. Indicative pronouns ეს *this* and ის *that*

• The pronoun **ის** designates the personal pronouns *he* or *she*. It also functions as the indicative pronoun *that*, and is paired with another indicative pronoun **ეს** *this*. **ეს** *this* and **ის** *that* are *nominative (or direct) forms* of the pronouns.

Direct Forms of the Indicative Pronouns
ეს (this) and ის (that)

ეს ბინა	this apartment	ის ბინა	that apartment
ეს ოთახი	this room	ის ოთახი	that room
ეს გაზეთი	this newspaper	ის გაზეთი	that newspaper

If the noun following these pronouns is in any case other than the nominative (for example, dative/accusative, genitive, etc.) or has a postposition, the pronouns **ის** *that* and **ეს** *this* will change to **ამ** and **იმ** respectively. They are called *indirect forms* of the indicative pronouns.

Indirect Forms of the Indicative Pronouns
ამ (this) and იმ (that)

იმ ბინას	this apartment	ამ ბინას	that apartment
იმ ოთახში	in this room	ამ ოთახში	in that room
იმ გაზეთზე	on this newspaper	ამ გაზეთზე	on that newspaper

Examples:

გურამი **ამ ბინას** ქირაობს.
Gurami is renting **this apartment**.

პაატა **იმ სახლში** ცხოვრობს.
Paata lives **in that house**.

შენი გაზეთი **ამ მაგიდაზეა.**
Your newspaper is **on this table.**

ჩემი კომპიუტერი **იმ ოთახშია.**
My computer is **in that room**.

Exercises

I. Fill in the blanks with the correct ending of the verb of motion. You should use the prefix მი- + დი- + the appropriate ending.

1. ქეგინი ბაზარში   _____

2. გამარჯობა, ლალი. სად   _____

3. მე და ქაკლინი დღეს კინოში   _____

4. თამაზი და ქეგინი ბაკნში   _____

5. თქვენ ბაზარში   _____

6. მე და ლალი სახლში   _____

II. In the sentence below, underline inseparable units and change the word order. You should come up with at least four possible versions.

ირაკლი იტალიურ ენას არ სწავლობს.
Irakli does not study the Italian language.

1. _____

2. _____

3. _____

4. _____

III. Conjugate orally the verbs below, referring to the verb chart given in the Grammar section I of this lesson:

    შე-ვ-დი-ვარ   I am going in (or into)

    ა-ვ-დი-ვარ   I am going up

    ჩა-ვ-დივარ   I am going down, I am arriving to

IV. Translate the following sentences into Georgian using the interrogative pronouns სად *where*, ვინ *who*, and ვისი *whose*. Choose any word order explained in this lesson.

A.

1. Where is Kevin?   _____

2. Where is your friend?   _____

3. Where is the toilet (restroom)? _____

B.

1. Who is that man?   _____

2. Who is going to the market? _____

3. Who does not speak English? _____

C.

1. Whose book is this?   _____

2. Whose computer is this?   _____

3. Whose bedroom is this?   _____

V. Fill in the blanks with the direct or indirect forms of the indicative pronouns:

1. (ეს, ამ) _____ სახლში თამაზი ცხოვრობს. _____ მისი საწოლი ოთახია.

2. (ის, იმ) _____ ხაჭაპური ძალიან გემრიელია.

3. (ეს, ამ) _____ ჩემი მაგიდაა. _____ მაგიდაზე ჩემი კომპიუტერია.

4. (იმ, ის) _____ გერმანული ბანკია. _____ ბანკში მე ვმუშაობ.

5. (ეს, ამ, ის, იმ) _____ ბინაში სამი ოთახია, _____ ბინაში ორი ოთახი.

6. (ეს, ამ, ის, იმ) _____ მაღაზია _____ მაღაზიაზე უფრო დიდია.

Lesson 5

გაკვეთილი მეხუთე

The farmers' market

ბაზარი

 **ბაზარი**

ქევინი და ლალი ბაზარში არიან და სურსათს ყიდულობენ.

ლალი:	ქევინ, რა გინდა იყიდო?
ქევინი:	ყველაფერი: ქათამი, ყველი, ბოსტნეული, ხილი.
ლალი:	ხორცი არ გინდა?
ქევინი:	არა, მე ხორცს არა ვჭამ.
ლალი:	ვეგეტარიანელი ხარ?
ქევინი:	არა, ქათამს და თევზს ვჭამ.
ლალი:	კარგი. მოდი, ჯერ ყველი ვიყიდოთ. **დია,** ყველი რა ღირს?
გამყიდველი:	კილო ხუთი ლარი.
ლალი:	ძალიან ძვირია.
გამყიდველი:	კარგი, ოთხი და ნახევარი. რამდენი გინდა?
ლალი:	ერთი კილო მომეცი.
ქევინი:	ლალი, აი, კარგი ვაშლია. მოდი, ეს **ვაშლი** ვიყიდოთ.
ლალი:	დეიდა, ვაშლი რა ღირს?
გამყიდველი:	კილო ლარნახევარი.
ქევინი:	ორი კილო მომეცი. აი, **ბატონო,** სამი ლარი.
ლალი:	ეხლა ბოსტნეული ვიყიდოთ. რა ბოსტნეული გინდა?
ქევინი:	კიტრი, პამიდორი, მწვანე ლობიო და ბადრიჯანი.
ლალი:	აი, ეს კარგი პამიდორია და იაფიც არის, კილო ორი ლარი.
ქევინი:	პამიდორი ბევრი არ მინდა. ოთხი ცალი საკმარისია.
ლალი:	დია, ოთხი პამიდორი მინდა.
გამყიდველი:	აირჩიე, **შვილო,** რომელი გინდა.
ლალი:	აი, ეს ოთხი. მგონი კილოზე ცოტა მეტია, არა?
გამყიდველი:	**არა უშავს,** ოთხად წაიღე.
ლალი:	მადლობთ, დია.

The farmers' market

Kevin and Lali are at the farmers' market and are buying produce.

Lali:	Kevin, what do you want to buy?
Kevin:	Everything: chicken, cheese, vegetables, fruit.
Lali:	You don't want meat?
Kevin:	No, I don't eat meat.
Lali:	Are you a vegetarian?
Kevin:	No, I eat chicken and fish.
Lali:	OK. Let's buy cheese first. Sir, (*lit.*: uncle) how much is the cheese?
Salesperson:	Five *lari*.
Lali:	It's too expensive.
Salesperson:	OK, four and a half. How much do you want?
Lali:	Give me one kilo.
Kevin:	Lali, here, (look) what nice apples. Let's buy these apples.
Lali:	Miss, how much are the apples?
Salesperson:	*Lari* and a half for a kilo.
Kevin:	Give me two kilos. Here, Miss (or Sir), three lari.
Lali:	Let's now buy vegetables. What kind of vegetables do you want?
Kevin:	Cucumbers, tomatoes, green beans and eggplants.
Lali:	Here, these are good tomatoes and cheap too, two laris for a kilo.
Kevin:	I don't want too many tomatoes. Four is enough.
Lali:	Sir, I want four tomatoes.
Salesperson:	Choose, child, which ones you want.
Lali:	Here, these four. Seems like it is a little over a kilo, isn't it?
Salesperson:	That's OK, take it for four (*lari*).
Lali:	Thank you, Sir.

Vocabulary

Georgian	Transcription	Meaning
სურსათი	[sursati]	produce
გინდა იყიდო *opt.*	[ginda iq'ido]	you want to buy
ყველაფერი	[q'velaperi]	everything
ქათამი	[katami]	chicken
ქათამს *dat./acc.*	[katams]	
ყველი	[q'veli]	cheese
ბოსტნეული	[bost'neuli]	vegetable(s)
ხილი	[xili]	fruit
ხორცი	[xor<u>ts</u>i]	meat *(unless specified, e.g. chicken, etc., it implies red meat)*
ვეგეტარიანელი	[veget'arianeli]	vegetarian
თევზი	[tevzi]	fish
თევზს *dat./acc.*	[tevzs]	
ჯერ	[jer]	first of all, before anything else
ვიყიდოთ *opt.*	[viq'idot]	let's buy, shall we buy
ძვირი	[<u>dz</u>viri]	expensive
ასე ძვირი	[ase <u>dz</u>viri]	so expensive
ნახევარი	[naxevari]	half
რამდენი	[ramdeni]	how much
მომეცი	[mome<u>ts</u>i]	give me
ვაშლი	[va<u>sh</u>li]	apple
ლარნახევარი	[larnaxevari]	*lari* and a half (ლარ+ნახევარი)
ეხლა (*or* ახლა)	[exla]	now
კიტრი	[k'it'ri]	cucumber
პამიდორი	[p'amidori]	tomato
მწვანე	[m<u>ts</u>'vane]	green
ლობიო	[lobio]	beans
ბადრიჯანი	[badrijani]	eggplant
იაფი	[iapi]	cheap
იაფიც	[iapi<u>ts</u>]	cheap too, cheap as well

ბევრი	[bevri]	many, much
ცალი	[tsali]	piece *(always used after numerals)*
საკმარისი	[sak'marisi]	enough
დია	[dzia]	*here*: Sir (*lit.*: uncle)
აირჩიე *aor./imp.*	[airchie]	(you) choose
მგონი	[mgoni]	seems like, looks like, I think
ცოტა	[tsot'a]	a little, few
მეტი	[met'i]	more
წაიღე *aor./imp.*	[ts'aighe]	(you) take

 Idiomatic Expressions and Culture Notes

- ბაზარი The *farmers' market* in Georgia, as in any Middle Eastern country, is a colorful and noisy place. In Tbilisi, farmers' markets are particularly colorful. People from different regions of the country and of various ethnicities mill around, while buyers try to bargain down the price. This is also the best place to practice colloquial Georgian.

- დია or ბიძია, literally *uncle*, is used when addressing an older man, a stranger, or a blood relative. It should not be used in formal, polite conversation.

- ვაშლი is the singular form of the word *apple*. When referring to an unspecified quantity of any produce such as fruits, vegetables, etc., the singular form of nouns should be used: კიტრი *cucumber*, პამიდორი, *tomato*, ბადრიჯანი *eggplant*, etc.

- ბატონო is, literally, the vocative case of *master*. (The *vocative case* is used when one is addressing someone or something.) If not followed by a personal name, the word ბატონო can be used when addressing either men or women.

- **შვილო** is the vocative case of **შვილი** *child*. This is how an older person would address a younger one, regardless of whether the addressee is male or female.

- **არა უშავს.** Depending on the situation, this idiomatic expression may mean *it's OK, just fine, no big deal, don't worry about it.*

Grammar

I. Interrogative pronouns **რა** *what*, **რომელი** *which one*, **როგორი** *what kind*

Although in some cases these pronouns may be interchangeable, **რა** *what*, **რომელი** *which one*, **როგორი** *what kind* are not synonymous. They function as qualifiers and form a tripartite unit with both the noun to which they refer and the verb which follows.

რა *what* like its English counterpart, may be followed by a verb or a noun:

რა არის ეს?
What is this?

რა გაზეთს კითხულობ?
What newspaper are you reading?

In the latter case, while the question does not refer to the specific qualities of some persons, objects, or species, the noun being modified by **რა** *what* must be named or otherwise identified.

Questions	**Possible Answers**
რა ენას სწავლობ?	**ქართულ ენას.**
What language do you study?	[The] Georgian language.
რა წიგნს კითხულობ?	**ფოლკნერის რომანს.**
What book are you reading?	A novel by Faulkner.
რა ფილმი გადის?	**ამერიკული ვესტერნი.**
What film are they showing?	An American Western.

რომელი *which one* implies a choice among several possibilities, and, just like როგორი *what kind*, it is followed either by a noun or the **enclitic -ა** *is*:

Questions	Possible Answers
რომელ სართულზე ცხოვრობ? On **which floor** do you live?	მეორეზე. On the second.
რომელია შენი კალამი? **Which one is** your pen?	წითელი. The red one.
რომელი ვაშლი ვიყიდოთ? **Which apples** should we buy?	ეს ვაშლი. These apples.
რომელია შენი ბინა? **Which one is** your apartment?	ეს ბინა. This apartment.

როგორი *what kind* refers to *specific qualities* of persons, things or species and, like რომელი *which one*, it is followed by a noun or by **enclitic -ა**.

Questions	Possible Answers
დღეს **როგორი ამინდია?** [Today **what kind weather is?**] How is the weather today?	საკმაოდ კარგი. Pretty good.
როგორია ჩემი ხაჭაპური? [**What kind is** my khachapuri?] How is my khachapuri?	ძალიან გემრიელი! Very delicious!
როგორი ჩაი გინდა? [**What kind** tea you want?] What kind of tea do you want?	მწვანე ჩაი. Green tea.

Interrogative **როგორი** *what kind* should not be confused with **როგორ** *how*. **როგორ** *how* is always followed by a verb, and functions as an adverb, i.e. it modifies the verb. If followed by a monosyllabic verb like ვარ *I am* or ხარ *you are*, **euphonic -ა** (not **enclitic -ა** that stands for *is*) will be added at the end.

Questions	Possible Answers
თამაზი **როგორ** ლაპარაკობს ინგლისურად? **How** does Tamazi speak English?	ძალიან კარგად. Very well.
გამარჯობა, ზურიკო. **როგორა** ხარ? Hello, Zuriko. **How** are you?	კარგად, გმადლობ. Fine, thank you.
როგორ არის ქართულად tomato? [**How** is in Georgian *tomato*?] How do you say *tomato* in Georgian?	პამიდორი. [pamidori].

II. Demonstrative, comparative and superlative adjectives

- **Regular forms**

  In Georgian, just as in English, there are demonstrative (**კარგი** *good*), comparative (**უკეთესი** *better*), and superlative (**საუკეთესო** *the best*) adjectives. The majority of comparative and superlative adjectives are formed by using the word **უფრო** *more* for comparative adjectives, and **ყველაზე** *most* for superlative adjectives.

Dem.	Com.	Sup.
დიდი big, large	უფრო დიდი bigger, larger	ყველაზე დიდი biggest, largest
პატარა small *(in size or age)*	უფრო პატარა smaller	ყველაზე პატარა smallest
ლამაზი beautiful	უფრო ლამაზი more beautiful	ყველაზე ლამაზი most beautiful
ძნელი difficult	უფრო ძნელი more difficult	ყველაზე ძნელი most difficult
ადვილი easy	უფრო ადვილი easier	ყველაზე ადვილი easiest

- **Irregular forms**
  A few adjectives have both regular and irregular comparative
  and superlative forms. These forms are mostly interchangeable,
  although irregular forms are more frequently used in reference to
  abstract concepts or in fixed phrases.

Dem.	Com.	Sup.
კარგი	უფრო კარგი = უკეთესი	ყველაზე კარგი = საუკეთესო
good	better	best, outstanding
ბევრი	უფრო ბევრი = მეტი	ყველაზე ბევრი = უმეტესი
many	more	most, the majority
ცუდი	უფრო ცუდი = უარესი	ყველაზე ცუდი = ყველაზე უარესი
bad	worse	worst
ცოტა	უფრო ცოტა = ნაკლები	ყველაზე ცოტა = ყველაზე ნაკლები
little	less	least

ეს **ყველაზე კარგი** ქართული გაზეთია.
This is the **best** Georgian newspaper.

ყველაზე ბევრი სტუდენტი ამ კურსზე სწავლობს.
The **greatest number** of students is enrolled in this course (*lit.*:
study in this course).

სტუდენტების **უმეტესი** ნაწილი ლაპარაკობს ესპანურად.
The **majority** of the students speaks Spanish.

The most common forms of comparison require the postposition **-ზე**.
When two nouns or pronouns are being compared, the second noun
or pronoun should be in the dative case, dropping the dative case
marker **-ს** and adding the postposition **-ზე**. The word **უფრო** *more*
may be omitted, since the postposition **-ზე** indicates that two items
are being compared.

Examples:

ეს ბინა   თამაზის ბინა**ზე**   (უფრო) დიდია.
1st noun   compared to 2nd noun + **-ზე** (more) adjective
this apartment   Tamazi's apartment   (more) large is
This apartment is **larger than** Tamazi's apartment.

ინგლისური ენა ფრანგულ**ზე** (უფრო) ადვილია.
The English language is easier than French.

ქეთინო ლალი**ზე** (უფრო) მაღალია.
Ketino is taller than Lali.

შენ ჩემ**ზე** კარგად ლაპარაკობ ინგლისურად.
You speak English better than I (do).

რუსიკო შენ**ზე** მაღალია.
Rusiko is taller than you.

Exercises

I. Fill in the blanks with interrogatives: რა, როგორი, რომელი, როგორ. Look at the answers for clues, and remember that the use of English and Georgian *how* does not always coincide.

1. - _____ ენას სწავლობს ქეთინო?
   - ფრანგულს.
2. - _____ ვაშლია უფრო გემრიელი?
   - ეს ვაშლი.
3. - _____ ლაპარაკობს ნინო იტალიურად?
   - ძალიან კარგად.
4. - _____ არის შენი ოთახი?
   - ის არის ჩემი ოთახი.
5. - _____ პური გინდა, ჩვეულებრივი?
   - არა, თონის პური.
6. - _____ არის ინგლისურად *გემრიელი*?

II. Fill in the blanks with the boldfaced comparative or superlative adjectives.

1. თბილისი _____ **largest** ქალაქია
   (city) საქართველოში.

2. შენი და ლალიზე _____ **smaller**
   არის, არა?

3. დღეს ამინდი (weather) _____ **worse**
   არის.

4. ამერიკის _____ **the most beautiful**
   ქალაქია სან-ფრანცისკო.

5. ის ქალი _____ **outstanding** ექიმია
   (doctor).

6. ჩემი ძმა თამაზზე _____ **tall.**

7. ეს _____ **shortest** გზაა (road).

8. მე ერთი კილო პამიდორი არ მინდა,
   _____ **less** მომეცი.

9. ეს ვაშლი _____ **cheaper.**

10. ეს _____ **the best** სკოლაა.

III. Fill in the blanks with words from the dialogue in this lesson:

1. ლალი: ქევინ, _____ იყიდო?

2. ქევინი: ყველაფერი: ქათამი, _____,
           ბოსტნეული, _____.

3. ლალი: _____ არ გინდა?

4. ქევინი: არა, მე ხორცს არ _____.

5. ლალი: _____ ხარ?

6. ქევინი: არა, ქათამს და _____ ვჭამ.

Lesson 6

გაკვეთილი მეექვსე

Renting an apartment

ბინის დაქირავება

ბინის დაქირავება

თამაზი და ქევინი თამაზის მეგობრის, რუსუდანის კარზე აკაკუნებენ.

რუსუდანი:	თამაზ, შენა? გამარჯობა.
თამაზი:	გამარჯობა, **რუსიკო**. **გაიცანი**, ეს არის ჩემი მეგობარი, ქევინი.
რუსუდანი:	გამარჯობათ. ძალიან სასიამოვნოა. მობრძანდით. თქვენ გინდათ ბინა იქირაოთ, არა?
ქევინი:	არა. მომავალ კვირას ჩემი მეგობარი, ემილი ჰანჯერი ჩამოდის ამერიკიდან და ბინას მისთვის ვქირაობ.
რუსუდანი:	გასაგებია. რამდენი ხნით გინდათ იქირაოთ?
ქევინი:	ერთი წლით.
რუსუდანი:	დიდი ბინა გინდათ?
ქევინი:	არა, მხოლოდ **ერთოთახიანი** ბინა.
რუსუდანი:	ჩემი ბინა სწორედ ერთოთახიანია.
ქევინი:	რამდენი იქნება თვიური გადასახადი?
რუსუდანი:	ასორმოცდაათი დოლარი.
ქევინი:	ძალიან კარგი. აქედან ტრანსპორტი კარგად დადის?
რუსუდანი:	ძალიან კარგად. მეტრო "**დელისი**" პირდაპირ სახლის წინ არის. აქვე ჩერდება ავტობუსები და **მარშრუტკები**. ტაქსის გაჩერებაც ახლოა.
ქევინი:	გასაგებია. პირველი თვის ქირა დღეს გინდათ?
რუსუდანი:	კარგი იქნება.
ქევინი:	**დოლარებში გინდათ** თუ ლარებში?
რუსუდანი:	თუ თქვენთვის სულერთია, დოლარებში.
ქევინი:	კი, ბატონო. აი ასორმოცდაათი დოლარი.
რუსუდანი:	გმადლობთ. აი, გასაღები. სამშაბათისთვის ბინა მზად იქნება.

Renting an apartment

Tamazi and Kevin are knocking at the door of Tamazi's friend, Rusudani's (apartment).

Rusudani: Tamaz, is that you? Hi.

Tamazi: Hi, Rusiko. Let me introduce to you, this is my friend, Kevin.

Rusudani: Hello. Nice to meet you. Please come in. You want to rent the apartment, right?

Kevin: No. Next week my friend Emily Hunter is arriving from America, and I want to rent an apartment for her.

Rusudani: I see. For how long do you want to rent the apartment?

Kevin: For a year.

Rusudani: Do you want a large apartment?

Kevin: No, just a one-room apartment.

Rusudani: My apartment is exactly one room.

Kevin: What will the monthly payment be?

Rusudani: A hundred and fifty dollars.

Kevin: Very good. Is there good public transportation from here?

Rusudani: (It's) very good. The subway (station) *Delisi* is right in front of the house. Buses and mini-buses stop right here. The taxi stand is also close by.

Kevin: I see. Do you want the first month's rent today?

Rusudani: That would be nice.

Kevin: Would you like (the payment) in dollars or in lari?

Rusudani: If it's OK with you, in dollars.

Kevin: Sure. Here are 150 dollars.

Rusudani: Thank you. Here is the key. By Tuesday the apartment will be ready.

ქევინი: მომავალ კვირას ემილი უკვე აქ იქნება.
             შეიძლება?

რუსუდანი: რასაკვირველია.

ქევინი: დიდი მადლობა. ნახვამდის.

რუსუდანი: ნახვამდის.

Kevin: Next week Emily will be here. OK?

Rusudani: Of course.

Kevin: Thank you very much. Good-bye.

Rusudani: Good-bye.

Vocabulary

დაქირავება	[dakiraveba]	renting, to rent
უნდა *pres.*	[unda]	(s/he) wants
უნდა იქირაოს *opt.*	[unda ikiraos]	wants to rent
მეგობრის(ა)თვის	[megobristvis]	for a friend
კარი	[k'ari]	door
აკაკუნებენ *pres.*	[ak'ak'uneben]	(they) knock, are knocking (at)
შენა (შენ+ა)	[shena]	is that you?
გინდათ იქირაოთ *opt.*	[gindat ikiraot]	(you) want, wish to rent
მომავალი	[momavali]	next, coming
მომავალ კვირას	[momaval k'viras]	next Sunday
ჩამოდის *pres.*	[chamodis]	arrives, is arriving
მისთვის	[mistvis]	for him/her
გასაგებია	[gasagebia]	I see (*lit.*: it is clear)
რამდენი ხნით *instr.*	[ramdeni xnit]	for how long
ერთი წლით *instr.*	[erti ts'lit]	for one year
მხოლოდ	[mxolod]	only
ერთოთახიანი	[ertotaxiani]	one-room (apartment)
ერთ(ი)+ოთახ(ი)+იანი		
სწორედ	[sts'ored]	precisely, exactly
იქნება *fut.*	[ikneba]	(s/he, it) will be
თვიური	[tviuri]	monthly
გადასახადი	[gadasaxadi]	payment, fee
ასორმოცდაათი	[asormotsdaati]	hundred and fifty
დოლარი	[dolari]	dollar
აქედან	[akedan]	from here
ტრანსპორტი	[t'ransp'ort'i]	transportation (cars, buses, etc.)
დადის *pres.*	[dadis]	(s/he) walks, walks around

მეტრო	[met'ro]	subway
პირდაპირ	[p'irdap'ir]	straight
წინ	[ts'in]	in front of
აქვე	[akve]	right here
ჩერდება *pres.*	[cherdeba]	stops, is stopping
ავტობუსები *pl.*	[avt'obusebi]	buses
ავტობუსი *sing.*	[avt'obusi]	bus
ტაქსი	[t'aksi]	taxi
ტაქსის *gen.*	[t'aksis]	
გაჩერება	[gachereba]	(bus) stop
გაჩერებაც	[gacherebats]	(bus) stop too
პირველი	[p'irveli]	first
თვე	[tve]	month
თვის *gen.*	[tvis]	
ქირა	[kira]	rent (payment)
თქვენთვის	[tkventvis]	for you
გასაღები	[gasaghebi]	key
სამშაბათის(ა)თვის	[samshabatis(a)tvis]	by Tuesday
იქნება *fut.*	[ikneba]	(s/he) will be
რასაკვირველია	[rasak'virvelia]	of course
მადლობა	[madloba]	thank
დიდი მადლობა	[didi madloba]	thank you very much

 Idiomatic Expressions and Culture Notes

* რუსიკო *Rusiko* is a diminutive of the name რუსუდანი *Rusudani*. Diminutives are used like nicknames; Tamazi addresses Rusudani in this way because he is her friend.

* გაიცანი means literally *get acquainted*. This is a standard formula of introduction. In formal situations, the more polite plural form გაიცანით is used.

- ერთოთახიანი ბინა is a *studio apartment*. From the Soviet era on, apartments have been described not by the number of bedrooms, but by the total number of rooms. ორთოთახიანი ბინა is a two-room apartment.

- დელისი *Delisi* is a subway station in Tbilisi, at a place which was formerly a small village of that name near the city.

- მარშრუტკები [mar<u>sh</u>rut'k'ebi] *mini-buses* is a plural form of მარშრუტკა [mar<u>sh</u>rut'k'a] *mini-bus*. It is actually a Russian word for mini-buses, and is widely used in spoken Georgian. Like regular buses, they run along a fixed route but are faster and make fewer stops. The fare is higher, but many people prefer to take a *mar<u>sh</u>rutka* if they are in a hurry and cannot afford a taxi.

- დოლარებში გინდათ *you want (it) in dollars*; in Georgia, the only accepted currency is *lari*. However, in some private business deals, especially when renting or selling an apartment, foreign currency is also accepted and indeed is often preferred.

- სულერთია means *all the same, doesn't make any difference*; თუ თქვენთვის სულერთია means *if it's OK with you* (lit.: *if it is the same for you*).

Grammar

I. Genitive case

The genitive case of Georgian nouns conveys the same possessive relationship as the English preposition *of* or *'s*: *time of day, taste of honey, day's work, my friend's sister*. The ending of the genitive case is -ის or -ს, depending on the final vowel of the nouns in the nominative case.

	-ი	-ა	-ე	-ო
nom.	სახლ-ი	კაბა	ხე	მეტრო
gen.	სახლ-ის	კაბ-ის	ხ-ის	მეტრო-ს
	house	dress	tree	subway

- The word order for nouns in genitive case constructions is similar to the English only when *'s* is used. While in English both *of* and *'s* can sometimes be omitted, in Georgian the genitive case must always be used.

სახლის გასაღები	a house key (*lit.*: key of a house)
კაბის სახელო	sleeve of a dress
ხის კარი	wooden door (*lit.*: door of a tree)
მეტროს სადგური	subway station

Syncope (collapsible vowels). Some but not all nouns lose the vowels -ა, -ე, -ო in the genitive case if these vowels are followed by -ლ, -მ, -ნ, -რ at the end of the word. There is no precise rule as to which nouns should be syncopated. If you are not sure just ignore the syncopation rule; you will gradually get the hang of it.

Nom.	Syncopation Gen.	Translation
მეგობ-არ-ი	მეგობრ-ის	of a friend
მეზობ-ელ-ი	მეზობლ-ის	of a neighbor
წ-ელ-ი	წლ-ის	of a year
საპ-ონ-ი	საპნ-ის	soap

Postposition -თვის *for* is added to nouns with the genitive case.

noun	noun + gen. -ის + -თვის	translation
მეგობარი	მეგობრ-ის-თვის	**for** a friend
ჩემი შვილი	ჩემი შვილ-ის-თვის	**for** my child
მისი და	მისი დ-ის-თვის	**for** his/her sister

- If added to a noun designating time, -თვის should be translated as either *for* or *by*.

time noun	noun + gen. -ის + -თვის	translation
კვირა	კვირ-ის-თვის	by (for) Sunday
ხვალ	ხვალ-ის-თვის	by (for) tomorrow
ორი საათი	ორი საათ-ის-თვის	by (for) two o'clock

- In order to facilitate pronunciation, sometimes (especially in spoken forms) the **euphonic** -ა is inserted before the postposition -თვის. For example: მეგობრისათვის, სამშაბათისათვის, ხვალისათვის, etc.

Personal names with -თვის *for.* Personal names that do not lose their final -ო have the same ending -ს both in the genitive and dative/accusative cases. (See Borrowed Nouns and Personal Names in Georgian, page 27.)

Nom.	Gen./Dat.	Post. -თვის (for)	Translation
თამაზ-ი	თამაზ-ი-ს	თამაზ-ი-ს-თვის	for Tamazi
ნან-ა	ნანა-ს	ნანა-ს-თვის	for Nana
ერეკლ-ე	ერეკლ-ე-ს	ერეკლ-ე-ს-თვის	for Erekle
მარ-ო	მარ-ო-ს	მარო-ს-თვის	for Maro
ნუნუ	ნუნუ-ს	ნუნუ-ს-თვის	for Nunu

Pronouns with -თვის *for.* Unlike English usage, the postposition should be used not with personal pronouns (*me, you, us,* etc.), but *with possessive pronouns* (*my, your, ours,* etc.) without the ending -ო.

Possessive Pronouns with -თვის (for)

Singular		Plural	
ჩემ-ი	ჩემ-თვის	ჩვენი	ჩვენ-თვის
my	for me	our	for us
შენ-ი	შენ-თვის	თქვენი	თქვენ-თვის
your	for you	your	for you
მის-ი	მის-თვის	მათი	მათ-თვის
his/her	for him/her	their	for them

Interrogative pronoun ვისი *whose* can also have the postposition -თვის *for* and thus becomes ვის-თვის *for whom.*

ვისთვის აკეთებ ამ ხაჭაპურს?
For whom are you making this *khachapuri?*

ვისთვის ქირაობ ამ ბინას?
For whom are you renting this apartment?

ვისთვის არის ეს ჩაი?
For whom is this tea?

II. Instrumental case

Instrumental case endings are -ით or -თი depending on the final vowel. Notice in the chart below that the final vowels -ო and -უ are not dropped before the instrumental case ending.

	-ი	-ა	-ე	-ო	-უ
nom.	ფეხ-ი	კაბ-ა	ხ-ე	მეტრ-ო	კუ
instru.	ფეხ-ით	კაბ-ით	ხ-ით	მეტრო-თი	კუ-თი
	foot	dress	tree	subway	turtle

* Nouns in the instrumental case may have a variety of grammatical functions. Most often they indicate *the instrument with which an action is performed.*

ბაზარში **ავტობუსით** მიდიხარ?
Do you go to the market **by bus**?

ამ **დანით** პურს ვჭრი.
With this knife I cut bread.

ბაზარში **ფეხით** მიდიხარ?
Are you going to the market **on foot**?

Syncope (the loss of the vowels -ა, -ე, -ო) occurs in the instrumental case in the same way as in the genitive. Like in the genitive, the qualifiers—adjectives, numerals, pronouns—that modify nouns in the instrumental case do not drop their final -ი.

Nom. Case	Syncopation Instrumental Case	Translation
წითელი ფანქ-არ-ი	წითელი ფანქრ-ით	with a red pencil
კარგი საპ-ონ-ი	კარგი საპნ-ით	with good soap
ერთი წ-ელ-ი	ერთი წლ-ით	for one year

გია შავი ფანქრით ხატავს. (ფანქ-ა-რი)
Gia paints with a black pencil.

ხელები ამ საპნით დაიბანე. (საპ-ო-ნი)
Wash your hands with this soap.

* When used in the instrumental case, nouns designating time indicate the intended duration of an action.

ლონდონში ერთი წლით მივდივარ.
I am going to London **for a year.**

ეს წიგნი ორი დღით მინდა.
I want this book **for two days.**

Remember that it is not a serious grammatical mistake to ignore syncopation rules when nouns are in the singular form. However, it is desirable to memorize gradually which nouns get syncopated. This rule is more strictly applied when these nouns are in the plural.

III. Plural forms of nouns

The plural form of nouns has the ending -ები.

noun ending	-ი	-ა	-ე	-ო	-უ
sing.	კაც-ი	ბინ-ა	ხე	გოგო	რუ
	man	apartment	tree	girl	creek
pl.	კაც-ები	ბინ-ები	ხე-ები	გოგო-ები	რუ-ები
	men	apartments	trees	girls	creeks

Nouns that have syncopation in the genitive, instrumental, and adverbial cases have the plural marker -ები added to their syncopated stems.

Singular	Plural	Translation
მეგობ-ა-რი	მეგობრ-ები	friends
წ-ე-ლი	წლ-ები	years
ფანქ-ა-რი	ფანქრ-ები	pencils
მეზობ-ე-ლი	მეზობლ-ები	neighbors

Exercises

I. Use the words given in parentheses to translate the English phrases below. Syncopating vowels are in boldface and underlined.

1. woman's dress (ქალი, კაბა)

   _____

2. a friend's letter (მეგობ**ა**რი, წერილი)

   _____

3. the key of an apartment (ბინა, გასაღები)

   _____

4. Gia's house (გია, სახლი)

   _____

5. Nunu's friend (ნუნუ, მეგობარი)

   _____

6. a neighbor's cat (მეზობ**ე**ლი, კატა)

   _____

II. Translate the words in parentheses into Georgian to complete the sentences.

A.

1. ეს (for me) _____ სულერთია.
   It does not matter to me.

2. ეს (for him/her) _____ სულერთი არ
   არის.
   This is not OK with him/her.

3. (For you) _____ შაბათი უკეთესია?
   Is Saturday better for you *(sing.)*?

4. (For us) _____ ეს მანქანა ძალიან
ძვირია.
For us this car is too expensive.

5. (For them) _____ ეს ახალი ამბავია.
This is news for them.

6. (For you) _____ წერილია.
There is a letter for you *(pl.)*.

B.
1. ეს კაბა (for Manana) _____ კარგი
იქნება.
This dress will be nice for Manana.

2. ამ ბინას (for Emily) _____ ქირაობ?
Are you renting this apartment for Emily?

3. (For tomorrow) _____ ბევრი საქმე
მაქვს.
I have a lot to do for tomorrow.

4. ეს საჩუქარი (for my sister) _____
ვიყიდე.
I bought this gift for my sister.

C.
1. (For whom) _____ აკეთებ ყავას?
For whom are you making coffee?

2. (For whom) _____ გინდა ეს წიგნი?
For whom do you want this book?

III. Put the words in parentheses in the instrumental case.

1. შენ უნივერსიტეტში (მანქანა) _____
   მიდიხარ?
   Do you go to the University by car?

2. მე ყოველთვის (შავი კალ-ა-მი) _____
   ვწერ.
   I always write with a black pen.

3. თამაზი ჩაის (შაქ-ა-რ-ი) _____ სვამს.
   Tamazi drinks tea with sugar.

4. კინოში როგორ წავიდეთ, (მეტრო) _____ თუ
   (ტაქსი)
   _____?
   How should we go to the movie (theater), by the subway or taxi?

IV. Put the nouns below into the plural. Syncopating vowels are printed in boldface and underlined.

1. ქალი   _____
2. საჩუქ**ა**რი   _____
3. მეზობ**ე**ლი   _____
4. კიბე   _____
5. საქმე   _____
6. კუ   _____
7. გოგო   _____
8. კალ**ა**მი   _____
9. სახელი   _____
10. ბაბ**ა**რ-ი   _____
11. მწერ**ა**ლი   _____
12. ბიჭი   _____

Lesson 7

გაკვეთილი მეშვიდე

At the bookstore

წიგნების მაღაზიაში

წიგნების მაღაზიაში

ქევინი:	ბოდიში, ქალბატონო, ქართულ-ინგლისური ლექსიკონი ხომ არა გაქვთ?
გამყიდველი:	**როგორ არა.** ლექსიკონები ამ თაროზეა. აი, ამაში ორივე ლექსიკონია: ინგლისურ-ქართული და ქართულ-ინგლისური.
ქევინი:	მაჩვენეთ, თუ შეიძლება. მე სწორედ ასეთი ლექსიკონი მინდა.
გამყიდველი:	კიდევ რამე ხომ არ გნებავთ?
ქევინი:	დიახ, **ქართული ხალხური სიმღერების სიდი** მინდა, თუ გაქვთ.
გამყიდველი:	რასაკვირველია. **კომპაქტდისკები** იმ თაროებზეა. ქართული ხალხური სიმღერები ბევრი გვაქვს: **"რუსთავი," "ერისიონი," "ბიჭები."** თქვენ რომელი გნებავთ?
ქევინი:	სამივეს ავიღებ. რა ღირს?
გამყიდველი:	"ერისიონი" და "რუსთავი" თითო ხუთი ლარი ღირს, "ბიჭები" სამი ლარი და ორმოცდაათი თეთრი.
ქევინი:	**პაპლეტ გონაშვილის** სიდი ხომ არა გაქვთ?
გამყიდველი:	სამწუხაროდ გაყიდულია. იცით, აქვე ახლოს კიდევ არის წიგნების მაღაზია. იქ იქითხეთ, ეგებ აქვთ.
ქევინი:	სად არის ის მაღაზია?
გამყიდველი:	აქედან ხელმარჯვნივ, ამ ქუჩის ბოლოში.
ქევინი:	დიდი მადლობა. ფული აქ უნდა გადავიხადო?
გამყიდველი:	დიახ, ოცდაცამეტი ლარი და ორმოცდაათი თეთრი.
ქევინი:	აი, ორმოცი ლარი. სამწუხაროდ ხურდა არა მაქვს.
გამყიდველი:	არა უშავს. აი, ექვსი ლარი და ორმოცდაათი თეთრი.
ქევინი:	გმადლობთ. ნახვამდის.

At the bookstore

Kevin:	Excuse me, Madam, do you have a Georgian-English dictionary?
Salesperson:	Of course. Dictionaries are on this shelf. In this one here, there are both dictionaries: English-Georgian and Georgian-English.
Kevin:	Let me have a look, please. I want exactly this kind of a dictionary.
Salesperson:	Is there anything else you would like?
Kevin:	Yes, I want some Georgian folk songs, if you have any.
Salesperson:	Of course. Compact disks are here, on these shelves. We have a variety of Georgian folk songs: *Rustavi*, *Erisioni*, *Boys*. Which one would you like?
Kevin:	I'll take all three. How much do they cost?
Salesperson:	*Erisioni* and *Rustavi* both cost five lari, *Boys* three lari and fifty tetri.
Kevin:	Do you have a CD of Hamlet Gonashvili by any chance?
Salesperson:	Unfortunately, it's sold out. There is another bookstore nearby. You could ask there, they may have (it).
Kevin:	Where is that bookstore?
Salesperson:	Just to the right from here, at the end of this street.
Kevin:	Thank you very much. Should I pay here?
Salesperson:	Yes, thirty-three lari and fifty tetri.
Kevin:	Here's forty lari. Unfortunately, I don't have (any) small change.
Salesperson:	It's OK. Here's six lari and fifty tetri.
Kevin:	Thank you. Good-bye.

Vocabulary

წიგნი	[ts'igni]	book
წიგნები *pl.*	[ts'ignebi]	
ლექსიკონი	[leksik'oni]	dictionary
ამაში (ამ+ euphonic ა+ში)	[amashi]	for this, in this one
თითო	[tito]	each
მაჩვენეთ *aor./imp.*	[machvenet]	show me
ასეთი	[aseti]	this kind, like this
კიდევ	[k'idev]	more, one more, another
რამე	[rame]	something
ხალხური *adj.*	[xalxuri]	folk
სიმღერა	[simghera]	song
სიმღერები *pl.*	[simgherebi]	
სხვადასხვა	[sxvadasxva]	variety
რომელი	[romeli]	which one
სამივე	[samive]	all three
სამივეს *dat.*	[samives]	
ავიღებ *fut.*	[avigheb]	I will take
სამწუხარო	[samts'uxaro]	unfortunate
სამწუხაროდ	[samts'uxarod]	unfortunately
გაყიდული	[gaq'iduli]	sold out
იკითხეთ *pl. & aor./imp.*	[ik'itxet]	(you) ask
ეგებ	[egeb]	may be
აქედან	[akedan]	from here
მარჯვნივ	[marjvniv]	to the right
მარცხნივ	[martsxniv]	to the left
უნდა გადავიხადო *opt.*	[unda gadavixado]	(I) should pay
ოცდაცამეტი	[otsdatsamet'i]	thirty-three
ხურდა	[xurda]	small change

Idiomatic Expressions and Culture Notes

- **როგორ არა** literally means *why not*. It could also mean *of course*, especially in response to questions with the negative particle **არ** or **არა**.

- **გნებავთ** is a polite form of *you wish*.

- **ქართული ხალხური სიმღერები** Georgian folk songs are famous for their polyphonic complex structure. Music lovers all over the world admire this unique art for its rich sound orchestration.

- **სიდი** is a phonetic transliteration of the English abbreviation for compact disc, CD. This is one of the many newly borrowed words, especially in the fields of computer technology, banking, marketing, and pop culture, that have inundated the languages of the former Soviet Union, including Georgian.

- **კომპაქტდისკები** is another newcomer to modern Georgian, the plural form of **კომპაქტდისკი** *compact disc*. **-ი** is the nominative ending.

- **რუსთავი, ერისიონი, ბიჭები** are popular singing groups whose programs consist exclusively of Georgian folk songs.

- **ჰამლეტ გონაშვილი** Hamlet Gona<u>sh</u>vili was a legendary singer of Georgian folk songs in the 1970s and 1980s.

Grammar

I. Stating *yes/no* questions with ხომ არ, ხომ არა

In Georgian, questions requiring a *yes* or *no* answer are often asked in the negative. The negative particles **არ** or **არა** in combination with the auxiliary particle **ხომ** make the question sound more polite or tentative. **ხომ არ** or **ხომ არა** are always placed right before the verb.

ხომ itself does not have any meaning, but together with არ or
არა can be translated as *by any chance*; *is it possible*; *could you*;
may I, etc.

შენ ხომ არა გაქვს ჩემი ლექსიკონი?
Do you have my dictionary (by any chance)?

ფოსტაში ხომ არ მიდიხარ?
Are you going to the post office (by any chance)?

ნუნუ ბიბლიოთეკაში ხომ არ არის?
(Can it be that) Nunu is in the library?

ხომ არ იცით, რომელი საათია?
May I ask you what time it is?

სიგარეტი ხომ არა გაქვს?
Do you have a cigarette?

II. Auxiliary particle კი

კი is another frequently used and versatile auxiliary particle that
may have a variety of meanings.

• It may function as the English *one* when it replaces a previously
used noun and its qualifiers. If კი is used, the verb that follows it
is usually omitted.

ეს სიდი ხუთი ლარი ღირს, ეს კი სამი.
This CD costs five lari, this one (costs) three.

ეს ჩემი ლექსიკონია, ის კი შენი.
This is my dictionary, that one (is) yours.

ეს გიას ტელეფონის ნომერია, ეს კი ლალის.
This is Gia's phone number; that one (is) Lali's.

• კი may contrast or oppose two statements, situations, persons, etc.
In such cases, კი may be translated as *but, and, however, while*.

გუშინ ცუდად ვიყავი, დღეს კი კარგად ვარ.
Yesterday I was not feeling well, but today I am fine.

გუშინ კარგი ამინდი იყო, დღეს კი წვიმს.
Yesterday was fine weather, but today it's raining.

ნინო კარგად ლაპარაკობს ფრანგულად, გია კი ცუდად.
Nino speaks French well, however Gia (speaks) it badly.

III. Cardinal and ordinal numbers

Cardinal numbers from one to ten were introduced in the chapter "Useful Words & Expressions." The rest of the numbers are built on these basic numbers.

Below are the numbers from 11 to 20. They are constructed according to the formula *ten (and) one more, ten (and) two more*, and so on. The word **მეტი** means *more*.

11	თერთმეტი	თ + ერთ(ი) + მეტი
12	თორმეტი	თ + ორ(ი) + მეტი
13	ცამეტი	assimilation of თ + ს = ც + მეტი
14	თოთხმეტი	თ + ოთხ + მეტი
15	თხუთმეტი	თ + ხუთ(ი) + მეტი
16	თექვსმეტი	თ + ექვს(ი) + მეტი
17	ჩვიდმეტი	assimilation of თ + შ = ჩ + მეტი
18	თვრამეტი	თ + ვრა + მეტი; here რვ has shifted to ვრ
19	ცხრამეტი	(თ) + ცხრა + მეტი
20	ოცი	

Ordinal numbers are formed by dropping the final vowel and adding the prefix მე- and the suffix -ე to cardinal numbers up to 20. The only exception is *first*: პირველი.

	Cardinal numbers		Ordinal numbers	
1	ერთი	one	პირველი	first
2	ორ-ი	two	მე-ორ-ე	second
3	სამ-ი	three	მე-სამ-ე	third
8	რვ-ა	eight	მე-რვ-ე	eighth
9	ცხრ-ა	nine	მე-ცხრ-ე	ninth
11	თერთმეტ-ი	eleven	მე-თერთმეტ-ე	eleventh
13	ცამეტი	thirteen	მე-ცამეტ-ე	thirteenth
17	ჩვიდმეტი	seventeen	მე-ჩვიდმეტ-ე	seventeenth

| 19 ცხრამეტი | nineteen | მე-ცხრამეტ-ე | nineteenth |
| 20 ოცი | twenty | მე-ოც-ე | twentieth |

Nouns after numbers are always in the singular form. Thus, we have:

Correct		***Incorrect***
ხუთი ლარი	five *lari*	*ხუთი ლარები
ათი თეთრი	10 *tetri*	*ათი თეთრები

- The verb following the *singular form of a noun* is also in the *singular*. Note in the paired sentences below that the verbs in Georgian (in boldface) are sometimes singular and sometimes plural, even though the subjects (underlined) of these verbs are all plural.

ჩემი სამი ძმა ბათუმში **ცხოვრობს**.
My three brothers **live** in Batumi.
ჩემი ძმები ბათუმში **ცხოვრობენ**.
My brothers **live** in Batumi.

ამ კურსზე ოცი სტუდენტი **სწავლობს**.
There are 20 students (**studying**) in this course.
სტუდენტები ქართულს **სწავლობენ**.
The students **study** Georgian.

დღეს ათი ტურისტი გორში **მიდის**.
Today 10 tourists **are going** to Gori.
ხვალ ტურისტები გორში **მიდიან**.
Tomorrow tourists **are going** to Gori.

ნინოს ორი მეზობელი ამერიკელია.
Nino's two neighbors **are** Americans.
ნინოს მეზობლები ამერიკელები **არიან**.
Nino's neighbors **are** Americans.

IV. Time of day

In contrast to English, which expresses the half hour with reference to the preceding hour and by using the cardinal number (e.g., 1:30

is *one thirty* or *half past one*), Georgian also uses cardinal numbers, but expresses the time as thirty minutes of the *coming* hour, i.e. *half of two* (i.e. halfway to the second hour). Notice below the difference between the English and Georgian way of telling time:

Time		Translation
2:30	სამის ნახევარი	half past two (*lit.*: half of **three**)
7:30	რვის ნახევარი	half past seven (*lit.*: half of **eight**)
11:30	თორმეტის ნახევარი	half past eleven (*lit.*: half of **twelve**)

The only exception is half past twelve when the ordinal number is used; instead of *half of one*, it is *half of the first*: პირველის ნახევარია.

V. Weights and volumes

Although in Georgian the genitive case is used much more often than in English, it is *omitted* when weight and volume are specified. Nouns following the numbers, as always, are in the singular.

In the examples below we have რძე *milk*, ჩაი *tea*, შაქარი *sugar* instead of რძის, ჩაის, შაქრის (the genitive forms of these nouns):

ერთი ბოთლი რძე	a bottle of milk
ორი ჭიქა ჩაი	two cups of tea
სამი კოვზი შაქარი	three spoons of sugar
ერთი ჭიქა ღვინო	a glass of wine
ორი ნაჭერი ნამცხვარი	two pieces of pastry

Exercises

I. Insert ხომ არ or ხომ არა in the proper place and translate the questions below into English.

1. იცი, მანანა სად არის?

_____

2. ბაზარში მიდიხართ?

_____

3. ქართული ხალხური სიმღერები გაქვთ?

4. თქვენ ბინას აქირავებთ?

5. ის კაცი შენი მეზობელი არის?

6. თინას ძმა ამ ბანკში მუშაობს?

II. Translate the following sentences into English, paying attention to the various possible meanings of კი.

1. მე ქართველი ვარ, ჩემი მეგობარი კი ამერიკელია.

2. ლალი ინგლისურად კარგად ლაპარაკობს, ფრანგულად კი არა.

3. ემილი ერთოთახიან ბინას ქირაობს, ნინო კი ოროთახიანს.

4. ეს კომპაქტდისკი ძვირია, ის კი იაფი.

III. Circle the correct form of the verbs in parentheses and translate the sentences into English.

1. ჩემი ორი მეგობარი ხვალ იტალიაში (მიდის, მიდიან).

2. თინა და ლალი ამ მაღაზიაში (მუშაობს, მუშაობენ).

3. ეს გოგონები იმ სახლში (ცხოვრობს, ცხოვრობენ).

_____

4. ეს სამი ბიჭი ძალიან კარგად (მღერის, მღერიან)
ქართულ ხალხურ სიმღერებს.

_____

5. რუსუდანის ქალიშვილი ამ სკოლაში (სწავლობს,
სწავლობენ).

_____

6. შაბათს თბილისში ხუთი ამერიკელი ექიმი (ჩამოდის,
ჩამოდიან).

_____

IV.

A. Read the numerals below and write down the corresponding cardinal numbers.
Example: სამი   3

1. ოცი   _____   5. ცხრამეტი   _____
2. ჩვიდმეტი   _____   6. ცამეტი   _____
3. თოთხმეტი   _____   7. თორმეტი   _____
4. თერთმეტი   _____   8. თექვსმეტი   _____

B. Translate into English the ordinal numbers listed below.

1. მეთორმეტე   _____   5. მეოთხე   _____
2. მეთექვსმეტე   _____   6. მეხუთ   _____
3. მეათე   _____   7. მეთხუთმეტე   _____
4. მეშვიდე   _____   8. მეთვრამეტე   _____

V. Write the following times in Georgian.

1. It is half past three.   _____

2. It is half past one.   _____

3. It is half past six.   _____

4. It is half past twelve.   _____

5. It is half past eight.   _____

6. It is half past eleven.   _____

Lesson 8

გაკვეთილი მერვე

At the bank

ბანკში

 **ბანკში**

ქევინს ანგარიში აქვს "ქართულ ბანკში."

ქევინი:	გამარჯობათ.
ოპერატორი:	გამარჯობათ. **რით შემიძლია გემსახუროთ?**
ქევინი:	მინდა ფული გავიტანო ჩემი ანგარიშიდან.
ოპერატორი:	კი, ბატონო. გაქვთ **ბანკის ბარათი და პირადობის მოწმობა?**
ქევინი:	დიახ. აი, ინებეთ.
ოპერატორი:	რამდენი გნებავთ გაიტანოთ?
ქევინი:	სამასი ლარი.
ოპერატორი:	აი, თქვენი ქვითარი. **ფულს სალაროში მიიღებთ.**

ქევინი:	გმადლობთ.
მოლარე:	**როგორ გნებავთ ფული გაიტანოთ,** ლარებში თუ დოლარებში?
ქევინი:	ლარებში.
მოლარე:	კი, ბატონო. ინებეთ.
ლალი:	ქევინ, გამარჯობა!
ქევინი:	ლალი! გამარჯობა. შენც ამ ბანკში გაქვს ანგარიში?
ლალი:	არა, ოცი ევრო მაქვს და ლარებში **მინდა გადავცვალო.**
ქევინი:	გუშინ დავრეკე თქვენთან და სახლში არ იყავი.
ლალი:	ჩვენი ტელეფონი დროებით გამორთულია. შენ არა გაქვს ჩემი **მობილურის** ნომერი?
ქევინი:	არა, არა მაქვს.
ლალი:	აი, ჩაიწერე: რვა-შვიდი-შვიდი, თერთმეტი, ოცდაორი, ორმოცი.
ქევინი:	ეხლა რას აკეთებ? თუ დრო გაქვს, მოდი, ყავა დავლიოთ.
ლალი:	სიამოვნებით.

At the bank

Kevin has an account at the Georgian Bank.

Kevin: Hello.
Bank teller: Hello. What can I do for you?
Kevin: I would like to withdraw some money.
Bank teller: Yes, sir. Do you have a bank card and an ID?

Kevin: Yes. Here you are.
Bank teller: How much do you want to withdraw?
Kevin: Three hundred *lari*.
Bank teller: Here is your receipt. You will get the money at the cashier's office.
Kevin: Thank you.
Cashier: What currency would you like, dollars or *lari*?

Kevin: *Lari*.
Cashier: Yes, sir. Here you are.
Lali: Kevin, hello!
Kevin: Lali, hello! Do you also have an account in this bank?

Lali: No, I have twenty Euros and want to change them to *lari*.
Kevin: I called your place yesterday and nobody answered.
Lali: Our telephone is temporarily disconnected. Don't you have my cell phone number?
Kevin: No, I don't.
Lali: Here, write it down: eight-seven-seven, eleven, twenty-two, forty.
Kevin: What are you doing now? If you have time, let's have coffee.
Lali: With pleasure.

Vocabulary

ბანკი	[bank'i]	bank
ანგარიში	[angari<u>sh</u>i]	account
ოპერატორი	[op'erat'ori]	bank teller
მინდა გავიტანო *opt.*	[minda gavit'ano]	I want to withdraw
ანგარიშიდან	[angari<u>sh</u>idan]	from (my) account
ბარათი	[barati]	card
მოწმობა	[mo<u>ts</u>'moba]	document
ქვითარი	[kvitari]	receipt
გნებავთ *pres. (pol. form)*	[gnebavt]	do you wish
სალარო	[salaro]	cashier's office
მიიღებთ *fut.*	[mii<u>gh</u>ebt]	you will receive
გინდათ გადაიტანოთ *opt.*	[gindat gait'anot]	you wish to withdraw
ინებეთ *(a pol. formula)*	[inebet]	here you are
ევრო	[evro]	Euro
მინდა გადავცვალო *opt.*	[minda gadav<u>ts</u>valo]	I want to exchange
დავრეკე *aor.*	[davrek'e]	I called
თქვენთან	[tkventan]	at your place
არავინ	[aravin]	nobody
პასუხობდა *imperf.*	[p'asuxobda]	was answering
დროებით	[droebit]	temporarily
გამორთული	[gamortuli]	disconnected
მობილური	[mobiluri]	cell phone
ნომერი	[nomeri]	number
ჩაიწერე *aor./imp.*	[<u>chaits</u>'ere]	write it down
ყავა	[q'ava]	coffee
დავლიოთ *opt.*	[davliot]	(let's) drink

Idiomatic Expressions and Culture Notes

- რით შემიძლია გემსახუროთ literally means: *with what (how) can I serve you?* It is a standard formula used to address a customer.

- ბანკის ბარათი is a bank card that can be used to withdraw money only from either your bank or from an ATM machine, a relative novelty in Georgia. So far, personal checks and credit cards are not available, and all purchases are therefore made in cash.

- პირადობის მოწმობა are individual personal identity cards issued to citizens of Georgia by the government. Since not everyone owns a car and, therefore, not everyone has a driver's license, these ID cards are presented whenever proof of identity is required.

- ფულს მიიღებთ სალაროში *you will get the money at the cashier's*: In Georgian banks, the teller only verifies your ID and fills out a withdrawal form; money is given out at the cashier's.

- როგორ გნებავთ ფული გაიტანოთ *how* (i.e.: *in what currency*) *do you want to take out your money?* At several major banks in Tbilisi and other cities, you can withdraw money in the currency of your choice: dollars, Euro or *lari*.

- მინდა გადავცვალო ...: *I want to exchange* ...: Money can be exchanged either in a bank or at one of many currency exchange booths that can be found in almost any supermarket or store.

- მობილური is an abbreviated form of მობილური ტელეფონი *cell phone*. They are as ubiquitous in Georgia as anywhere in the U.S.

Grammar

I. Future and imperfect (narrative past) tenses of 1st conjugation verbs

In order to form the *future tense* of 1st conjugation verbs, you should add a *preverb* (verbal prefix) to *the conjugated forms of the verb in the present tense*. There are a variety of different preverbs, and the only way to know which preverb should be used with which verb is to memorize them, as is the case in German or Russian. The person markers for the future tense are the same as in the present tense.

To form the *past* (or *imperfect*) *tense* no preverb is required; instead a different ending is added to the present-tense forms.

The following chart gives the present, future and imperfect (past) forms of a 1st conjugation verb, აკეთებ *you do, make*.

1st conjugation verb
აკეთებ (you do, make)

		Present	Future	Imperfect
Sing.				
1st	მე	ვ-აკეთ-ებ	გა-ვ-აკეთ-ებ	ვ-აკეთ-ებ-დი
2nd	შენ	აკეთ-ებ	გა-აკეთ-ებ	აკეთ-ებ-დი
3rd	ის	აკეთ-ებ-ს	გა-აკეთ-ებ-ს	აკეთ-ებ-და
Pl.				
1st	ჩვენ	ვ-აკეთ-ებ-თ	გა-ვ-აკეთ-ებ-თ	ვ-აკეთ-ებ-დი-თ
2nd	თქვენ	აკეთ-ებ-თ	გა-აკეთ-ებ-თ	აკეთ-ებ-დი-თ
3rd	ისინი	აკეთ-ებ-ენ	გა-აკეთ-ებ-ენ	აკეთ-ებ-დნენ

You can see in the chart above that the preverb for the *future* tense for აკეთებ *you do, make* is გა- and that the person markers for the present and future are the same.

The present/future stem formant (PFSF) First conjugation verbs may have different endings in the present and future tenses such as -ებ, -ობ, -ავ, -ამ, -ი. These are called the *present/future stem formant* or PFSF. The PFSF is present in all three tenses—present, future, and imperfect. If you look at the conjugation table above for აკეთებ *you do, make*, you'll see that the PFSF is -ებ and it is present in all three tenses.

Some verbs have no PFSF; for example: წერ *you write* or ჭამ *you eat*. However, their conjugation patterns and person markers follow those of the verb აკეთებ *you do, make*. Below is the present, future, and imperfect conjugations of the verb ხარჯავ *you spend* with PFSF -ავ and preverb და-. Notice the similarity of person markers in the conjugations of ხარჯავ *you spend* and აკეთებ *you do, make* (see previous chart):

1st conjugation verb
ხარჯავ (you spend)

Sing.		Present	Future	Imperfect
1st	მე	ვ-ხარჯ-ავ	და-ვ-ხარჯ-ავ	ვ-ხარჯ-ავ-დი
2nd	შენ	ხარჯ-ავ	და- ხარჯ-ავ	ხარჯ-ავ-დი
3rd	ის	ხარჯ-ავ-ს	და- ხარჯ-ავ-ს	ხარჯ-ავ-და
Pl.				
1st	ჩვენ	ვ-ხარჯ-ავ-თ	და-ვ-ხარჯ-ავ-თ	ვ-ხარჯ-ავ-დი-თ
2nd	თქვენ	ხარჯ-ავ-თ	და- ხარჯ-ავ-თ	ხარჯ-ავ-დი-თ
3rd	ისინი	ხარჯ-ავ-ენ	და- ხარჯ-ავ-ენ	ხარჯ-ავ-დნენ

Verbs with multiple preverbs. Some verbs may have *several* preverbs. Preverbs modify the meaning of verbs in a way similar to some English prepositions. Thus, the English verb *to get* has different meanings in the following examples: *to get in*; *get out*; *to get over with*.

Here are some examples of verbs with multiple preverbs:

გა-აკეთ-ებ	(you) will do, make
შე-აკეთ-ებ	(you) will repair
გადა-აკეთ-ებ	(you) will change, remake, alter something
და-დ-ებ	(you) will put (down), place something
შე-დ-ებ	(you) will put, place something into (a drawer, oven, hole, etc.)
გადა-დ-ებ	(you) will put aside, postpone
გა-იხდი	(you) will take off (coat, shoes)
მო-იხდი	(you) will take off (head gear)
გადა-იხდი	(you) will pay (bills)

As the examples above indicate, some preverbs may function in a way similar to postpositions indicating direction of the action (*put on, put in*, etc.) but *preverbs do not replace postpositions.* In the sentences below preverbs და- and მე- do not eliminate the necessity of the postpositions -ზე *on* or -ში *into, to.*

მე ფულს მაგიდაზე დავდებ და რძეს კი მაცივარში შევდებ.
I **will put** the money **on** the table and the milk **into** the refrigerator.

რუსიკო ამ მაღაზიაში ხშირად მედის.
Rusiko often **goes to** this store.

Function of the future tense. The future tense of Georgian verbs has basically the same function as the English future tense, i.e., to express action in future time. As in English, you can also express action in the *immediate future* by using verbs in the present tense.

Pres.:   ბინის ქირას როდის იხდი?
         When are you going to pay the rent?

Fut.:   ბინის ქირას როდის გადაიხდი?
         When will you pay the rent?

Pres.:   ხვალ მე სადილ არ ვაკეთებ.
         I am not going to make dinner tomorrow.

Fut.:   ხვალ მე სადილს არ გავაკეთებ.
         I will not make dinner tomorrow.

Function of the imperfect tense. The imperfect *(narrative past)* tense designates actions in the past that occurred frequently, habitually, or for certain periods of time.

ჩემი დები ამ სკოლაში სწავლობდნენ.
My sisters **studied** in this school. *(for a period of time in the past)*

მამაჩემი სათვალეს არ ატარებდა.
My father **did not wear** eyeglasses. *(a habit)*

ბინის ქირას თვის ბოლოს ვიხდიდი.
I **paid** (my) rent at the end of the month. *(an habitual action)*

- The imperfect may also convey the idea of continuous action that was not completed, stressing the process of the action rather than its result.

გუშინ მთელი დღე წერილებს **ვწერდი**.
I **was writing** letters all day yesterday.

გასულ ზაფხულს სად **ისვენებდი?**
Where **were** you **vacationing** last summer?

ისინი ამ ხიდს ერთი წელი **აშენებდნენ**.
They **were building** this bridge for a year.

II. Future and imperfect tenses of 3rd conjugation verbs

The conjugation pattern of 3rd conjugation verbs in the *imperfect* is similar to that of 1st conjugation verbs.

The *future* tense, however, is different. Instead of a preverb, all 3rd conjugation verbs will have the vowel ო- prefixed to the stem of the verb. Also, the PFSF in the future tense will change: the PFSF of these verbs (the majority of them have -ობ, and a few of them have -ი or -ებ) will be replaced with the ending -ებ.

3rd conjugation verb
ლაპარაკობ (you speak)

	Present	Future	Imperfect
Sing.			
1st	ვ-ლაპარაკ-ობ	ვ-ო-ლაპარაკ-ებ	ვ-ლაპარაკ-ობ-დი
2nd	ლაპარაკ-ობ	ო-ლაპარაკ-ებ	ლაპარაკ-ობ-დი
3rd	ლაპარაკ-ობ-ს	ო-ლაპარაკ-ებ-ს	და-ლაპარაკ-ობ-და
Pl.			
1st	ვ-ლაპარაკ-ობ-თ	ვ-ო-ლაპარაკ-ებ-თ	ვ-ლაპარაკ-ობ-დი-თ
2nd	ლაპარაკ-ობ-თ	ო-ლაპარაკ-ებ-თ	ლაპარაკ-ობ-დი-თ
3rd	ლაპარაკ-ობ-ენ	ო-ლაპარაკ-ებ-ენ	ლაპარაკ-ობ-დნენ

- Two 3rd conjugation verbs, ვ-მუშა-ობ *I work* and ვ-ქირა-ობ *I rent* have stems ending in a vowel, and therefore the consonant -ვ- is inserted before the ending -ებ in the future tense to facilitate

pronunciation. With this exception, these verbs faithfully follow
the conjugation pattern of the 3rd conjugation.

3rd conjugation verbs ending in a vowel

Present		Future	
ვ-მუშა-ობ	I work	ვ-ი-მუშა-ვ-ებ	I will work
ვ-ქირა-ობ	I rent	ვ-იქირა-ვ-ებ	I will rent

Note: You may refer to Appendix II for a more detailed explanation of conjugation patterns and their use.

III. Future and imperfect tenses for the verb *to be*

In Georgian, as in almost every language, the verb *to be* (**ხარ** *you
are*) is irregular, that is, *it has different roots in every tense*. The best
way to learn them is to memorize the forms in the three most frequently used tenses: present, past, and future.

ხარ (you are)

	Present		Imperfect (Past)		Future	
	Sing.	Pl.	Sing.	Pl.	Sing.	Pl.
1st	ვარ	ვარ-თ	ვ-იყავი	ვ-იყავი-თ	ვ-იქნები	ვ-იქნები-თ
2nd	ხარ	ხარ-თ	იყავი	იყავი-თ	იქნები	იქნები—თ
3rd	არის	არიან	იყო	იყვ-ნენ	იქნება	იქნები-ან

გუშინ სად **იყავი**?
Where **were** you yesterday?

ირაკლი და ნანა გასულ კვირას ჩვენთან **იყვნენ**.
Irakli and Nana visited us (**were** at our place) last week.

სამშაბათს ისინი აქ **იქნებიან**.
On Tuesday they **will be** here.

ამ საღამოს სად **იქნები**?
Where **will** you **be** tonight?

IV. Suffix -იანი approximates the meaning of the preposition *with*. It is added to nouns in the genitive case, but without the case ending.

მარილ-ი (salt)	მარილ-იანი (salt-with)	**მარილიანი** ყველი (cheese **with salt**)	salty cheese
შაქარ-ი (sugar)	შაქრ-იანი (sugar-with)	**შაქრიანი** ყავა (coffee **with sugar**)	coffee with sugar
კარაქ-ი (butter)	კარქ-იანი (butter-with)	**კარაქიანი** პური (bread **with butter**)	bread with butter
ქარ-ი (wind)	ქარ-იანი (wind-with)	**ქარიანი** ამინდი (weather **with wind**)	windy weather
შხამ-ი (poison)	შხამ-იანი (poison-with)	**შხამიანი** სოკო (mushroom **with poison**)	poisonous mushroom
მზ-ე (sun)	მზ-იანი (sun-with)	**მზიანი** დღე (day **with sun**)	sunny day

Exercises

I. **Fill in the blanks with verbs in the required tenses:** present, future or imperfect. Verbs in parentheses are given in the **second person singular** form of the *future* tense. Fill in the correct form for the subject of the sentence. The number indicates the conjugation group to which the verb belongs.

1. თამაზ, გუშინ რას _____
(გა-ა-კეთებ, 1st)?
Tamaz, what were you doing yesterday?

2. საქართველოში ორი წელი _____
(ი-ცხოვრებ, 3rd).
I lived in Georgia for two years.

3. ქეთინო უნივერსიტეტს როდის _____
(და-ამთავრებ, 1st).
When will Ketino graduate (finish) the university?

4. ჩვენ შუაღამემდე _____
(ი-მუშავებ, 3rd).
We were working till midnight.

5. ადრე რუსიკო ხორცს _____, ეხლა კი არ
_____ (შე-ჭამ, 1st).
In the past, Rusiko ate meat, but now she does not eat (it).

6. თამრიკო დღეს პირველ საათზე _____
(და-რეკავ, 1st).
Tamriko will call at one o'clock today.

7. გურამი და გია ეზოში ფეხბურთს
_____ (ი-თამაშებ, 3rd).
Gurami and Gia are playing football in the yard.

8. ლია და ზაზა კარგად _____
ინგლისურად (ი-ლაპარაკებ, 3rd).
Lia and Zaza speak English well.

9. მანანასთან როდის _____
(და-რეკავ, 1st)?
When will you call Manana?

10. ისინი დილის შვიდ საათზე _____
(ი-საუზმებ, 3rd).
They have breakfast at seven in the morning.

11. ემილისთან ი-მეილს როდის _____
(გა-გზავნი, 1st)?
When will you send an e-mail to Emily?

12. ირაკლი ამ სიტყვებს ხშირად _____
(გა-იმეორებ, 1st).
Irakli often repeated these words.

II. The verbs below are given in the second person singular form. Conjugate them in the future and imperfect tenses referring to the chart given in the Grammar section of this lesson. The preverbs (in boldface) of the 1st conjugation verbs are in parentheses.

The 1st conjugation	Future	Imperfect
(**და**)-ამთავრ-ებ (you finish, graduate)	_____	_____
(**და**)-კარგ-ავ (you lose)	_____	_____
(**გა**)-გზავნ-ი (you close)	_____	_____
(**შე**)-ჭამ (you eat)	_____	_____

The 3rd conjugation

	Future	Imperfect
სადილ-ობ (you dine)	_____	_____
ხუმრ-ობ (you joke)	_____	_____
ფიქრ-ობ (you think)	_____	_____
თამაშ-ობ (you play)	_____	_____

III. Fill in the blanks with appropriate forms of the verb *to be*.

1. ჩვენ თქვენთან რვის ნახევარზე _____ .
   We'll be at your place at half past seven.

2. შენ ხვალ დილით სად _____ სახლში თუ
   სკოლაში?
   Where will you be tomorrow morning, at home or in school?

3. გუშინ ჩვენ კინოში _____ და
   საინტერესო ფილმი ვნახეთ.
   Yesterday we were at the movie and saw an interesting film.

4. გუშინ რა დღე _____ პარასკევი თუ
   შაბათი?
   What day was yesterday, Friday or Saturday?

5. მომავალ კვირას ქეთინო უკვე თბილისში
   _____ .
   Next week Ketino will be already in Tbilisi.

6. თქვენ უკვე _____ ექიმთან?
Have you seen the doctor already? (*lit.*: Have you been at the doctor's?)

7. ათ საათამდე სახლში _____ , მერე
ბანკში მივდივარ.
I'll be at home till ten, after that I"ll go to the bank.

8. გუშინ პარასკევი _____ , დღეს შაბათია.
Yesterday was Friday, today is Saturday.

IV. Add the suffix -იანი to the words in parentheses and put them in the blanks.

1. წელს როგორი _____ ზაფხულია!
(წვიმა, rain)
What a rainy summer (we have) this year!

2. ეს თინიკოს _____ წიგნია.
(სურათები, pictures)
This is Tiniko's picture book.

3. გუშინ _____ ამინდი იყო.
(ქარი, wind)
It was a windy day yesterday.

4. შენ არ გიყვარს _____ ჩაი?
(ლიმონი, lemon)
Don't you like tea with lemon?

5. ეს სუპი ძალიან _____ არის.
(მარილი, salt)
This soup is very salty.

6. რა ლამაზი _____ ღამეა!
(მთვარე, moon)
What a beautiful moonlit night!

Lesson 9

გაკვეთილი მეცხრე

In the cafeteria

კაფეტერია

კაფეტერია

ქევინი და ლალი კაფეტერიაში არიან.

ქევინი: მე მშია. შენ არ გშია? მოდი ვჭამოთ. უკვე ორის
           ნახევარია.
ლალი: მეც მშია. ხაჭაპური და ყავა ავიღოთ.
ქევინი: ხაჭაპურს და სალათს მეც ავიღებ. სუპი არ გინდა?

ლალი: არა, სუპი არ მინდა.
კევინი: ყავასთან ნამცხვარი?
ლალი: მინდა, მაგრამ დიეტაზე ვარ.
ქევინი: შენ? დიეტაზე? შენ დიეტა არ გჭირდება.
ლალი: შენ ასე ფიქრობ?
ქევინი: დარწმუნებული ვარ.
ლალი: კარგი, ერთ ნაჭერ ნამცხვარსაც ავიღებ. ავიღოთ
           ერთი ბოთლი ცივი ჩაი?
ქევინი: უსათუოდ. ეს ცივი ჩაი ლიმონათზე უკეთესია.
მოლარე: ეს ორი ერთად?
ქევინი: დიახ, ერთად. რამდენია?
მოლარე: თორმეტი ლარი და სამოცდაათი თეთრი.
ქევინი: ლალი, აი, ფანჯარასთან თავისუფალი მაგიდაა.
ლალი: რა გემრიელი ხაჭაპურია!
ქევინი: ყავა როგორია?
ლალი: ყველაფერი ძალიან გემრიელია. დიდი მადლობა,
           ქევინ. სხვათა შორის, მომავალ კვირას თამაშის
           დაბადების დღეა. შენ და ემილის გახსოვთ, არა?
ქევინი: რასაკვირველია, გვახსოვს, უსათუოდ მოვალთ.

In the cafeteria

Kevin and Lali are in a cafeteria.

Kevin: I am hungry. Aren't you hungry? Let's eat. It's already half past one.

Lali: I am hungry too. Let's have *khachapuri* and coffee.

Kevin: I'll also have (take) *khachapuri* and salad. Don't you want soup?

Lali: No, I don't.

Kevin: (How about) a cake with (your) coffee?

Lali: I'd love to, but I'm on a diet.

Kevin: You? On a diet? You don't need a diet.

Lali: You think so?

Kevin: I am sure (of it).

Lali: OK, I'll have a piece of cake too. Shall we have a bottle of iced tea?

Kevin: By all means. This iced tea is better than lemonade.

Cashier: These two together?

Kevin: Yes, together. How much is it?

Cashier: Twelve lari and seventy tetri.

Kevin: Lali, over there, there's a free table at the window.

Lali: What delicious *khachapuri*!

Kevin: How's the coffee?

Lali: Everything is delicious. Thank you, Kevin. By the way, next Sunday is Tamazi's birthday. You and Emily remember (that), don't you?

Kevin: Of course, we remember. We'll be sure to come over.

Vocabulary

Georgian	Transcription	Meaning
კაფეტერია	[k'apet'eria]	cafeteria
მშია *pres.*	[mshia]	I am hungry
(მოდი) ვჭამოთ *opt.*	[modi vch'amot]	let's eat
სალათი	[salati]	salad
ავიღებ *fut.*	[avigheb]	I will take (*in the sense of* have, order)
სუპი	[sup'i]	soup
ნამცხვარი	[namtsxvari]	pastry
დიეტა	[diet'a]	diet
გჭირდება *pres.*	[gch'irdeba]	(you) need
ასე	[ase]	so, this way, this manner
ფიქრობ *pres.*	[pikrob]	(you) think
დარწმუნებული	[darts'munebuli]	sure, convinced
ნაჭერი	[nach'eri]	piece
ბოთლი	[botli]	bottle
ცივი	[tsivi]	cold
ლიმონათი	[limonati]	lemonade
ფანჯარასთან	[panjarastan]	near window, at the window
თავისუფალი	[tavisupali]	free, vacant, unoccupied
მაგიდა	[magida]	table
ყველაფერი	[q'velaperi]	everything
მომავალ კვირას	[momaval k'viras]	next week
დაბადების დღე	[dabadebis dghe]	birthday
გახსოვს *pres.*	[gaxsovs]	(you) remember

 ## Idiomatic Expressions and Culture Notes

- კაფეტერია is a type of self-service eatery that is gradually gaining popularity, especially among the young, while older people frequent traditional restaurants. No wine is served in cafeterias.

- გასულ კვირას may mean *last week* or *last Sunday*. The exact meaning is usually indicated by the context. Similarly, მომავალ კვირას could be *next week* or *next Sunday*.

- ცივი ჩაი literally, *cold tea*, is a Georgian variety of iced tea. It is produced and sold in bottles like lemonade. You can find delicious cold tea of various flavors in any food store.

- სხვათა შორის means *by the way*.

- დაბადების დღე *birthday*: Surprise birthday parties are unfamiliar to Georgians. Usually the person celebrating his or her birthday invites his/her friends and relatives. The guests are expected to bring small gifts: flowers, a book, a bottle of wine, a little trinket of some kind. Not to bring anything is a forgivable sin.

Grammar

I. Negative particles არ and ვერ

There are two types of negation in Georgian: არ and ვერ.

არ is used in two cases:
- First of all, it is used in **simple statements** referring to things not done habitually or commonly: *Gia does not work at this bank* or *Alice does not live here any more.* არ is also used to express an obvious or well known fact. For example: *Lions do not live in the North Pole* and *Sea water is not drinkable* would mean, simply, that this is "the way things are."

- Secondly, არ is used when a statement refers to **an intentional decision** not to do something. The sentence *Today I am not going to the office* would imply that I have decided not to go to the office today (I have other urgent things to attend to; I am meeting someone at the airport, etc.).

ვერ always means that some **external factor** prevents the subject from doing something. It does not refer to a deliberate refusal to do something. Using **ვერ** in the statement *I am not going (= cannot go) to the office today* implies there is an *obstacle* preventing me from going there (I am not well; my car broke down, etc.).

A.

მე ქართულად **არ** ვლაპარაკობ.   I don't speak Georgian.
(A simple statement that I don't know the language, I've never studied it.)

მე ქართულად **ვერ** ვლაპარაკობ.   I cannot speak Georgian.
*(***ვერ*** implies I may know a little Georgian, but not well enough to speak.* My poor knowledge is an external factor preventing me from speaking.*)*

B.

დღეს სადილს **არ** ვაკეთებ.   I am not making dinner today.
(I could make it if I wanted to, but I don't intend to because I've been invited out to a restaurant.)

დღეს სადილს **ვერ** ვაკეთებ.   I can't make dinner today.
(There is an external obstacle—I don't have the time, or the ingredients—rendering me incapable of doing the task.)

II. 4th conjugation verbs

About three dozen Georgian verbs have a conjugation pattern that identifies them as verbs of the 4th conjugation (see Appendix II and III). The majority of them denote feelings, sensations, or states of mind:

მინდა I want	**მიყვარს** I love
მშია I am hungry	**მახსოვს** I remember
მიხარია I am glad	**შემიძლია** I can

The person markers of this conjugation differ from those of all other groups, the 1st, 2nd or 3rd conjugations. Therefore, we will use the **1st person singular present** as a base form for these verbs.

There are basically two conjugation patterns of 4th conjugation verbs. They are illustrated by the two charts below, the first one for the verbs **მაქვს** *I have* (referring to something *inanimate*) and **მყავს**

I have (referring to something *animate*); and the second for the verbs
მინდა *I want* and მიხარია *I am glad.*

4th conjugation verbs

				მყავს (I have *s.th. animate*)	
	მაქვს (I have *s.th.* inanimate)				
	Sing.	**Pl.**		**Sing.**	**Pl.**
1st	მე	მ-აქვს	ჩვენ	გვ-აქვს	მ-ყავს	გვ-ყავს
2nd	შენ	გ-აქვს	თქვენ	გ-აქვ-თ	გ-ყავს	გ-ყავ-თ
3rd	მას	ა-ქვს	მათ	აქვ-თ	*(მ-)ყავს	*(მ-)ყავ-თ

*The 3rd person marker მ- is in parentheses because it is routinely dropped in the spoken language.

4th conjugation verbs

	მინდა (I want)			მიხარია (I'm glad)	
	Sing.	**Pl.**		**Sing.**	**Pl.**
1st	მე	მი-ნდა	ჩვენ	გვი-ნდა	მი-ხარია	გვი-ხარია
2nd	შენ	გი-ნდა	თქვენ	გი-ნდა-თ	გი-ხარია	გი-ხარია-თ
3rd	მას	უ-ნდა	მათ	უ-ნდა-თ	უ-ხარია	უ-ხარია-თ

Notice that in both of these charts **the 3rd person pronouns (*he/ she* and *they*) are not in the nominative case but in the dative**; instead of ის there is **მას** and instead of ისინი we have **მათ**. This "anomaly" is the distinguishing feature of all the 4th conjugation verbs.

Therefore, as the examples below clarify, the subject-object relation of these verbs differs from that of all other conjugations; *the subject* (noun, pronoun, or personal name) *is always in the dative*, while the *direct object* (noun, pronoun or personal name) *is in the nominative case*. However, in practical terms, this rule is relevant only when *the subject is in the third person, both in singular and plural forms*. First and second person pronouns მე, შენ, ჩვენ, and თქვენ have the same form both in the nominative and dative case and therefore, they do not change.

Pay attention to the case of the subjects and objects in the sentences below:

კევინს *(subj./dat.)* უნდა შენი ტელეფონის ნომერი *(dir. obj./nom.)*
Kevin wants your telephone **number.**

ჩემს მეგობრებს *(subj.dat.)* არა აქვთ **შენი მისამართი** *(dir. obj./nom.).*
My friends do not have **your address**.

ამ კაცს *(subj./nom.)* **სამი ვაჟი** *(dir. obj./nom.)* (ჰ)ყავს.
This man has **three sons**.

მათ *(subj./dat.)* **სამოთახიანი ბინა** *(dir. obj./nom.)* აქვთ.
They have a **three-room apartment**.

ნუნუს და ქეთინოს *(subj./dat.)* კარგად ახსოვთ ეს ამბავი *(dir. obj./nom.).*
Nunu and **Ketino** remember **this event** well.

III. Verbs მაქვს *to have (s.th. inanimate)* and მყავს *to have (s.th. animate)*

The Georgian equivalents for the verb *to have* are strictly differentiated: **მაქვს** refers to having something *inanimate* and **მყავს** to something *animate*. Since these verbs are monosyllabic in the present tense, in negative sentences არა (not არ) should be used with these verbs.

თამაზის ხვალ დაბადების დღე აქვს.
Tamazi has his birthday tomorrow.

შენ გაქვს ჩემი ლექსიკონი?
Do you have my dictionary?

გიას ცოლი არა (ჰ)ყავს.
Gia does not have a wife. *(he is not married)*

თამრიკოს ორი კატა (ჰ)ყავს.
Tamriko has two cats.

ჩვენ დღეს დრო არა გვაქვს.
We don't have time today.

მე ბევრი მეგობარი მყავს.
I have many friends.

*When one is referring to a car (*a steel horse*), however, მყავს should be used.

გურამს ახალი მანქანა (ჰ)ყავს.
Guram has a new car.

შენ რა მანქანა გყავს, ფორდი თუ ტოიოტა?
What (kind of) car do you have, a Ford or a Toyota?

Exercises

I. **Fill in the blanks with negative particles არ(ა) or ვერ.**

1. ჩემი მეგობარი _____ ლაპარაკობს
   ფრანგულად.
   My friend does not speak French.

2. თინა გერმანულს სწავლობდა, მაგრამ კარგად _____
   ლაპარაკობს.
   Tina studied German but she does not speak it well.

3. წელს მე ამერიკაში _____ მივდივარ, ფული
   არა მაქვს.
   This year, I can't go to America, I don't have money.

4. ემილის ქართულ-ინგლისური ლექსიკონი _____
   აქვს.
   Emily does not have a Georgian-English dictionary.

5. თამაზის _____ ყავს ძმა, მაგრამ ყავს ერთი და.
   Tamazi does not have a brother but has a sister.

6. დღეს მე _____ ვარ კარგად და თქვენთან
   _____ მოვალ.
   I am not feeling well today and won't be able to come to
   your place.

II. Conjugate in the present tense orally or in writing the following two groups of 4th conjugation verbs: the first (A) follows the conjugation pattern of **მაქვს**; the second (B) follows the conjugation pattern of **მინდა**.

A.
მშია (I am hungry) _____

მახსოვს (I remember) _____

მჭირდება (I need) _____

B.
მიყვარს (I love, like) _____

მირჩევნია (I prefer) _____

III. Fill in the blanks with the words (nouns, pronouns, and personal names) given in parentheses in correct cases (nominative or dative).

1. (ლამარა) _____ უყვარს (ტკბილი ჩაი) _____.
   Lamara likes sweet tea.

2. (შენ) _____ (როგორი პური) _____ გინდა?
   What kind of bread do you want?

3. (ის) _____ უნდა (ოროთახიანი ბინა) _____.
   He wants a two-room apartment.

4. (ისინი) _____ ახსოვთ (ჩვენი მისამართი) _____?
   Do they remember our address?

5. (მე) _____ (ოცი დოლარი)
_____ მჭირდება.
I need twenty dollars.

6. (თქვენ) _____ გიყვართ (ოპერა)
_____?
Do you like opera?

IV. Fill in the blanks with correct forms of the verb *to have*.
Remember that this verb has two different forms whether
referring to something animate or inanimate.

1. რუსიკოს ახალი ტელევიზორი _____.
Rusiko has a new TV.

2. მე _____ ორი და და ერთი ძმა.
I have two sisters and a brother.

3. ჩვენ ძველი თეთრი მაზდა _____.
We have an old white Mazda.

4. მზიას ბევრი მეგობარი _____.
Mzia has many friends.

5. თქვენ დღეს დრო _____?
Do you *(pl.)* have time today?

6. მათ სამოთახიანი ბინა _____.
They have a three-room apartment.

Lesson 10

გაკვეთილი მეათე

Transportation

ტრანსპორტი

ტრანსპორტი

ქევინი და ლალი კაფეტერიიდან ქუჩაში გამოდიან.

ლალი: ნახვამდის, ქევინ, კარგად იყავი.

ქევინი: **ერთი წუთით**, ლალი. ხომ არ იცი, აქ ახლოს არის აფთიაქი?

ლალი: კი, არის. ფეხით ათ-თხუთმეტ წუთში მიხვალ.

ქევინ: **გითხრა მართალი**, მეჩქარება. ეგებ ტაქსი გავაჩერო?

ლალი: ტაქსი რად გინდა?! აქედან ავტობუსიც მიდის, და მეტროც.

ქევინი: მარშრუტკა არ მიდის?

ლალი: მიდის, მაგრამ ავტობუსით ან მეტროთი ჯობია. **მარშრუტკით მგზავრობა** 40 ან 50 თეთრი ღირს, ავტობუსით კი მხოლოდ ოცი.

ქევინი: სხვათა შორის, მე ყოველთვის მარშრუტკით. ვმგზავრობ. საჭიროა ავტობუსში ბილეთი ან ჟეტონი ვიყიდო?

ლალი: არა, ჟეტონი მხოლოდ მეტროშია საჭირო. ფული მძღოლს მიეცი.

ქევინი: როგორც მარშრუტკაში?

ლალი: ხო, როგორც მარშრუტკაში. **ხურდა** გაქვს?

ქევინი: არა, არა მაქვს. უსათუოდ საჭიროა?

ლალი: არა უშავს; ლარი მიეცი და მძღოლი ხურდას დაგიბრუნებს.

ქევინი: ავტობუსის გაჩერება სად არის?

ლალი: აი, იქ, გაზეთების ჯიხურთან. ჩაჯექი ოც ან ორმოცდაათ ნომერ ავტობუსში და მესამე გაჩერებაზე ჩამოდი.

ქევინი: გასაგებია. ეხლა სად მიდიხარ?

ლალი: **ინტერნეტ კლუბში**. ერთ მეგობარს **იმეილი** მინდა გავუგზავნო.

ქევინი: აჰა, **კარგად**, ლალი, ნახვამდის.

Transportation

Kevin and Lali come out of the cafeteria.

Lali: Good-bye, Kevin, take care.

Kevin: Just a minute, Lali. Do you know if there is a drugstore near here?

Lali: Yes, there is. On foot you'll get there in ten or fifteen minutes.

Kevin: To tell the truth, I'm in a hurry. Maybe I should take a taxi?

Lali: Why do you need a taxi?! From here, buses and the subway both go (that way).

Kevin: Doesn't the *marshrutka* go there?

Lali: It does, but a bus or subway is better. A ride in a *marshrutka* costs forty or fifty *tetri*, while on a bus (it's) only twenty.

Kevin: By the way, I always take the *marshrutka.* Is it necessary to buy a ticket or a token on the bus?

Lali: No, a token is required only in the subway. Give the money to the driver.

Kevin: As in a *marshrutka*?

Lali: Yes, as in a *marshrutka.* Do you have small change?

Kevin: No, I don't. Is it absolutely necessary?

Lali: It's OK, pay with lari, and the driver will give back the change.

Kevin: Where is the bus stop?

Lali: Over there, by the newspaper stand. Get on bus number twenty or fifty, and get off at the second stop.

Kevin: I see. Where are you going now?

Lali: To an Internet Club. I want to send an e-mail to a friend.

Kevin: Well, take care, Lali, good-bye.

Vocabulary

გამოდიან	[gamodian]	(they) come out, are coming out
აფთიაქი	[aptiaki]	drugstore
ფეხით *instru.*	[pexit]	on foot
ფეხი *nom.*	[pexi]	foot
მიხვალ *fut.*	[mixval]	(you) will get to
მეჩქარება *pres.*	[mechkareba]	I am in a hurry
გავაჩერო *opt.*	[gavachero]	(I) should stop, flag down, hail (a taxi)
რად	[rad]	what for
წასვლა *verbal n.*	[ts'asvla]	going
ჯობია	[jobia]	it's better
მგზავრობა	[mgzavroba]	travel, traveling
ყოველთვის	[q'oveltvis]	always
ვმგზავრობ *pres.*	[vmgzavrob]	I travel
საჭირო	[sach'iro]	necessary, required
ბილეთი	[bileti]	ticket
ჟეტონი	[zhet'oni]	token
მძღოლი	[mdzgholi]	driver
მიეცი *aor./imp.*	[mietsi]	(you) give
როგორც	[rogorts]	just like, similar to
დაგიბრუნებს *fut.*	[dagibrunebs]	(s/he) will return (something)
გაჩერება	[gachereba]	stop, stopping (*here:* bus stop)
გაზეთი	[gazeti]	newspaper
ჯიხური	[jixuri]	booth, stand
ჩაჯექი *aor./imp.*	[chajeki]	(you) get on
მესამე	[mesame]	third
ჩამოდი *aor./imp.*	[chamodi]	(you) get off
ინტერნეტკლუბი	[int'ernet'k'lubi]	Internet club
იმეილი	[imeili]	e-mail
გავუგზავნო *opt.*	[gavugzavno]	(should) send (him/her/them)

Idiomatic Expressions and Culture Notes

- გრანსპორგი *transportation*. In Tbilisi, the most accessible and cheapest forms of transportation are the subway and the bus. Season tickets have not yet been introduced in Georgia, and it is advisable to keep small change or one *lari* bill handy, especially if you are in a hurry to get off the bus.

- ერთი წუთით means *just a minute*.

- გითხრა მართალი means *to tell you the truth*.

- მარშრუგკით მგზავრობა literally means *travel by marshrutka*, but it can be understood as *marshrutka fare*; ავგობუსით მგზავ-რობა means *bus fare*, etc.

- ხურდა means *change (money)* or *small change (coins)*.

- ინგერნეგ კლუბი *Internet clubs* have mushroomed throughout the former Soviet republics to accommodate those who do not have personal computers. They provide access to the Internet, computer games, and sometimes classes for their customers. In some of these clubs one can have coffee, tea, and pastry.

- იმეილი *e-mail* is one of many English words referring to computer technology that have "invaded" languages all over the world.

- კარგად is the abbreviation of კარგად იყავი *be well, take care*.

Grammar

I. Interrogative and relative pronouns

In Georgian there are two sets of pronouns: interrogative and relative. The former are used in questions *(interrogative sentences)*, and the latter in regular narrative sentences. Often but <u>not always</u>, relative pronouns can be translated into English as *whatever, whoever, whenever*, etc.

interrogative pronouns		relative pronouns	
რა	what ... ?	რაც	what/whatever
როდის	when ... ?	*როდესაც/	when/
		როცა	whenever
სად	where ... ?	სადაც	where/
			wherever
როგორ	how ... ?	როგორც	whatever way/
			as far as
ვინ	who ... ?	ვინც	whoever
რამდენი	how many/	რამდენიც	as many as,
	much ... ?		as much as

*The pronoun **როდესაც** *when, whenever* has a shorter form—**როცა**—that is frequently used in spoken forms.

A.
რა *(interrogative)* ავიღოთ?
What shall we have?
რაც *(relative)* შენ გინდა.
Whatever you like.

B.
როდის *(int.)* მიდიხარ სამსახურში?
When do you go to work (to your office)?

როდესაც *(rel.)* შენ დარეკე, მე უკვე სახლიდან გავდიოდი.
When you called, I was already leaving home.

როდის *(int.)* მიდიხარ ლონდონში?
When are you going to London?

როცა *(rel.)* დისერტაციას დავამთავრებ.
Whenever/When I finish my dissertation.

C.
სად ცხოვრობ?
Where do you live?
სადაც შარშან ვცხოვრობდი.
Where I lived last year.

სადაც *(rel.)* შენ მუშაობ, იქ ახლოს დიდი უნივერმაგია.
Where you work, there is a big department store nearby.

D.

როგორ *(int.)* წავიდეთ ნინოსთან, ფეხით თუ ავტობუსით?

How shall we go to Nino, on foot (shall we walk) or by bus?

როგორც *(rel.)* გინდა.

As you wish (**whatever way, however** you wish).

როგორც ვიცი, მერი ახლა საქართველოშია.

As far as I know, Mary is in Georgia now.

E.

ვინ *(int.)* არის ის კაცი?

Who is that man?

ვინც *(rel.)* დღეს აქ არ არის, ამ გაკვეთილს ვერ ისწავლის.

Whoever is not here today *(he/she)* won't be able to learn this lesson.

F.

რამდენი წლის ხარ?

How old (of **how many** years) are you?

ოცი წლის.

Twenty (of twenty years).

წითელი ფანქარი გაქვს?

Do you have a red pencil?

რამდენიც გინდა.

As many as you want.

II. Genitive case postpositions -დან *from (s.th.)* and -გან *from (s.o.)*

- **-დან** corresponds to the English preposition *from*. It is added to nouns in the genitive case (with the nouns losing the final **-ს** of the genitive case ending).

Nom.	Gen.	-დან (from)	Translation
ბანკი	ბანკ-ის	ბანკ-ი-დან	**from** the bank
სახლი	სახლ-ის	სახლ-ი-დან	**from** home
ფანჯარა	ფანჯრ-ის	ფანჯრ-ი-დან	**from** the window
კიბე	კიბ-ის	კიბ-ი-დან	**from** the stairs

ლალი ბანკიდან სახლში მიდის.
Lali is going home from the bank.

შენ სახლიდან რეკავ?
Are you calling from home?

არა, ბიბლიოთეკიდან.
No, from the library.

ამ ფანჯრიდან ლამაზი ხედია.
There is a beautiful view from this window.

- **-გან6** also means *from*, but in reference only to *persons*. It is added to nouns in the genitive case without the nouns dropping the final **-ს** of the genitive case ending.

Nom.	Gen.	-გან6 (from s.o.)	Translation
კაცი	კაც-ის	კაც-ის-გან6	**from** (the) man
და	დ-ის	დის-გან6	**from** (his) sister
მეგობარი	მეგობრ-ის	მეგობრ-ის-გან6	**from** (his) friend
მარინა	მარინა-ს	მარინა-ს-გან6	**from** Marina

ეს საჩუქარი ჩემი მეგობრისგან6 არის.
This gift is from my friend.

კევინმა დისგან6 წერილი მიიღო.
Kevin received a letter from (his) sister.

ემილი რუსიკოსგან6 ბინას ქირაობს.
Emily is renting an apartment from Rusiko.

- **Postposition -გან6** can be added to possessive pronouns (*my, your, ours,* etc.) with their nominative ending **-ი** dropped.

Possessive Pronouns with -გან6 (from, one of)
Singular

ჩემ-ი	my	ჩემ-გან6	from me
შენ-ი	your	შენ-გან6	from you
მის-ი	his/her	მის-გან6	from him/her

Plural

ჩვენ-ი	our	ჩვენ-გან	from us
თქვენ-ი	your	თქვენ-გან	from you
მათ-ი	their	მათ-გან	from them

აი, ეს საჩუქარი **ჩვენგან** არის.
This gift, here, is from us.

მისგან წერილები ხშირად მოდის.
Letters come from him often.

შენგან ამას არ ველოდი.
I didn't expect this from you.

III. Dative/accusative case postposition -თან *with (s.o.), near (a place), at (s.o.'s place)* with nouns and pronouns

In Lesson 3 the postposition -თან was used with personal names. It is added to nouns in the same way.

The case ending -ს of the dative/accusative case is dropped only if the noun in the nominative case ends with -ი. Nouns ending with vowels -ა, -ე, or -უ will maintain the -ს ending followed by the postposition -თან.

Nom.	Dat./Acc.	-თან (with)	Translation
სტუდენტ-ი	სტუდენტ-ს	სტუდენტ-თან	with a student
სკოლა	სკოლა-ს	სკოლა-ს-თან	near (a) school
კიბე	კიბე-ს	კიბე-ს-თან	near (at) the stairs
რუ	რუ-ს	რუ-ს-თან	near a creek

- When added to pronouns, -თან can be translated as *at my place, at my apartment, at my house, where I live.*

ჩემ-თან	**at** (to) my place	ჩვენ-თან	**at** (to) our place
შენ-თან	**at** (to) your place	თქვენ-თან	**at** (to) your place
მას-თან	**at** (to) his/her place	მათ-თან	**at** (to) their place

A.

ჩვენთან როდის მოდიხარ?
When are you coming to see us (to our place)?

თქვენთან შაბათს მოვდივარ.
I'll come over to see you (to your place) on Saturday.

B.

ნათელა შენთან არის?
Is Natela with you (at your place)?

არა, თინასთან არის.
No, she is with Tina (at her place).

C.

შენთან დავრეკე, მაგრამ სახლში არ იყავი.
I called you (at your place, apartment, etc.), but you weren't at home.

IV. Interrogative pronoun ვისი (*whose*) can also have the
postpositions **-გან** *from* and **-თან** *to*. They are added to its
stem **ვის-** with the final **-ი** dropped.

ვის-გან from whom   ვის-თან to whom, to whose place

ვისთან used with the word **ერთად** *together* in the phrase **ვისთან
ერთად** means *together with whom*.

ეს წერილი **ვისგან** არის?
From whom is the letter?

ვისთან რეკავ?
To whom *(lit.: to whose place)* are you calling?

ვისთან ერთად მიდიხარ თეატრში?
(Together) with whom are you going to the theater?

Exercises

I. Fill in the blanks with appropriate interrogative pronouns (რა, როგორ, სად, ვინ როდის, როგორი, რამდენი) or relative pronouns (რაც, როგორც, სადაც, ვინც, როცა, როგორიც).

1. დღეს _____ პური ვიყიდოთ, თონის პური თუ ჩვეულებრივი?
   Which bread should we buy, oven-baked bread or a regular one today?

2. ყველაფერი, _____ ქეთინომ თქვა, მართალია.
   Everything that (whatever) Ketino said is true.

3. _____ ჩიკაგოდან დავბრუნდები, დაგირეკავ შენთან.
   When I return from Chicago, I will call you.

4. იტალიაში _____ მიდიხარ?
   When are you leaving for Italy?

5. იქ, _____ ჩვენი სახლი იყო, ეხლა ახალი მაღაზიაა.
   There, where our house stood, now there is a new store.

6. ხომ არ იცი, _____ არის ჩემი სათვალე?
   Do you know by any chance where my eyeglasses are?

7. _____ ცხოვრობს ამ ბინაში?
   Who lives in this apartment?

8. _____ ვიცი, ირაკლი ეხლა ამერიკაშია.
   As (far as) I know, Irakli is in America now.

II. Add -დან or -გან to the words (nouns, personal names, and pronouns) in parentheses and put them in the blanks.

1. მე (სახლი) _____ გავდივარ დილის
   რვა საათზე.
   I leave (go out of) the house at 8 o'clock in the morning.

2. (ზურაბი) _____ მოდიხარ?
   Are you coming from Zurabi?

3. მამაშენი როდის ჩამოდის (ჩიკაგო)
   _____?
   When is your Dad coming back from Chicago?

4. ეხლა მე ჩემი (მეგობარი) _____
   ვრეკავ.
   Right now, I am calling from my friend's place.

5. ეს წიგნი (ვისი) _____ არის?
   From whom is this book?

6. ეს საჩუქარი (მათი) _____ არის.
   This gift is from them.

III. Add postposition -თან to the personal names and pronouns in parentheses and put them in the blanks.

1. გუშინ ჩვენ (მანანა) _____ვიყავით.
   Yesterday we were at Manana's place.

2. ერთი საათის წინ ეთერი (at my place)
   _____ იყო.
   An hour ago, Eteri was at my place.

3. ჩვენი სახლი (ბაზარი) _____ ახლოა.
   Our house is close to (near) the market.

4. (To us, to our place) _____ რატომ არ
რეკავ?
Why don't you call us?

5. მე მინდა (მეგობრები) _____
ვილაპარაკო ამ თემაზე.
I want to speak with (my) friends on this topic.

6. დღეს მერაბი (ექიმი) _____მიდის.
Today Merabi is going to (see) a doctor *(to the doctor's place)*.

IV. Add the postposition -გან or -თან to the pronoun ვისი.

1. (With whom) _____ ლაპარაკობ?
With whom are you speaking?

2. (From whom) _____ მოდიხარ, თინასგან?
From whom are you coming, from Tina?

3. (With whom) _____ ერთად მუშაობ ამ
პროექტზე?
Together with whom are you working on this project?

Lesson 11

გაკვეთილი მეთერთმეტე

Khachapuri

ხაჭაპური

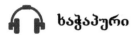 **ხაჭაპური**

ემილი ლალისთან არის და ხაჭაპურის გაკეთებას სწავლობს.

ლალი: ყველაფერი მზად არის. მოდი დავიწყოთ. აიღებ
         ერთ ჭიქა **ბორჴომს** ან სხვა მინერალურ წყალს.
         დაუმატებ ცოტ-ცოტა ფქვილს და კარგად მოზელავ.

ემილი: ფქვილი რამდენი უნდა?

ლალი: დაახლოვებით სამი ჭიქა ან ცოტა მეტი. ცომი
         რბილი უნდა იყოს.

ემილი: როგორი ფქვილია საჭირო?

ლალი: ჩვეულებრივი პურის ფქვილი. გააკეთებ ცომის
         გუნდას და გააბრტყელებ. დააყრი გახეხილ ან
         დაფხვნილ ყველს, ცომის ნაპირებს შუაში შეკრავ
         და მერე ისევ გააბრტყელებ.

ემილი: ეს რა ყველია?

ლალი: ეს **ჭყინტი ყველია**. შეგიძლია **სულგუნი** იხმარო.
         თუ ყველი ძალიან მარილიანია, წყალში დაალბობ.
         ამასობაში გააცხელებ ღუმელს, ტაფაზე ცოტა
         ფქვილს მოაყრი, ზედ დადებ ყველიან ცომს და
         შედებ ღუმელში.

ემილი: ღუმელი ძალიან ცხელი უნდა იყოს?

ლალი: საკმაოდ ცხელი. ხაჭაპური თხუთმეტ ან ოც წუთში
         მზად იქნება. თუ ბორჴომი არა გაქვს, შეგიძლია
         მაწონი იხმარო, მაგრამ მაშინ ჩაუმატებ ერთ
         კვერცხს, ცოტა გამდნარ კარაქს და სოდას.

ემილი: სოდა რამდენი?

ლალი: დაახლოვებით ერთი ჩაის კოვზი. **იცი რა**, მგონი
         მაწონი მაქვს. მოდი, კიდევ ერთი ხაჭაპური
         მაწვნით გავაკეთოთ.

ემილი: ოჰ, რა კარგი იქნება!

Khachapuri

Emily is at Lali's place learning how to make *khachapuri*.

Lali: Everything is ready. Let's start. You'll take one cup of *Borjomi* or other mineral water. Add the flour little by little and knead it well.

Emily: How much flour does it need?

Lali: Approximately three cups or a little more. The dough should be soft.

Emily: What kind of flour is needed?

Lali: Regular bread flour. You'll make a ball of dough and flatten it. Spread grated or minced cheese on top of it, pinch together the outer edges of the dough in the center, and flatten it.

Emily: What kind of cheese is this?

Lali: This is *fresh cheese*. You can use *sulguni* as well. If the cheese is too salty, soften it in water. Meanwhile, heat the oven, sprinkle a little bit of flour on a large skillet, place the dough with cheese on it, and place it in the oven.

Emily: Should the oven be very hot?

Lali: Pretty hot. The *khachapuri* will be ready in twenty or twenty-five minutes. If you don't have *Borjomi*, you can use yogurt, but then you'll add one egg, a little bit of melted butter, and baking soda.

Emily: How much soda?

Lali: About one teaspoonful. You know what; I think I have some yogurt. Let's make one more *khachapuri* with yogurt.

Emily: Oh, that will be so good!

Vocabulary

გაკეთება *verbal n.*	[gak'eteba]	making
დავიწყოთ *opt.*	[davi<u>ts'</u>q'ot]	(shall we, let's) start
აიღებ *fut.*	[ai<u>gh</u>eb]	(you) will take
ჭიქა	[<u>ch</u>'ika]	cup, glass
მინერალური	[mineraluri]	mineral
დაუმატებ *fut.*	[daumat'eb]	(you) will add
ცოტ-ცოტა	[<u>ts</u>ot'-<u>ts</u>ot'a]	little-by-little
ფქვილი	[pkvili]	flour
მოზელავ *fut.*	[mozelav]	(you) will knead
ცოტა	[<u>ts</u>ot'a]	a little, little bit
ცომი	[<u>ts</u>omi]	dough
რბილი	[rbili]	soft
გააკეთებ *fut.*	[gaak'eteb]	(you) will make
გუნდა	[gunda]	ball (of dough or snow)
შუაში	[<u>shuash</u>i]	in the middle
გააბრტყელებ *fut.*	[gaabrt'q'eleb]	(you) will flatten
ზედ	[zed]	on it, on top of it
დააყრი *fut.*	[daaq'ri]	(you) will spread, sprinkle
გახეხილი	[gaxexili]	grated
დაფხვნილი	[dapxvnili]	crumbled
ნაპირი	[nap'iri]	edge, shore (of a river or sea)
შეკრავ *fut.*	[<u>sh</u>ek'rav]	(you) will tie
მერე	[mere]	afterwards, after
ისევ	[isev]	again
იხმარო *opt.*	[ixmaro]	(you) use
მარილიანი	[mariliani]	salty
დაალბობ *fut.*	[daalbob]	(you) will soften, soak
ამასობაში	[amasoba<u>sh</u>i]	meanwhile
გააცხელებ *fut.*	[gaa<u>ts</u>xeleb]	(you) will heat up
ტაფა	[t'apa]	skillet
დადებ *fut.*	[dadeb]	(you) will put (on)
ყველიანი	[q'veliani]	with cheese, cheesy
შედებ *fut.*	[<u>sh</u>edeb]	(you) will put in
ცხელი	[<u>ts</u>xeli]	hot
საკმაოდ ცხელი	[sak'maod <u>ts</u>xeli]	rather hot

მაშინ	[ma<u>sh</u>in]	then, what then, in that case
კვერცხი	[k'ver<u>ts</u>xi]	egg
გამდნარი	[gamdnari]	melted
კარაქი	[k'araki]	butter
სოდა	[soda]	soda (baking soda)
კოვზი	[k'ovzi]	spoon

 Idiomatic Expressions and Culture Notes

- ხაჭაპური *khachapuri* can be bought or ordered at various diners, bakeries, and special *khachapuri* stands in Tbilisi and other cities. Homemade *khachapuri* with a personal touch, however, still holds a special place at the dinner table. A recipe offered in this lesson is one of many varieties you can obtain from Georgian friends and from many cookbooks.

- ბორჯომი *Borjomi*. Named after a small health resort famous for its natural mineral springs and beautiful scenery in central Georgia, *Borjomi* is the most popular Georgian mineral water. Since the nineteenth century, this has been a favorite spa and summer vacation place. Many consider *Borjomi* mineral water beneficial for treating stomach ulcers and other ailments.

- ჭყინტი ყველი is a type of *fresh cheese* somewhat similar to fresh mozzarella.

- სულგუნი is a type of Georgian *white gourmet cheese*.

- მაწონი *yogurt*. This word has an irregular declination: the vowel -ო- is changed to the consonant -ვ- in the genitive (მაწ-ვ-ნ-ის), instrumental (მაწ-ვ-ნ-ით) and adverbial (მაწ-ვ-ნ-ად) cases. მაწვნის სუპი *yogurt soup* is another Georgian delicacy.

- იცი რა? Means *you know what?*

Grammar

I. Optative tense

The optative is the most versatile form of the verb. It conveys a *modality* of action, that is, *how* some action is done, whether with intention, necessity, possibility, or desirability, etc. (see Appendices II and III).

Optative forms of 1st and 3rd conjugation verbs are formed from their future tense. The endings of the present/future tense, (as you may recall, the *present/future stem formant* or PFSF) whether -ებ, -ავ, -ამ or -ი, are dropped and replaced by *optative endings*. If a verb does not have any PFSF, the optative endings are added directly to its root.

Below is a conjugation chart of two verbs (გა-)ა-კეთ-ებ *you do, make* and (და-)წერ *you write*, one with PFSF -ებ, and the other with zero PFSF.

1st Conjugation
გა-ა-კეთ-ებ (you will make)

	Future	Optative
Sing.		
1st	გა-ვ-ა-კეთ-ებ	გა-ვ-ა-კეთ-ო
2nd	გა-ა-კეთ-ებ	გა-ა-კეთ-ო
3rd	გა-ა-კეთ-ებ-ს	გა-ა-კეთ-ოს
Pl.		
1st	გა-ვ-ა-კეთ-ებ-თ	გა-ვ-ა-კეთ-ოთ
2nd	გა-ა-კეთ-ებ-თ	გა-ა-კეთ-ოთ
3rd	გა-ა-კეთ-ებ-ენ	გა-ა-კეთ-ონ

და-წერ (you will write)

	Future	Optative
Sing.		
1st	და-ვ-წერ	და-ვ-წერ-ო
2nd	და-წერ	და-წერ-ო
3rd	და-წერ-ს	და-წერ-ოს
Pl.		
1st	და-ვ-წერ-თ	და-ვ-წერ-ოთ
2nd	და-წერ-თ	და-წერ-ოთ
3rd	და-წერ-ენ	და-წერ-ონ

Notice that the optative endings are -ო for the first and second person singular forms and -ოთ for their plural forms. The 3rd person form has -ოს in its singular form and -ონ in plural.

The 3rd conjugation verbs have exactly the same endings in the optative tense as the verbs of the 1st conjugation. However, *in the future tense they always have a* -ებ *ending* (see Lesson 8). Like 1st conjugation verbs, 3rd conjugation verbs in the optative drop the ending -ებ.

3rd Conjugation
საdiლ-ობ (you dine)

Sing.	Future	Optative
1st	ვ-ი-საdiლ-ებ	ვ-ი-საdiლ-ო
2nd	ი-საdiლ-ებ	ი-საdiლ-ო
3rd	ი-საdiლ-ებ-ს	ი-საdiლ-ოს
Pl.		
1st	ვ-ი-საdiლ-ებ-თ	ვ-ი-საdiლ-ოთ
2nd	ი-საdiლ-ებ-თ	ი-საdiლ-ოთ
3rd	ი-საdiლ-ებ-ენ	ი-საdiლ-ონ

მღერ-ი (you sing)

Sing.	Future	Optative
1st	ვ-ი-მღერ-ებ	ვ-ი-მღერ-ო
2nd	ი-მღერ-ებ	ი-მღერ-ო
3rd	ი-მღერ-ებ-ს	ი-მღერ-ოს
Pl.		
1st	ვ-ი-მღერ-ებ-თ	ვ-ი-მღერ-ოთ
2nd	ი-მღერ-ებ-თ	ი-მღერ-ოთ
3rd	ი-მღერ-ებ-ენ	ი-მღერ-ონ

• Optative tense with 4th conjugation verbs

Optative verbs often follow 4th conjugation verbs in sentences. In such case, verbs in the optative should be translated into English in their infinitive form.

- In the examples below, verbs in the optative come after the 4th conjugation verb **მინდა** *I want* with which they *do not form inseparable units*. However, in negative sentences the negative particle **არ-** precedes the verb **მინდა** and forms an inseparable unit with it. Remember also, that with verbs in the optative the *direct object is always in the nominative* and *the subject (whether noun or pronoun) is in the dative/accusative* case, just as with verbs of the 4th conjugation.

1. ჩემს ძმას   უნდა   **იყიდოს**   ახალი მანქანა.
   My brother   wants   **to buy**   a new car.
   (subj./dat.)   *(d.o./nom.)*
   მას   <u>არ უნდა</u>   **იყიდოს**   ახალი მანქანა.
   He   <u>does not want</u>   **to buy**   a new car.
   (sub./dat.)   *(d.o./nom.)*

2. ლალის   უნდა   **დახატოს**   ჩემი პორტრეტი.
   Lali   wants   **to paint**   my portrait.
   (subj./dat.)   *(d.o./nom.)*
   მას   <u>არ უნდა</u>   **დახატოს**   ჩემი პორტრეტი.
   She   <u>does not want</u>   **to paint**   my portrait.
   (subj./dat.)   *(d.o./nom.)*

3. ემილის და   უნდათ   **გააკეთონ**   ხაჭაპური.
      ლალის
   Emily and Lali   want   **to make**   a khachapuri.
   (subj./dat.)   *(d.o./nom.)*
   მათ   <u>არ უნდათ</u>   **გააკეთონ**   ხაჭაპური.
   They   <u>do not want</u>   **to make**   a khachapuri.
   (subj./dat.)   *(d.o./nom.)*

- As mentioned before (see Lesson 9), the first and second person pronouns—**მე** *I*, **ჩვენ** *we*, **შენ** *you* (sing.), **თქვენ** *you* (pl.)—*have the same form both in the dative and nominative cases.* Therefore they are not affected by 4th conjugation verbs. When used with verbs in the optative, these pronouns are frequently omitted, especially in interrogative sentences. The 4th conjugation verb and the verb in optative do not form inseparable unit and can be split as in the examples below.

1. (მე) მინდა **ვისწავლო** ქართული ენა.
   (I, *subj.*) want **to study** the Georgian language. *(d.o./nom.)*

   (მე) მინდა ქართული ენა **ვისწავლო.**
   (I, *subj.*) want the Georgian language *(d.o./nom.)* **to study.**

2. (შენ) არ გინდა ეს ფილმი **ნახო?**
   (You, *subj.*) don't want this film *(d.o.)* **to see?**

   (შენ) არ გინდა **ნახო** ეს ფილმი?
   (You, *subj.*) don't want **to see** this film *(d.o.)?*

- In order to express the ability to do something, verbs in the optative should be placed after the 4th conjugation verb **შემიძლია** *I can, I could*. This verb has a somewhat different conjugation pattern; its person markers, although exactly the same as the rest of 4th conjugation verbs, are preceded by the prefix **შე-**.

შემიძლია (I can, am able)

		Singular		Plural
1st	მე	შე-**მი**-ძლი-ა	ჩვენ	შე-**გვი**-ძლი-ა
2nd	შენ	შე-**გი**-ძლი-ა	თქვენ	შე-**გი**-ძლი-ა-თ
3rd	მას	შე-**უ**-ძლი-ა	მათ	შე-**უ**-ძლი-ა-თ

1. მანანას შეუძლია **გააკეთოს** გემრიელი ხაჭაპური.

   Manana can **make** a delicious khachapuri.
   (subj./dat.) *(d.o./nom.)*

   მას შეუძლია გემრიელი ხაჭაპური **გააკეთოს.**
   She can a delicious khachapuri. **make.**
   (subj./dat.) *(d.o./nom.)*

2. შეგიძლია **დარეკო** ზაზასთან?
   Can you **call** Zaza (to Zaza's
                    place)?
   (could you)   *(ind. obj.)*

   შეგიძლია მასთან **დარეკო?**
   Can you   him   **call?**
   (could you) (ind. obj.)

3. (მე)   არ შემიძლია **ვიმუშავო**   შენთან.
   (I, subj.) cannot   **work**   with you.

   (მე)   არ შემიძლია შენთან   **ვიმუშავო.**
   I *(subj.)* cannot   with you   **work.**

- Verbs in the optative may express suggestion or invitation to do something if placed after the verb **მოდი** *let's* (*lit.:* come) or its plural form **მოდით**, used when addressing more then one person. In both cases *verbs in optative should be in plural form.* They do not form inseparable units with either **მოდი** or **მოდით.** Moreover, both these words can be omitted, in which case the suggestion or invitation will sound a little more forceful.

A.
(მოდი) **ავიდოთ** პიცა.
(მოდი) პიცა **ავიდოთ.**
Let's (you and I) **have** (*lit.:* take) pizza.

(მოდი) **დავურეკოთ** ქეთინოს.
(მოდი) ქეთინოს **დავურეკოთ.**
Let's **call** Ketino.

(მოდი) **ვილაპარაკოთ** ქართულად.
(მოდი) ქართულად **ვილაპარაკოთ.**
Let's **speak** in Georgian.

B.

(მოდით) დავისვენოთ ცოტა.
(მოდით) ცოტა დავისვენოთ.
Let's **have** a little rest.

(მოდით) ვისადილოთ ეხლა.
(მოდით) ეხლა ვისადილოთ.
Let's **have** dinner now.

(მოდით) ვნახოთ ხვალ ეს ფილმი.
(მოდით) ხვალ ეს ფილმი ვნახოთ.
Let's **see** this movie tomorrow.

- The verb *to go* is irregular in Georgian (see Appendix III), and its optative form for 1st person plural is წავიდეთ *let's go*, a frequently used form in invitation formulas. While წა- is the most neutral prefix, it may be replaced with any of the prefixes that have more specific directional meaning: მი- (მივიდეთ *let's get to*), ჩა- (ჩავიდეთ *let's go down*), შე- (შევიდეთ *let's go in*), etc. (see Lesson 4 and/or Appendix III). These optative forms are often used after the verb მოდი(თ) *come, let's go* in singular or plural form. While in English it may sound redundant (*come, let's go*), it makes perfect sense in Georgian.

მოდი კინოში წავიდეთ.
(Come) let's (you and I) go to a movie.

მოდით მცხეთაში წავიდეთ.
(Come) let's (all of us) go to Mtskheta.

მოდით თამაზისთან მივიდეთ.
Let's (all of us) go over to Tamazi.

მოდი ამ წიგნების მაღაზიაში შევიდეთ.
Let's (you and I) go (in)to this bookstore.

- Optative forms of verbs can be used independently in *interrogative* sentences. In this case they may convey invitation as well as hesitation or uncertainty to do something. In English sentences of this type, auxiliaries like *shall* or *should* are used.

დავლიოთ ჩაი?
Shall we have (drink) tea?

დავიწყოთ გაკვეთილი?
Shall we start the class (lesson)?

დავრეკო გიასთან?
Should I call Gia?

ვიყიდო ეს კაბა?
Should I buy this dress?

Exercises

I. The verbs listed below are in the 2nd person singular of the future tense. Use them to fill in the blanks putting them in the appropriate optative form.

შე-ი-ტან	(you will) deposit, take in(to)
ი-ყიდ-ი	(you will) buy
და-რეცხ-ავ	(you will) wash (laundry, dishes, etc.)
ისწავლ-ი	(you will) see
გა-ა-კეთ-ებ	(you will) send
ი-ქირავ-ებ	(you will) rent

1. ხვალ მე მინდა ამ ბანკში ფული

   _____.

   Tomorrow I want to deposit money at the bank.

2. კევინს უნდა ქართული სიმღერების სიდი

   _____.

   Kevin wants to buy a CD of Georgian songs.

3. მას უნდა დღეს სარეცხი

   _____.

   She wants to wash (her) laundry today.

4. ჩემ(ს) დას უნდა ინგლისში

_____.

My sister wants to study in England.

5. ჩვენ გვინდა დღეს ქართული სადილი

_____.

We want to make a Georgian dinner today.

6. მათ უნდათ ბინა მეტრო დელისთან

_____.

They want to rent an apartment near the metro station Delisi.

II. Fill in the blanks with the appropriate form of the verb *can*.

1. თქვენ _____ ეს წერილი გააგზავნოთ?
Can you send this letter?

2. შენ არ _____ ემილისთან დარეკო?
Can't you call Emily?

3. სამწუხაროდ, მე არ _____ ეს
დოკუმენტი გადავთარგმნო.
Unfortunately, I cannot translate this document.

4. მას _____ ეს წიგნი ამ მაღაზიაში
იყიდოს.
He can buy this book in this bookstore.

III. Translate the sentences putting the verbs listed below (given in the future tense, 2nd person singular) in the appropriate optative form.

ა-იღ-ებ (you will) take, have
ი-საუზმ-ებ (you will) have breakfast
გა-ყიდ-ი (you will) sell

1. _____.
   Let's have (take) coffee and cake.

2. _____.
   Let's have breakfast.

3. _____.
   Let's sell our old car.

IV. Translate the sentences below using the expression *let's go*.

1. Let's (you and I) go to the opera tomorrow.
   _____.

2. Let's (all of us) go to Gia (Gia's place) today.
   _____.

3. Let's (you and I) go now to the market.
   _____.

V. Translate the following sentences using the verbs listed below in the appropriate optative form.

ი-თამაშ-ებ   (you will) play
და-ხურ-ავ   (you will) close
ი-ყიდ-ი   (you will) buy

1. ფეხბურთი _____ ?

2. _____ ჩვენი ანგარიში ამ ბანკში?

3. _____ თონის პური?

Lesson 12

გაკვეთილი მეთორმეტე

A Birthday

დაბადების დღე

დაბადების დღე

ქევინი და ემილი თამაზისთან სტუმრად მოვიდნენ. თამაზის დედა, ქალბატონი თინა კარს აღებს.

ქ-ნი თინა: ქევინ, ემილი, შემოდით, შემოდით. ჩვენ უკვე თამადა ავირჩიეთ.

თამაზი: ქევინ, ემილი, მოდით, ჩემს გვერდით დასხედით. დღეს გურამია ჩვენი თამადა.

ქევინი: თამაზ, გილოცავ დაბადების დღეს. აი, ეს პატარა საჩუქარი ჩვენგან.

თამაზი: ო, დიდი მადლობა! რატომ შეწუხდით?

გურამი: მეგობრებო, დავლიოთ თამაზის სადღეგრძელო. ემილი, თქვენი ჭიქა რატომ არის ცარიელი?

ემილი: ბოდიში, მაგრამ მე ღვინოს არ ვსვამ.

ქ-ნი თინა: მაშ ღვინოს ნუ დალევ. წვენი ან ლიმონათი დალიე.

ემილი: გმადლობთ, წვენს სიამოვნებით დავლევ.

გურამი: თამაზ, გისურვებ ბედნიერებას და კარგად ყოფნას ყველა შენი ახლობლებით.

ქევინი: თამაზ, გისურვებ ბედნიერებას და წარმატებას.

ემილი: თამაზ, გილოცავ. მრავალს დაესწარი!

გურამი: ყველამ დალია? თამაზ, ეხლა შენი ჯერია.

თამაზი: დიდი მადლობა, მეგობრებო, თქვენი კეთილი სურვილებისთვის. ყველას გაგვიმარჯოს!

ქ-ნი თინა: ემილი, აი, გასინჯეთ, რა გემრიელი საცივია.

ემილი: გმადლობთ, ქალბატონო თინა. უკვე გავსინჯე. ხაჭაპურს ავიღებ.

ლალი: მოდით ეხლა ვიცეკვოთ. მე ახალი სიდი მაქვს.

გურამი: არა, ჯერ ვიმღეროთ. ქევინ, შენ რა სიმღერა გიყვარს?

ქევინი: მაშ მრავალჟამიერი ვიმღეროთ.

A Birthday

Kevin and Emily come to Tamazi's apartment. Tamazi's mother, Ms. Tina (Shonia), opens the door.

Ms. Tina: Kevin, Emily, come in, come in. We've already chosen the *tamada*.

Tamazi: Kevin, Emily, come over here, sit next to me. Today Gurami is our *tamada*.

Kevin: Tamaz, happy birthday. This is a little gift from us.

Tamazi: Oh, thank you! Why did you bother to do that?

Gurami: Friends, let's drink a toast to Tamazi. Emily, why is your glass empty?

Emily: I apologize, but I don't drink wine.

Ms. Tina: In that case don't drink wine. Drink some juice or lemonade.

Emily: Thank you, I'd love to have some juice.

Gurami: I want, Tamaz, to wish you happiness and wellbeing with all your loved ones.

Kevin: Tamaz, I wish you happiness and success.

Emily: Tamaz, congratulations. Many happy returns!

Gurami: Did everyone drink? Tamaz, now it's your turn.

Tamazi: Thank you very much, my friends, for your kind words. Let victory be ours!

Ms. Tina: Emily, here, try this delicious *satsivi*.

Emily: Thank you, Ms. Tina, I've already had some. I'll have some *khachapuri*.

Lali: Let's dance now. I have a new CD.

Gurami: No, let's sing first. Kevin, which song do you like?

Kevin: Then let's sing *Mravalzhamieri*.

Vocabulary

ავირჩიეთ *aor.*	[avir<u>ch</u>iet]	(we) chose
ჩემს გვერდით	[<u>ch</u>ems gverdit]	by my side, next to me
დასხედით *aor./imp.*	[dasxedit]	(you) sit down
გილოცავ	[gilo<u>ts</u>av]	I congratulate you *(fixed expression)*
საჩუქარი	[sa<u>ch</u>ukari]	gift
სადღეგრძელო	[sad<u>gh</u>egr<u>dz</u>elo]	a toast *(to s.o.)* (*lit.*: for long days)
ცარიელი	[<u>ts</u>arieli]	empty
ნუ	[nu]	don't *(used in requests not to do s.th.)*
წვენი	[<u>ts</u>'veni]	juice
გისურვებ *pres./fut.*	[gisurveb]	I wish you
ბედნიერება	[bedniereba]	happiness
ყოფნა *verbal n.*	[q'opna]	being
ყველა	[q'vela]	all, everybody, everyone
ახლობელი	[axlobeli]	a loved one, a relative
ახლობლები *pl.*	[axloblebi]	loved ones, relatives
წარმატება	[<u>ts</u>'armat'eba]	success
ჯერი	[jeri]	turn
ჩემი ჯერია	[cemi jeria]	my turn
შენი ჯერია	[<u>sh</u>eni jeria]	your turn
კეთილი	[k'etili]	kind
სურვილი	[survili]	wish
სურვილები *pl.*	[survilebi]	wishes
ვიცეკვოთ *opt.*	[vi<u>ts</u>ekvot]	(let's) dance
ახალი	[axali]	new
ჯერ	[jer]	first *(before doing something else)*
ვიმღეროთ *opt.*	[vim<u>gh</u>erot]	(let's) sing

Idiomatic Expressions and Culture Notes

- **ქალბატონი თინა** *Ms. Tina.* In English, Ms. Tina sounds awkward; this is, however, the proper form for addressing a woman. As mentioned in the section "Borrowed Words and Personal Names in Georgian" (page 27), Georgians address each other by their first names.

- **ქ-ნი** is an abbreviated form of **ქალბატონი** *Miss or Madam.* For **ბატონი** *Sir or Mister,* an abbreviated form is **ბ-ნი**.

- **თამადა** *toastmaster.* The *tamada* is the toastmaster chosen by guests at a festive dinner or *supra* **სუფრა** in Georgian. Traditionally, the *tamada* was always a man. Sometimes, however, a woman may also be given the task of being the *tamada*. Rules of *supra* are rather elaborate, and toasts are offered in a fixed order. Georgians never drink wine without a toast.

- **სადღეგრძელო** *toast.* The main function of the *tamada* is to make sure that the rules of the *supra* are observed. It is the *tamada* who offers the topic of each toast, and only after he drinks his toast must the guests one by one raise their glasses, each elaborating further on the topic proposed by the *tamada*. Men must stand up when giving a toast and hold the glass in the right hand. It is considered very rude to eat or drink while the *tamada* is giving his toast. After the traditionally required toasts (for the host and hostess, for parents, for children, for siblings, etc.), the *tamada* honors every person present at the *supra* with a toast. Toasts can be made on more general subjects as well: Georgia, love, friendship, etc. The final toast is for the *tamada*. This toast is raised by one of the guests, thus signaling the end of the *supra*. No *supra* is complete without singing, and it is a part of the ritual to sing a few Georgian folk songs in-between toasts.

- **მაშ** is an auxiliary word equivalent to the English *then, in that case, so,* etc.

- საღ იყავით აქამდე means *where have you been (all this time)*?!

- გილოცავ დაბადების დღეს *Happy Birthday*. გილოცავ literally means: *I bless (something) for you*. It can be used for various occasions: გილოცავ ახალ წელს *Happy New Year*; გილოცავ შობას *Happy (Merry) Christmas*, and so forth.

- რატომ შეწუხდით means literally *why did you trouble yourselves (to do something)*. It is a polite formula implying gratitude and appreciation for something.

- ყველა შენი ახლობლებით means *with all your loved ones*.

- მრავალს დაესწარი *many happy returns*; lit.: *may you attend many more*, i.e. may you attend many more of your birthdays. The formula is used in wishing a happy New Year, or in reference to other festive days.

- საცივი *sat̲sivi* is a gourmet Georgian dish, turkey or chicken in spicy walnut sauce.

- გაგვიმარჯოს is a fixed formula that literally means: *let us be victorious*.

- მრავალჟამიერი *Mravalzhamieri* is one of the most famous of Georgian folk songs sung at *supra*.

Grammar

I. Aorist tense

The aorist refers to action that was carried out in the past but, in contrast to the imperfect, the aorist tense indicates completion of the action and not its continuity or frequency. Thus, the sentence *I was writing a letter* should be translated into Georgian with the verb in the *imperfect* tense. However, in the sentence *I wrote a letter* (it's finished and ready to be sent), the verb must be in the aorist tense.

Lesson Twelve 195

Aorist forms of 1st and 3rd conjugation verbs are formed from
their future tense. Just like with optative forms, the endings of the
future tense, whether -ებ, -ავ, -ამ or -ი, are replaced by the aorist
endings.

Below are the charts of 1st and 3rd conjugation verbs in future, aorist
and optative tenses.

1st Conjugation
სინჯავ (you try, taste)

	Future	Aorist	Optative
Sing.			
1st	გა-ვ-სინჯ-ავ	გა-ვ-სინჯ-ე	გა-ვ-სინჯ-ო
2nd	გა-სინჯ-ავ	გა-სინჯ-ე	გა-სინჯ-ო
3rd	გა-სინჯ-ავ-ს	გა-სინჯ-ა	გა-სინჯ-ოს
Pl.			
1st	გა-ვ-სინჯ-ავ-თ	გა-ვ-სინჯ-ე-თ	გა-ვ-სინჯ-ო-თ
2nd	გა-სინჯ-ავ-თ	გა-სინჯ-ე-თ	გა-სინჯ-ო-თ
3rd	გა-სინჯ-ავ-ენ	გა-სინჯ-ეს	გა-სინჯ-ონ

3rd Conjugation
მღერი (you sing)

	Future	Aorist	Optative
Sing.			
1st	ვ-ი-მღერ-ებ	ვ-ი-მღერ-ე	ვ-ი-მღერ-ო
2nd	ი-მღერ-ებ	ი-მღერ-ე	ი-მღერ-ო
3rd	ი-მღერ-ებ-ს	ი-მღერ-ა	ი-მღერ-ოს
Pl.			
1st	ვ-ი-მღერ-ებ-თ	ვ-ი-მღერ-ე-თ	ვ-ი-მღერ-ო-თ
2nd	ი-მღერ-ებ-თ	ი-მღერ-ე-თ	ი-მღერ-ო-თ
3rd	ი-მღერ-ებ-ენ	ი-მღერ-ეს	ი-მღერ-ონ

II. Irregular verbs

The majority of Georgian verbs conjugate like the verbs given in the charts shown above. However, there are some verbs that have irregular conjugation forms. These verbs should be learned individually (see appendix IV).

- The verb სვამ *you drink*, used in this lesson, sounds excessively formal and outdated in its future, aorist, and optative forms. Therefore, in these tenses *an entirely different verb is used.*

სვამ (you drink, *pres.*)

Person	Present	Imperfect
Sing.		
1st	ვ-სვ-ამ	ვ-სვ-ამ-დი
2nd	სვ-ამ	სვ-ამ-დი
3rd	სვ-ამ-ს	სვ-ამ-და
Pl.		
1st	ვ-სვ-ამ-თ	ვ-სვ-ამ-დი-თ
2nd	სვ-ამ-თ	სვ-ამ-დი-თ
3rd	სვ-ამ-ენ	სვ-ამ-დნენ

დალევ (you will drink, *fut.*)

Person	Future	Aorist	Optative
Sing.			
1st	და-ვ-ლევ	და-ვ-ლი-ე	და-ვ-ლი-ო
2nd	და-ლევ	და-ლი-ე	და-ლი-ო
3rd	და-ლევ-ს	და-ლი-ა	და-ლი-ოს
Pl.			
1st	და-ვ-ლევ-თ	და-ვ-ლი-ე-თ	და-ვ-ლი-ო-თ
2nd	და-ლევ-თ	და-ლი-ე-თ	და-ლი-ო-თ
3rd	და-ლევ-ენ	და-ლი-ეს	და-ლი-ონ

მე ყავას არ ვსვამ. *(pres.)*
I don't drink coffee.

ჩვენ ამ წყალს ვერ ვსვამდით. *(imp.)*
We couldn't drink this water.

რას **დალევ**, ჩაის თუ ყავას? *(fut.)*
What will you have *(drink)* tea or coffee?

დალიე თამაზის სადღეგრძელო? *(aor.)*
Did you drink a toast for Tamazi?

მოდი **დავლიოთ**. *(opt.)*
Let's have a drink. (*lit.*: Let's drink)

III. Ergative case

When 1st and 3rd conjugation verbs are used in the aorist tense, the subject of the sentence must be in the **ergative** case, not in the nominative as in the present, imperfect, and future tenses. Since 1st and 2nd person pronouns (**მე** *I*, **შენ** *you*, **ჩვენ** *we*, **თქვენ** *you pl.*) never decline, *this rule effectively applies only to the 3rd person singular and plural subjects, nouns and pronouns alike.*

- The ending of the ergative case is **-მა** for **-ი** ending nouns, and **-მ** for all others.

Nom.	Ergative	Translation
კაც-**ი**	კაც-**მა**	man
დედა	დედა-**მ**	mother
მეფე	მეფე-**მ**	king
გოგო	გოგო-**მ**	girl
ბუ	ბუ-**მ**	owl

- **All possessive pronouns and adjectives** ending with **-ი** should also be in the ergative when the nouns they modify are in the ergative case. Adjectives ending with vowels other than **-ი** remain unchanged.

nominative	ჩემ-**ი** უმცროს-**ი** და
ergative	ჩემ-**მა** უმცროს-**მა** დამ
translation	**my** younger sister

nominative	შენ-ი საინტერესო რომან-ი
ergative	შენ-მა საინტერესო რომან-მა
translation	**your** interesting novel

nominative	მის-ი მოკლე სტატია
ergative	მის-მა მოკლე სტატია-მ
translation	**his/her** short article

* The ergative case of personal names most often have the -მ ending.

თამაზი<u>მ</u> Tamazi<u>m</u>	რუსიკო<u>მ</u> Rusiko<u>m</u>
ლალი<u>მ</u> Lali<u>m</u>	ნუნუ<u>მ</u> Nunu<u>m</u>

In the relatively few names that lose the final -ი, the ergative ending will be -მა.

დავითმა *Davitma*	თამარ<u>მა</u> *Tamar<u>ma</u>*
არჩილ<u>მა</u> *Archilma*	იორამმა *Ioramma*

(See also *Borrowed Words and Personal Names in Georgian*, page 27.)

IV. The direct object with verbs in the aorist tense

In the aorist, just as in the optative, *the direct object will be in the nominative case*, not in the dative/accusative. Notice the case endings for the subjects and direct objects in the sentences below.

Tense	Subject	Direct Object	Verb
Present	ჩემი პატარა და	წერილს	წერს.
	[My little sister	a letter	is writing]
	(nom.)	*(dat./acc.)*	
	My little sister is writing a letter.		

Tense	Subject	Direct Object	Verb
Imperfect	ჩემი პატარა და [My little sister *(nom.)*	წერილს a letter *(dat./acc.)*	წერდა. was writing.]
	My little sister was writing a letter.		
Future	ჩემი პატარა და [My little sister *(nom.)*	წერილს a letter *(dat./acc.)*	დაწერს. will write.]
	My little sister will write a letter.		
Aorist	ჩემმა პატარა დამ [My little sister *(ergative case)*	წერილი a letter *(nom.)*	დაწერა. wrote.]
	My little sister wrote a letter.		
Optative	ჩემმა პატარა დამ [My little sister *(ergative case)*	წერილი a letter *(nom.)*	უნდა დაწეროს. should write.]
	My little sister should write a letter.		

V. Aorist with negation არ and ვერ

When used with the aorist tense, the negation არ usually implies a conscious decision not to do something, and sounds quite emphatic. For more neutral statements Georgians use the present perfect tense, which is not discussed in this book. You can get by if you use ვერ instead of არ to make the statement less emphatic.

A.
მე ეს ფილმი **არ ვნახე**.
I didn't see this film. *(I didn't want to.)*

მე ეს ფილმი **ვერ ვნახე**.
I was not able to see this film. *(i.e. I have not seen it.)*

B.

გიამ სკოლა **არ დაამთავრა**.
Gia **didn't graduate** from school. *(she decided to drop out)*

გიამ სკოლა **ვერ დაამთავრა**.
Gia **was not able to graduate** from school.

C.

შენ ეს რომანი რატომ **არ წაიკითხე**?
Why **didn't you read** this novel?

ძალიან გრძელია და **ვერ წავიკითხე**.
It's too long and I **couldn't read** it.

VI. Stating an order or request

The aorist tense is used to express an order or request to do something.

დალიე ეს წამალი.	**Drink** this medicine.
გაიმეორე ეს სიტყვა.	**Repeat** this word.
გააგზავნე ჩემი წერილი.	**Send** my letter.

To make your request sound polite, add phrases such as:

თუ შეიძლება	please, if possible
ძალიან გთხოვ	if I may ask
თუ არ შეგაწუხებთ	if it is no trouble for you

A very casual form of mild request can be expressed by putting **რა** right after the verb in the aorist tense. In this position **რა** corresponds to the English *would you* or *could you*. However, in formal situations the plural form of the aorist tense should be used.

V. Request in negative form

When asking someone **not** to do something, the negating particles არ and ნუ are used.

- არ is used with the *optative tense*. However, არ makes a request very strong, and should not be used in a formal situation.

- ნუ used with the *present tense* or *future tense* makes a request sound milder and more polite.

Pay attention to the case of the direct objects whch are in boldface in the following sentences:

Optative
არ გაიმეორო **ეს სიტყვა**! (*d.o., nom.*)
Don't repeat **this word**!

არ დალიო **ღვინო**! (*d.o., nom.*)
Don't drink **wine**!

Present
ნუ იმეორებ **ამ სიტყვას**. (*d.o., dat./acc.*)
(Please) don't repeat **this word**.

ნუ დალევ **ღვინოს**. (*d.o., dat./acc.*)
(Please) don't drink **wine**.

Exercises

I. **Put the following nouns and their qualifiers (pronouns, adjectives or numerals) in the ergative case.**

1. კარგი გოგონა _____

2. მისი პატარა ჭიქა _____

3. ორი დიდი მაგიდა _____

4. მაღალი ხე _____

5. შენი გრძელი სტატია   _____

6. მოკლე თეთრი კაბა   _____

II. **Put the 1st conjugation verbs in parentheses in the correct tenses**: present, imperfect, future, aorist, or optative, and fill in the blanks. All verbs are given in the future tense, 2nd person singular.

1. თამაზმ უნივერსიტეტი შარშან (და-ამთავრ-ებ)
_____.
Last year Tamazi graduated from the university.

2. ჩემი წერილი (გა-გზავნ-ი)
_____?
Did you send my letter?

3. ისინი ჩვენთან ორის ნახევარზე (და-რეკ-ავ)
_____.
They will call us at half past one.

4. ამ მანქანაზე ფული არ (და-ხარჯ-ავ)
_____.
Don't spend money on this car.

5. გუშინ თინამ ბაზარში საფულე (და-კარგ-ავ)
_____.
Yesterday Tina lost her purse at the market.

6. დღეს მე სახლი (და-ალაგ-ებ)
_____.
Today I cleaned (*tidied up*) the house.

III. **Put the 3rd conjugation verbs in parentheses in the correct tenses**: present, imperfect, future, aorist, or optative, and fill in the blanks. The verbs are given in the present tense, 2nd person singular.

1. მომავალ წელს გია ამ ბანკში (მუშა-ობ)
_____.
Next year, Gia will work in this bank.

2. ემილი ბინას ამ რაიონში (ქირა-ობ)

   _____.

   Emily is renting an apartment in this region (*this part of the city*).

3. მოდი, (ცეკვ-ავ) _____.

   Let's dance.

4. როცა ამერიკაში იყავი, რომელ შტატში (-ცხოვრ-ობ)

   _____?

   When you were in America, in which state did you live?

5. როცა ლალი პატარა იყო, ძალიან კარგად (ცეკვ-ავ)

   _____.

   When Lali was little, she danced very well.

6. ისინი ყოველთვის ექვსის ნახევარზე (სადილ-ობ)

   _____.

   They always have dinner at half past five.

IV. Put the subjects and objects in the following sentences in the correct cases. Pay attention to the verbal forms.

1. (ჩემი მეგობარი) _____ (საინტერესო

   სტატია) _____ დაწერა.

   My friend wrote an interesting article.

2. (რუსიკო და ნანა) _____ (სარეცხი)

   _____ დარეცხეს.

   Rusiko and Nana washed the laundry.

3. (ბავშვები) _____ ეზომში (ფეხბურთი)

   _____ თამაშობენ.

   The children are playing football in the yard.

4. არ გინდა (ყავა) _____ დალიო?

   Don't you want to have (*to drink*) coffee?

5. თამაზის (სტუმრები) _____ (ქართული
   სიმღერები) _____მღეროდნენ.
   Tamazi's guests were singing Georgian folk songs.

6. მე ჯერ (სადილი) _____ დავამთავრებ და
   მერე (ტელევიზორი) _____ ჩავრთავ.
   I will finish dinner first, and then will turn on the TV.

V. **Translate the sentences below using appropriate forms of
   request or order.**

1. Let's sing this song. _____

2. Don't sing this song! _____

3. Could you make coffee? _____

4. Please, don't make coffee, make tea. _____

5. Let's make *khachapuri*. _____

6. Shall we make *khachapuri*? _____

Lesson 13
გაკვეთილი მეცამეტე

Tbilisi, Vakhtang Gorgasali Square
თბილისი, ვახტანგ გორგასლის მოედანი

თბილისი, ვახტანგ გორგასლის მოედანი

თამაზი, ემილი და ქევინი **მთაწმინდის** პლატოზე არიან.

ემილი: რა ლამაზი ხედია!

თამაზი: აი, ის არის **ვახტანგ გორგასლის** მოედანი. ეს იყო ძველი თბილისის ცენტრი. მოედნის ერთ მხარეს არის **სიონის ტაძარი**, ქართველი ქრისტიანების მთავარი ეკლესია.

ქევინი: აქ მეჩეთიც იყო, არა?

თამაზი: ჰო, აქ ხიდთან იყო შიიტური მეჩეთი. მაგრამ ათას ცხრაას ორმოცდაათ წელს დაიწყეს ახალი ხიდის მშენებლობა და მეჩეთი დაანგრიეს. მოედანთან ახლოს, ბოტანიკური ბაღია. ხედავთ?

ემილი: ვიცი. მე იქ ვიყავი ორი კვირის წინ.

თამაზი: იქ, ბაღთან ახლოს, სუნიტური მეჩეთია. როცა შიიტური მეჩეთი დაანგრიეს, სუნიტები და შიიტები ამ მეჩეთში ერთად ლოცულობდნენ.

ქევინი: რას ამბობ, მართლა?! ეს მართლაც შესანიშნავია.

თამაზი: მოედანთან ახლოს არის ებრაული სინაგოგა და **სომხური ეკლესია. როგორც ხედავთ,** ეს ადგილი არის რელიგიური ტოლერანტობის სიმბოლო საქართველოში.

ემილი: მართლაც! ის დიდი ეკლესია მთაზე როდის ააშენეს?

თამაზი: ის არის სამების ტაძარი. მისი მშენებლობა ათას ცხრაას ოთხმოცდათექვსმეტ წელს დაიწყეს და ორი წლის წინ დაამთავრეს.

ქევინი: ვინ დააფინანსა ეს მშენებლობა?

თამაზი: მთელმა საქართველომ—კერძო პირებმა, ბიზნესმენებმა და სხვადასხვა ორგანიზაციებმა.

ემილი: მოდით, ჩვენი ექსკურსია გორგასლის მოედნიდან დავიწყოთ.

თამაზი: ძალიან კარგი. წავიდეთ.

Tbilisi, Vakhtang Gorgasali Square

Tamazi, Emily and Kevin are on Mtatsminda plateau.

Emily:	What a beautiful view!
Tamazi:	Down there is Vakhtang Gorgasali Square. This was the center of old Tbilisi. On one side of the square is Sioni Cathedral, the main church of Georgian Christians.
Kevin:	There was a mosque here too, wasn't there?
Tamazi:	Yes, here, near the bridge there was a Shiite mosque. But in 1950 they started building a new bridge and demolished the mosque. There is a Botanical Garden near the bridge. Do you see it?
Emily:	I know. I was there two weeks ago.
Tamazi:	There, near the Garden, there is a Sunni mosque. After (when) they demolished the Shiite mosque, the Shiites and the Sunnis prayed together in this mosque.
Kevin:	You don't say, really? This is truly remarkable.
Tamazi:	Near the square there are a Jewish synagogue and an Armenian church. As you see, this place is a symbol of religious tolerance in Georgia.
Emily:	Yes indeed! When did they build that big church on the hillside?
Tamazi:	This is Trinity Cathedral. Its construction was begun in 1996 and finished two years ago.
Kevin:	Who financed the building?
Tamazi:	All of Georgia—individuals, businessmen, and various organizations.
Emily:	Let's start our excursion with Gorgasali Square.
Tamazi:	Very well. Let's go.

Vocabulary

მოედანი	[moedani]	(city) square
პლატო	[p'lat'o]	plateau, flat top of a mountain
ხედი	[xedi]	view
ქრისტიანი	[krist'iani]	Christian
მთავარი	[mtavari]	main
მეჩეთი	[mecheti]	mosque
ხიდი	[xidi]	bridge
შიიტური	[shiit'uri]	Shiite
დაიწყეს *aor.*	[daits'q'es]	(they) started
მშენებლობა	[mshenebloba]	construction
დაანგრიეს *aor.*	[daangries]	(they) demolished
ბოტანიკური	[bot'anik'uri]	botanical
ბაღი	[baghi]	garden
ხედავთ *pres.*	[xedavt]	(you) see
სუნიტური	[sunit'uri]	Sunni
ლოცულობდნენ *imperf.*	[lotsulobdnen]	(they) prayed
მართლაც	[martlats]	indeed
შესანიშნავი	[shesanishnavi]	remarkable
ებრაული	[ebrauli]	Jewish *(referring to inanimate things)*
სინაგოგა	[sinagoga]	synagogue
სომხური	[somxuri]	Armenian *(referring to inanimate things)*
ეკლესია	[ek'lesia]	church
ადგილი	[adgili]	place
რელიგიური	[religiuri]	religious
ტოლერანტობა	[t'olerant'oba]	tolerance
სიმბოლო	[simbolo]	symbol
ააშენეს *aor.*	[aashenes]	(they) built
დაამთავრეს *aor.*	[daamtavres]	(they) competed, finished
დააფინანსა *aor.*	[daapinansa]	(s/he) financed
კერძო	[k'erdzo]	private

პირი	[p'iri]	person
ორგანიზაცია	[organiza<u>ts</u>ia]	organization
ექსკურსია	[eksk'ursia]	excursion

 Idiomatic Expressions and Culture Notes

- მთაწმინდა or literally *Holy Mountain* is the name of a high hill overlooking Tbilisi. In 1906 a cable railway to the top of the mountain was completed. The funicular road, visible from every point of the city, became the most recognizable landmark of Tbilisi, like the Empire State building in New York or the Eiffel Tower in Paris. Another name for the mountain is მამა დავითის მთა, or the *Mountain of St. David*. The name was given in honor of Father David, a revered sixth-century monk. According to legend, he lived in a cell that he had carved into the rocky slope of the mountain. In the ninth century, a church was built on the site of the legendary cell. Over the following years, the church was rebuilt and restored several times. Since the nineteenth century, the cemetery attached to the church has been the resting place of the most outstanding Georgian poets, writers, and other prominent personalities. Burial at the cemetery of the Holy Mountain (or Pantheon, as Georgians call it) was the highest posthumous honor, and was bestowed even during the Soviet period.

- ვახტანგ გორგასალი *Vakhtang Gorgasali* was a fifth-century ruler of Kartli, the heartland of present-day Georgia. He made Tbilisi the capital city of his kingdom. A well-known myth about Tbilisi's founding tells us that, during a hunting expedition, Vakhtang discovered hot sulfur springs in the forest and decided to build a city there. The name Tbilisi stems from the word თბილი *warm*. Until today, the famous public bathhouses of the city are supplied with the water from many underground hot springs which give off a distinctly detectable smell of sulfur. Vakhtang led long and often victorious battles against the Persians, who tried to impose their control over the land. Gorgasali or *wolf head* is actually a Persian name given to the king because of his helmet with a figure of a wolf on the top. Vakhtang became a folk hero admired for his military skill and courage.

- **სიონის ტაძარი** *Sioni Cathedral* is the seat of the supreme leader (Catholicos) of the Georgian Church. At present, His Holiness Ilia II holds the title.

- **სომხური ეკლესია** *Armenian Church.* Both Georgians and Armenians are Orthodox Christians. However, at the beginning of the sixth century the two groups split on the basis of theological considerations and have remained divided ever since.

- **როგორც ხედავთ** means *as you see.*

Grammar

I. Syncope in personal names

In Lesson 6, we discussed syncopation of vowels -ა, -ე, and -ო in the genitive case when they are followed by the consonants ლ, მ, ნ, and რ. The same rule applies to personal last names. Since the rule is often ignored in the spoken language, it is not a serious grammatical error if you forget to syncopate these vowels.

Nom.	გორგას-**ალ**-ი	წერეთ-**ელ**-ი	ამილახვ-**არ**-ი
Gen.	გორგას-**ლ**-ის	წერეთ-**ლ**-ის	ამილახვ-**რ**-ის

II. Impersonal constructions

In sentences where the subject is not specified, Georgian uses the verb in the 3rd person plural (*they*) form. This type of sentence can be translated into English using both active and passive forms.

ეს ხიდი ათი წლის წინ ააშენეს.
They built this bridge ten years ago.
This bridge was built ten years ago.

ქალაქის ცენტრში რამდენიმე ძველი შენობა **დაანგრიეს.**
They demolished several old buildings in the center of the city.
Several old buildings were demolished in the center of the city.

აქ ბაღის მშენებლობა **დაიწყეს.**
They started building a garden here.
(Building of) a garden has been started here.

III. Ergative case of pronouns

If the verb is in the aorist or optative tense, the pronouns (personal, indicative or interrogative) should be in the ergative case. However, only 3rd person pronouns (ის *he/she*, ისინი *they*) change in the ergative case; the rest (მე *I*, შენ *you*, ჩვენ *we*, თქვენ *you pl.*) have the same form as in the nominative case.

- The third person plural pronoun (*they*) has identical forms in the ergative and dative cases.

	I	you	he/she	we	you *(pl.)*	they
Nom.	მე	შენ	ის	ჩვენ	თქვენ	ისინი
Dat.	მე	შენ	მას	ჩვენ	თქვენ	მათ
Erg.	მე	შენ	მან	ჩვენ	თქვენ	მათ

მე დღეს ხაჭაპურს ვაკეთებ.
I am making a khachapuri today.
მე დღეს ხაჭაპური გავაკეთე.
I made a khachapuri today.

შენ ხატავ ამ პორტრეტს?
Are **you** painting this portrait?
შენ დახატე ეს პორტრეტი?
Did **you** paint this portrait?

ის საინტერესო სტატიას წერს.
He is writing an interesting article.
მან საინტერესო სტატია დაწერა.
He wrote an interesting article.

ისინი ფეხბურის კარგად თამაშობენ.
They play football well.
მათ ფეხბურთი კარგად ითამაშეს.
They played football well.

- Indicative pronouns ის *that* and ეს *this* will be in their indirect forms: ამ and იმ.

ეს ბიჭი კარგად მღერის.
This boy sings well.
ამ ბიჭმა კარგად იმღერა.
This boy sang well.

ის ბანკი პროცენტებს ზრდის.
That bank is increasing interest rates.
იმ ბანკმა პროცენტები გაზარდა.
That bank increased interest rates.

- The pronoun ვინ *who* does not change in the ergative case.

ვინ რეკავს ასე ადრე?
Who is calling so early?
ვინ დარეკა ამ დილით?
Who called this morning?

IV. Use of მინდა *I want* **and უნდა** *I should*

მინდა *I want* is a verb and it conjugates, i.e. changes its form, with various pronouns in singular and plural forms. უნდა *must, ought to, should* is an auxiliary like *shall* or *should* and it does not conjugate, but rather has the same form with all pronouns. Verbs in the optative tense preceded by უნდა *should* are translated as an infinitive.

Person	მინდა (I want)		უნდა (I should)	
Sing.				
1st	მე მინდა	I want	მე უნდა	I should
2nd	შენ გინდა	you want	შენ უნდა	you should
3rd	მას უნდა	he/she wants	მან უნდა	he/she should
Pl.				
1st	ჩვენ გვინდა	we want	ჩვენ უნდა	we should
2nd	თქვენ გინდათ	you want	თქვენ უნდა	you should
3rd	მათ უნდათ	they want	მათ უნდა	they should

As the chart above indicates, these two verbs have the same form in the 3rd person singular. However, the subject with **მინდა** *want* is in the *dative case*, while **უნდა** *should* requires the subject be in the *ergative case*.

Neither **მინდა** *want* nor **უნდა** *should* form inseparable units with the optative verbs they precede. However, more often than not, **უნდა** *should* is placed right before the verb in optative tense.

In order to understand the meaning of a sentence correctly, you should pay attention to the *case of the subject*.

მას *(dat.)* **უნდა** ბინის ქირა დღეს **გადაიხადოს**.
She wants to pay the rent today.

მან *(erg.)* ბინის ქირა დღეს **უნდა** გადაიხადოს.
She should (has to) pay the rent today.

The 3rd person plural pronoun **ისინი** *they* has the form **მათ** both for the dative and ergative cases. However, **უნდა** *should, ought to, must* will not have the plural marker **-თ** at the end of the verb since it does not decline.

მათ *(dat.)* **უნდათ** ფული ამ ბანკში შეიტანონ.
They want to deposit money in this bank.

მათ *(erg.)* ფული ამ ბანკში **უნდა** შეიტანონ.
They should deposit money in this bank.

V. The verb *to be*

The verb *to be* is one of the highly irregular verbs; *it has different roots in every tense*. In Lesson 8, the conjugations chart of its present, imperfect, and future tense was given. Here we add its aorist and optative forms.

ხარ (you are)

Person	Present	Imperfect/Aorist	Future	Optative
Sing.				
1st	ვარ	ვიყავი	ვიქნები	ვიყო
2nd	ხარ	იყავი	იქნები	იყო
3rd	არის	**იყო**	იქნება	იყოს
Pl.				
1st	ვართ	ვიყავით	ვიქნებით	ვიყოთ
2nd	ხართ	იყავით	იქნებით	იყოთ
3rd	არიან	**იყვნენ**	იქნებიან	**იყვნენ**

Note the boldfaced forms of **იყო** and **იყვნენ** in this chart. **იყო** for the 3rd person singular in imperfect/aorist tense coincides with the 2nd person singular form in optative. **იყვნენ** has the same form in the 3rd person plural imperfect/aorist and in optative.

In order to understand correctly the meaning of these forms, have in mind the following rule of thumb: **იყო** and **იყვნენ** are in the optative tense and should be translated as the infinitive *to be* only if they are preceded by verbs of the 4th conjugation (*want, can, etc.*) or the word **უნდა** (*must, have to, should*).

A. *To be* in the imperfect/aorist tense

წუმი ძმა შარშან იაპონიაში **იყო**.
My brother **was** in Japan last year.

ვინ **იყო** ის სიმპატიური კაცი?
Who **was** that nice man?

გასულ კვირას არჩილი და თინა *(sub./nom.)* ჩვენთან **იყვნენ**.
Last week Archili and Tina **were** at our place.

გუშინ ისინი თეატრში **იყვნენ**.
Yesterday they **were** in the theater.

B. *To be* in the optative tense

არ **გინდა** ხვალ ჩვენთან **იყო**?
Don't *you want* to be with us tomorrow?

როდის **უნდა იყო** სადგურში?
When *should* you be at the station?

სტუდენტები დილის 9 საათზე აქ **უნდა იყვნენ**.
The student *must* be here at 9 o'clock in the morning.

მათ **უნდათ** მომავალ წელს საქართველოში **იყვნენ**.
They *want* to be in Georgia next year.

* The verb *to be* and verbs of motion (**მივდივარ** *I am going,*
მიდიხარ *you are going,* etc.) do not have direct objects and do
not require the ergative case.

Exercises

**I. Fill in the blanks with personal pronouns in the appropriate
form.**

1. (ჩვენ) _____ უკვე ვისადილეთ.
   We already had dinner.

2. (ისინი) _____ უნივერსიტეტი ორი წლის
   წინ დაამთავრეს.
   They graduated from the university two years ago.

3. (შენ) _____ დღეს როდის გაიღვიძე?
   When did you wake up today?

4. (მე) _____ ახალი პროექტი დავიწყე.
   I started a new project.

5. (ის) _____ ბინა მეტროსთან ახლოს
   იქირავა.
   He (she) rented an apartment near the subway.

6. (თქვენ) _____ ემილის წერილი
გაუგზავნეთ, არა?
You sent a letter to Emily, didn't you?

II. **Fill in the blanks with appropriate forms of the verb მინდა**
want or the auxiliary უნდა should. Refer to the verb chart in
Grammar section IV in this lesson.

1. მან სასწრაფოდ _____ გაგზავნოს ეს
საბუთები საელჩოში.
She (he) should urgently send these documents to the embassy.

2. ამ საღამოს ჩვენ გიასთან _____
დავრეკოთ.
Tonight we want to call Gia.

3. _____ ქართული უკეთესად **ვისწავლო.**
I want (would like) to learn Georgian better.

4. დღეს შენ ეს წიგნები ბიბლიოთეკაში
_____ დააბრუნო.
Today you should return these books to the library.

5. მათ _____ ახალი კომპიუტერი
იყიდონ.
They want to buy a new computer.

6. მას არ _____ აქ დიდი ხანი
იმუშავოს.
She (he) does not want to work here for long.

7. მათ ბინის ქირა დღეს _____
გადაიხადონ.
They should pay the rent today.

8. ოპერის ბილეთები _____ ხვალ იყიდო.
You should buy opera tickets tomorrow.

**III. Fill in the blanks with appropriate forms of the verb *to be* in
the present, future, imperfect/aorist, or optative tense.**

1. სამშაბათს ემილი თბილისში _____.
   On Tuesday Emily will be here.

2. ეს _____ ჩვენი მუზეუმი.
   This is our museum.

3. გუშინ გია სკოლაში არ _____.
   Yesterday Gia was not in school.

4. ძალიან მინდა ახლა შენთან _____.
   I wish (want very much) to be with you right now.

5. სად _____ მანანა და ლია გასულ კვირას?
   Where were Manan and Lia last week?

6. მერაბი და მისი ცოლი სად _____?
   Where are Merabi and his wife?

7. მათ უნდათ რვა საათისთვის სახლში
   _____.
   They want to be at home by eight o'clock.

8. შაბათს უასათუოდ აქ უნდა _____.
   You must be here on Saturday by all means.

9. რამდენი ხანი _____ ამერიკაში?
   For how long will you *(pl.)* be in America?

10. მალე ისინიც ჩვენთან _____.
    Soon they too will be with us (at our place).

KEY TO EXERCISES

Lesson 1

I.

1. რა ლამაზია!   4. რა დიდია!
2. რა ცუდია!   5. რა უცნაურია!
3. რა სასიხარულოა!   6. რა პატარაა!

II.

1. გერმანული ბანკი
2. ქართული ღვინო
3. რუსი სტუდენტი
4. ფრანგი დიპლომატი
5. ამერიკული გაზეთი

III.

1. ესპანური	ესპანურად	in Spanish
2. პოლონური	პოლონურად	in Polish
3. არაბული	არაბულად	in Arabic
4. იტალიური	იტალიურად	in Italian

IV.

A.

1. მე კარგად ვლაპარაკობ ქართულად.
2. თქვენ ლაპარაკობთ იტალიურად?
3. მე ვლაპარაკობ არაბულად და პოლონურად.

B.

მე ამერიკელი სტუდენტი ვარ. ჩემი სახელია ჯონი, მე ვცხოვრობ და ვმუშაობ თბილისში. მე აქ ბინას ვქირაობ. მე ვლაპარაკობ ქართულად, მაგრამ ცუდად.

V.

1. თამაზი: ცხოვრობთ
2. ქევინი: ბინას
3. თამაზი: ამერიკელი, ინგლისელი

4. ქევინი: ამერიკელი
5. თამაზი: ლაპარაკობთ

Lesson 2

I.

A.

1. მე აქ არ ვცხოვრობ.
2. თქვენ სკოლაში არ მუშაობთ.
3. ქევინი გაზეთს არ კითხულობს.

B.

1. მე ქართველი სტუდენტი არა ვარ.
2. შენ დაკავებული არა ხარ?
3. ლალი აქ არ არის.

C.

1. დღეს ბანკი ღია არ არის.
2. კვირას სკოლა დაკეტილი არ არის.
3. თამაზი სახლში არ არის.

II.

1. ეს თამაზის სახლია.
2. ქევინი კარგი სტუდენტია
3. ლალი დაკავებულია.

III.

1. საათში   4. ჩიკაგოში
2. ქუჩაში   5. ბანკში
3. გაზეთში   6. პერუში

IV.

1. თამაზი: ხარ
2. ქევინი: კარგად
3. თამაზი: მეც, კინოში
4. ქევინი: კინოში, გადის
5. თამაზი: "რუსთაველში," ფილმი
6. ქევინი: სიამოვნებით
7. თამაზი: მზად იყავი
8. ქევინი: ვიქნები

Lesson 3

I.
1. ცხოვრობენ
2. სწავლობს
3. ვაკეთებ
4. კითხულობ
5. ლაპარაკობ
6. მუშაობენ

II.
1. ოთახი ოთახს ოთახში ოთახზე
2. კინო კინოს კინოში კინოზე
3. კვირა კვირას კვირაში კვირაზე
4. თვე თვეს თვეში თვეზე

III.
1. თამართან
2. ვასოსთან
3. მურმანთან
4. ქეთინოსთან
5. ლაშასთან
6. ნათელასთან

IV.
1. შენ სტუდენტი ხარ არა?
2. ლალი თქვენი დაა, არა?
3. ეს თქვენი ბინაა, არა?
4. თქვენ აქ ცხოვრობთ, არა?

V. Check on the conjugation of these verbs in Appendix III.

Lesson 4

I.
1. მიდის
2. მიდიხარ
3. მივდივართ
4. მიდიან
5. მიდიხართ
6. მივდივართ

II.
1. ირაკლი არ სწავლობს იტალიურ ენას.
2. იტალიურ ენას ირაკლი არ სწავლობს.
3. არ სწავლობს ირაკლი იტალიურ ენას.
4. არ სწავლობს იტალიურ ენას ირაკლი.

III. Check on the conjugation of these verbs in Appendix III.

IV.

A.

1. სად არის ქვეინი?   or   ქვეინი სად არის?
2. სად არის შენი მეგობარი? or   შენი მეგობარი სად არის?
3. სად არის საპირფარეშო? or   საპირფარეშო სად არის?

B.

1. ვინ არის ის კაცი?   or   ის კაცი ვინ არის?
2. ვინ მიდის ბაზარში?   or   ბაზარში ვინ მიდის?
3. ვინ არ ლაპარაკობს   or   ინგლისურად ვინ არ
     ინგლისურად?   ლაპარაკობს

C.

1. ვისია ეს წიგნი?   or   ეს წიგნი ვისია?
2. ვისია ეს კომპიუტერი? or   ეს კომპიუტერი ვისია?
3. ვისია ეს საწოლი ოთახი? or   ეს საწოლი ოთახი ვისია?

V.

1. ამ, ეს   4. ის, იმ
2. ის   5. ამ, იმ
3. ეს, ამ   6. ეს, იმ

Lesson 5

I.

1. რა or რომელ   4. რომელი
2. რომელი   5. როგორი
3. როგორ   6. როგორ

II.

1. ყველაზე დიდი   6. მდალია
2. პატარა   7. ყველაზე მოკლე
3. უარესი   8. ნაკლები
4. ყველაზე ლამაზი   9. უფრო იაფია
5. საუკეთესო   10. ყველაზე კარგი or საუკეთესო

III.

1. რა გინდა
2. ყველი, ხილი
3. ხორცი
4. ვჭამ
5. ვეგეტარიანელი
6. თევზს

Lesson 6

I.

1. ქალის კაბა
2. მეგობრის წერილი
3. ბინის გასაღები
4. გიას სახლი
5. ნუნუს მეგობარი
6. მეზობლის კატა

II.

A.

1. ჩემთვის
2. მისთვის
3. შენთვის
4. ჩვენთვის
5. მათთვის
6. თქვენთვის

B.

1. მანანასთვის
2. ემილისთვის
3. ხვალისთვის
4. ჩემი დისთვის

C.

1. ვისთვის
2. ვისთვის

III.

1. მანქანით
2. შავი კალმით
3. შაქრით
4. მეტროთი, ტაქსით

IV.

1. ქალები
2. საჩუქრები
3. მეზობლები
4. კიბეები
5. საქმეები
6. კუები
7. გოგოები
8. კალმები
9. სახელები
10. ბაზრები
11. მწერლები
12. ბიჭები

Lesson 7

I.

1. ხომ არ იცი მანანა სად არის?
2. ბაზარში ხომ არ მიდიხართ?
3. ქართული ხალხური სიმღერები ხომ არა გაქვთ?
4. თქვენ ბინას ხომ არ აქირავებთ?
5. ის კაცი შენი მეზობელი ხომ არ არის?
6. თინას ძმა ამ ბანკში ხომ არ მუშაობს?

II.

1. I am Georgian; my friend, however, is American.
2. Lali speaks English well but does not speak French.
3. Emily is renting a one-room apartment, and Nunu is renting a two-room one.
4. This CD is expensive, while that one is cheap.

III.

1. My two friends are leaving for Italy tomorrow. (მიდის)
2. Tina and Lali work in this store. (მუშაობენ)
3. These girls live in that house. (ცხოვრობენ)
4. These three boys sing Georgian folk songs very well. (მღერის)
5. Rusudan's daughter goes (studies) to this school. (სწავლობს)
6. On Saturday five American doctors will arrive in Tbilisi.
   (ჩამოდის)

IV.

A.

1. ოცი	20		5. ცხრამეტი	19
2. ჩვიდმეტი	17		6. ცამეტი	13
3. თოთხმეტი	14		7. თორმეტი	12
4. თერთმეტი	11		8. თექვსმეტი	16

B.

1. 12th   5. 4th
2. 16th   6. 5th
3. 10th   7. 15th
4. 7th   8. 18th

V.
1. ოთხის ნახევარია. 4. პირველის ნახევარია
2. ორის ნახევარია 5. ცხრის ნახევარია
3. შვიდის ნახევარია 6. თორმეტის ნახევარია

Lesson 8

I.
1. აკეთებდი
2. ვცხოვრებდი
3. ამთავრებს OR დაამთავრებს
4. ვმუშაობდით
5. ჭამდა, ჭამს
6. დარეკავს.

7. თამაშობენ.
8. ლაპარაკობენ
9. დარეკავ
10. საუზმობენ
11. გაგზავნი
12. იმღერებდა

II. Check on the conjugation of these verbs in Appendix III.

III.
1. ვიქნებით 5. იქნება.
2. იქნები 6. იყავით
3. ვიყავით 7. ვიქნები
4. იყო 8. იყო

IV.
1. წვიმიანი 4. ლიმონიანი
2. სურათებიანი 5. მარილიანი
3. ქარიანი 6. მთვარიანი

Lesson 9

I.
1. არ 4. არა
2. ვერ 5. არა
3. ვერ 6. არა, ვერ

II. Check on the conjugation of these verbs in Appendix III.

III.
1. ლამარას, ტკბილი ჩაი
2. შენ, პური
3. მას, ორმთახიანი ბინა
4. მათ, ჩვენი მისამართი
5. მე, ოცი დოლარი
6. თქვენ, ოპერა

IV.
1. აქვს   4. (პ)ყავს
2. მყავს   5. გაქვთ
3. გვყავს   6. აქვთ

Lesson 10

I.
1. როგორი (or რომელი)   5. სადაც
2. რაც   6. სად
3. როცა   7. ვინ
4. როდის   8. როგორც

II.
1. სახლიდან   4. მეგობრისგან
2. ზურაბისგან   5. ვისგან
3. ჩიკაგოდან   6. მათგან

III.
1. მანანასთან   4. ჩვენთან
2. ჩემთან   5. მეგობრებთან
3. ბაზართან   6. ექიმთან

IV.
1. ვისთან
2. ვისგან
3. ვისთან

Lesson 11

I.
1. შევიტანო
2. იყიდოს
3. დარეცხოს

4. ისწავლოს
5. გავაკეთოთ
6. იქირავონ

II.
1. შეგიძლიათ.
2. შეგიძლია

3. შემიძლია
4. შეუძლია

III.
1. მოდი ყავა და ნამცხვარი ავიღოთ.
2. მოდი ვისაუზმოთ.
3. მოდი გავყიდოთ ჩვენი ძველი მანქანა.

IV.
1. მოდი ხვალ ოპერაში წავიდეთ.
2. მოდით დღეს გიასთან მივიდეთ (or წავიდეთ).
3. მოდი ახლა ბაზარში წავიდეთ.

V.
1. ვითამაშოთ
2. დავხუროთ
3. ვიყიდოთ

Lesson 12

I.
1. კარგმა გოგონამ
2. მისმა პატარა ჭიქამ
3. ორმა დიდმა მაგიდამ

4. მაღალმა ხემ
5. შენმა გრძელმა სტატიამ
6. მოკლე თეთრმა კაბამ

II.
1. დაამთავრა
2. გააზავნე
3. დარეკავენ

4. დახარჯო
5. დაკარგა
6. დავალაგე

III.

1. იმუშავებს 4. ცხოვრობდი
2. ქირაობს 5. ცეკვავდა
3. ვიცეკვოთ. 6. სადილობენ

IV.

1. ჩემმა მეგობარმა, საინტერესო სტატია
2. რუსიკომ და ნანამ, სარეცხი
3. ბავშვები, ფეხბურთის
4. ყავა
5. სტუმრები, ქართულ სიმღერებს
6. სადილს, ტელევიზორს

V.

1. მოდი ეს სიმღერა ვიმღეროთ.
2. არ იმღერო ეს სიმღერა!
3. ყავა გააკეთე, რა? OR შეგიძლია ყავა გააკეთო?
4. ძალიან გთხოვ, ყავას ნუ აკეთებ, ჩაი გააკეთე.
5. მოდი ხაჭაპური გავაკეთოთ.
6. გავაკეთოთ ხაჭაპური?

Lesson 13

I.

1. ჩვენ 4. მე
2. მათ 5. მან
3. შენ 6. თქვენ

II.

1. უნდა 5. უნდათ
2. გვინდა 6. უნდა
3. მინდა 7. უნდა
4. უნდა 8. უნდა

III.

1. იქნება 6. არიან
2. არის 7. იყვნენ
3. იყო 8. იყო
4. ვიყო 9. იქნებით
5. იყვნენ 10. იქნებიან

GEORGIAN-ENGLISH GLOSSARY

Parts of speech for each entry are abbreviated and italicized. (Please refer back to the list of abbreviations on p. 17.) Syncopating vowels of nouns are printed in italics. All verbs (except for the verb *be*) are given in the present-tense, 2nd-person singular form, followed by the preverb that forms the future tense in parentheses. (The verb *be* is given in its verbal noun form ყოფნა.) The numbers and capital letters in parentheses following the English translations of the verbs indicate conjugation groups and subgroups. In addition, the aorist form of irregular verbs is given.

Sample entry:

ა-კეთ-ებ (გა-) *v.* (you) do, make, prepare, cook (1, A)

The abbreviation *v.* indicates the word is a verb; the second-person singular form is აკეთებ meaning *you make*; -ებ is the PFSF, i.e., the present/future stem formant; the addition of (გა-) to the present tense—გააკეთებ—creates the future tense, meaning *you will make*. The verb is of the 1st conjugation group, subgroup A (1, A). (All conjugation charts can be found in Appendix III.)

ა

აბაზანა *n.* bathroom

ა-ბრუნ-ებ (და-) *v.* (you) return (*s.th.*) (1, A)

ა-ბრტყელ-ებ (გა-) *v.* (you) flatten (1, A)

ა-გდ-ებ (გააგდა-) *v.* (you) throw away (1, C)

ა-გრძელ-ებ (გა-) *v.* (you) continue (1, A)

ადამიანი *n.* human being, person

ა-დარ-ებ (შე-) *v.* (you) compare (1, A)

ადგილი *n.* place

ადვილი *adj.* easy

ადვილად *adv.* easily

ადრე *adv.* early, earlier

ა-ვს-ებ (შე-) *v.* (you) fill, fill out (*s.th.*) (1, C)

ავტორი *n.* author

აზრი *n.* opinion, idea

აი here you are, here (it is), look

აივა-ნი *n.* balcony

ა-კაკუნ-ებ (და-) *v.* (you) knock (at) (1, A)

ა-კეთ-ებ (გა-) *v.* (you) do, make, prepare, cook (1, A)

ა-ლაგ-ებ (და-) *v.* (you) tidy up, clean up (1, A)

ა-ლბ-ობ (და-) *v.* (you) soften, soak (1, A)

ალბათ *adj.* probably
ამასობაში *adv.* meanwhile
ამაყი *adj.* proud
ამ საღამოს tonight
ამბავი *n.* event, fact, happening /
   ამბები *pl.* / ახალი ამბები *pl.*
   n. news
ამერიკა America
ამერიკელი *adj.* American
   (person)
ამერიკული *adj.* American
   (thing)
ა-მზად-ებ (მო-) *v.* (you) prepare
   (1, A)
ა-მთავრ-ებ *v.* (you) complete,
   finish, graduate (1, A)
ამინდი *n.* weather
ან or
ანგარიში *n.* account
ა-ნგრ-ევ (და-) *v.* you) demolish
   (1, *irr.*) /
   და-ა-ნგრი-ე *v. aor./imp.*
არავინ *pron.* nobody
არასოდეს *adv.* never
არაფ-ე-რი *n.* nothing
არჩევნები *pl. n.* elections
ასანთი *n.* lighter, matches
ასე *adv.* so, this way, this
   manner
ასეთი *adj.* this kind, like this
ასპირანტი *n.* graduate student
ა-სრულ-ებ (შე-) *v.* (you) fulfill,
   carry out (a task) (1, A)
ა-სწავლ-ი *v.* (you) teach (1, B)
ა-სწორ-ებ (გა-) *v.* (you) correct
   (1, A)
ა-სხ-ამ (და-) *v.* (you) pour (1) /
   და-ა-სხ-ი *v. aor./imp.*
ატ-ა-მი *n.* peach

ა-ცყობინ-ებ (შე-) *v.* (you)
   inform (1, A)
აფთიაქი *n.* drugstore
აქ *adv.* here / აქედან from
   here / აქვე right here
ა-ქირავ-ებ (გა-) *v.* (you) lease,
   rent out (1, A)
ა-ცხელ-ებ (გა-) *v.* (you) heat up
   (s.th.) (1, A)
ა-ცხ-ობ (გამო-) *v.* (you) bake
   (1, C)
აღდგომა *n.* Easter
ა-ღ-ებ, გა- *v.* (you) open (1, C)
აღმოსავლეთი *adj.* east
აღმოსავლეთ საქართველო
   East Georgia
ა-ყრი (და-) *v.* (you) spread,
   sprinkle (1, B)
ა-შენ-ებ *v.* (you) build (1, A)
ა-ჩერ-ებ, (გა-) *v.* to stop *(s.o.* or
   s.th.) (1, A)
ახლა *adv.* now
ახლობ-ე-ლი *adj./n.* loved one,
   relative
ახლო(ს) *adv.* near, nearby

ბ

ბადრიჯ-ა-ნი *n.* eggplant
ბაზ-ა-რი *n.* farmer's market
ბარგი *n.* luggage
ბაღი *n.* garden
ბედნიერი *adj.* happy
ბედნიერება *n.* happiness
ბევრი *adj.* many, much
ბეჭ-ე-დი *n.* ring / საქორწინო
   ბეჭედი wedding ring
ბიბლია *n.* bible
ბიზნესი *n.* business
ბიზნესმენი *n.* businessman

ბილეთი *n.* ticket
ბინა *n.* apartment, residence
ბიჭი *n.* boy
ბოდიში *n.* excuse (me)
ბოდიშს ვიხდი I apologize
ბოთლი *n.* bottle
ბოლო *adj.* last, final; *n.* end
ბოლოს *adv.* finally
ბოსტნეული *n.* vegetables
ბოტანიკური *adj.* botanical
ბრუნდ-ებ-ი (და-) *v.* (you) return
(from) (2, A)

გ
გადასახადი *n.* payment
გაზეთი *n.* newspaper
გათხოვილი *adj.* married
(woman)
გაკვეთილი *n.* lesson, tutorial
გამყიდველი *n.* salesperson
გამოთქმა *n.* expression
გამოცდილება *n.* experience
განათლება *n.* education
გარაჟი *n.* garage
გასაგები *adj.* clear, intelligible
გასაგებია *v.* I see
გასაღები *n.* key
გა-ქვს (you) have *(thing)*
გაყიდული *adj.* sold out
გაჩერება *n.* stop, stopping /
ავტობუსის გაჩერება bus stop
(lit.: a stop of bus)
გ-ახსოვს *v.* (you) remember
(4, A)
გი-რჩევნია *v.* (you) prefer
(4, B)
გი-ყვარს *v.* (you) love, like
(4, B)
გემრიელი *adj.* delicious, tasty

გემო *n.* taste
გერმანია Germany
გერმანელი *adj.* German
(person)
გერმანული *adj.* German *(thing)*
გე-შინია *v.* (you) are afraid
(4, C)
გე-ჩქარ-ებ-ა *v.* (you) are in a
hurry (4, C)
გვარი *n.* last name
გვერდი *n.* side; page
გვერდით *dat.* by the side, next
to *(s.th.* or *s.o.)*
გ-გზავნ-ი (გა-) *v.* (you) send
(1, B)
გი-ნდა *v.* (you) want (4, B)
(გ)მადლობა (თ) *v.* thank you
გნებავთ *v. pol.* (do) you wish
გოგო(ნა) *n.* girl
გრანტი *n.* grant, scholarship
გ-შია *v.* (you are) hungry (4)
გ-ჭირდება *v.* (you) need (4, B)
გ-ყავს *v.* (you) have *(person)*
(4, A)

დ
და *n.* sister; *conj.* and
და-ძმა *n.* siblings
დაბადება *n.* birth
დაბადების დღე birthday
დაბლა *adv.* below, down
დაკავებული *adj.* busy
დაკეტილი *adj.* closed, locked
დამთავრებული *adj.*
completed, finished
დანა *n.* knife
დარდი *n.* grief
დარდიანი *adj.* sad, grief
stricken

დასავლეთი *adj.* west
დასავლეთ საქართველო West
Georgia
დარწმუნებული *adj.* sure,
convinced
დ-ებ (და-) *v.* (you) put (on)
(1, C)
დ-ებ (შე-) *v.* (you) put in, into
(1, C)
დიდი *adj.* big, large, great
დედოფ-ა-ლი *n.* queen
დეიდა *n.* aunt, auntie
დეიდაშვილი *n.* cousin *(on
mother's side)*
დილა *n.* morning
დისერტაცია *n.* dissertation
დოლარი *n.* dollar
დრო *n.* time
დროებით *adv.* temporarily
დროშა *n.* flag, banner
დღე *n.* day
დღეს *adv.* today

ე
ებრაელი *adj.* Jewish *(person)*
ებრაული *adj.* Jewish *(thing)*
ეგება maybe, what if
ევრო *n.* Euro
ევროპა *n.* Europe
ეკლესია *n.* church
ეკრანი *n.* screen
ელჩი *n.* ambassador
ენა *n.* tongue, language
ერბოკვერცხი *n.* omelet
ერთად *adv.* together, together
with
ერთმანეთი each other
ექიმი *n.* doctor *(medical)*
ექსკურსია *n.* excursion

ეწევი *v.* (you) smoke (1) /
მოწიე *v.* *aor./imp.*
ეჭვი *n.* doubt
ეჭვ-ობ *v.* doubt (3, A)
ეხლა *adv.* now *(regional)*

ვ
ვალი *n.* debt, duty
ვაშლი *n.* apple
ვალუტა *n.* currency / უცხოური
ვალუტა foreign currency
ვარსკვლავი *n.* star /
კინოვარსკვლავი *n.*
movie star
ვარჯიში *n.* exercise
ვარჯიშ-ობ *v.* exercise (3, A)
ვეგეტარიანელი *adj.* vegetarian
ვერცხლი *n.* silver
ვერცხლის კოვზი silver spoon
ვინ *pron.* who
ვინმე *pron.* anybody, somebody

ზ
ზეგ *adv.* the day after tomorrow
ზეიმი *n.* celebration, festival,
holiday
ზეიმ-ობ *v.* (you) celebrate (3, A)
ზუსტი *adj.* precise, exact
ზუსტად *adv.* precisely, exactly

თ
თავისუფალი *adj.* free;
unoccupied
თამაში *n.* game, play
თამაშ-ობ *v.* (you) play (3, A)
თარო *n.* shelf / წიგნების
თარო book shelf
თარჯიმანი *n.* interpreter
თეატრი *n.* theater

თევზი *n.* fish
თეთრი *adj.* white; *n.* tetri
(Georgian currency / small
change)
თეფში *n.* plate
თვალი *n.* eye
თვე *n.* month
თვიური *adj.* monthly
თითი *n.* finger
თითო *adj.* each
თითქმის *adj.* almost
თუ or, if
თურმე *adv.* apparently
თქვენ *pron.* you
თქვენი *pron.* your
თხოვნა *n.* request

ი

იაფი *adj.* cheap
იატაკი *n.* floor
ი-ვიწ̌ყ-ებ (და-) *v.* (you) forget
(1, A)
ი-თვლ-ი (და-) *v.* (you) count
(1, D) / და-ი-თვალ-ე *v.*
aor./imp.
იმეილი *n.* e-mail
ინგლისელი *adj.* British
(person)
ინგლისური *adj.* English
(thing) / ინგლისურად in
English
ინდაური *n.* turkey
ინებეთ *v. pol.* here you are
ინტერნეტი *n.* Internet
ინტერნეტკლუბი *n.* Internet
club
ი-რჩ-ევ, (ა-) *v.* (you) chose (1) /
აირჩიე *v. aor./imp.*
ისევ again

ი-სვენ-ებ (და-) *v.* (you) rest,
relax
ისტორია *n.* history
ისტორიკოსი *n.* historian
იურისტი *n.* lawyer
ი-ღ-ებ (ა-) *v.* (you) take, pick up
(1, C)
ი-ღ-ებ (მი-) *v.* (you) receive
(1, C)
ი-ღვიძ-ებ (გა-) *v.* (you) wake up
(1, A)
იშვიათი *adj.* rare, unusual,
precious
იშვიათად *adv.* rarely,
infrequently
ი-ცვ-ამ, (ჩა-) *v.* get dressed (1) /
ჩა-იცვ-ი *v. aor./imp.*
იცი *v.* (you) know (1, E)
ი-ცნ-ობ (გა-) *v.* (you) meet
someone, are introduced (1, D) /
გაიცანი *v. aor./imp.*
ი-ძინ-ებ (და-) *v.* (you) fall asleep
(1, A)
ი-წ̌ყ-ებ (და-) *v.* (you) start (1, C)
ი-ხდ-ი (გა და-) *v.* (you) pay
(1, D) / გადა-ი-ხად-ე *v.*
aor./imp.
ი-ხდ-ი (გა-) *v.* (you) take off
(coat, shoes, etc.) (1, D) /
გა-ი-ხად-ე *v. aor./imp.*

კ

კაბა *n.* dress
კათალიკოსი *n.* Catholicos,
head of the Georgian Church
კამათი *n.* argument
კამათ-ობ *v.* (you) argue (3, A)
კანონი *n.* law / უკანონო *adj.*
illegal

კარაქი *n.* butter / კარაქიანი *adj.* with butter

კარგ-ავ (და-) *v.* (you) lose (1, A)

კარგი *adj.* good, nice

კარი *adj.* door

კარტოფილი *n.* potato

კარტოფილის პიურე mashed potatoes (*lit.*: mash of potato)

კატა *n.* cat

კაფეტერია *n.* cafeteria

კაცი *n.* man, human being

კბილი *n.* tooth

კეთილი *adj.* kind

კერძი *n.* dish *(food)*

კერძო *adj.* private

კვერცხი *n.* egg

კი *conj.* and, however, on the other hand

კი yes

კიდევ more, one more

კითხვა *n.* question

კითხულ-ობ *v.* (you) read, ask (1, F)

კილო *n.* kilogram *(short form)*

კინო *n.* movie, movie theater

კინოვარსკვლავი *n.* movie star

კინოფესტივალი *n.* film festival

კიტრი *n.* cucumber

კოვზი *n.* spoon / ვერცხლის კოვზი silver spoon

კომბოსტო *n.* cabbage

კომპაქტდისკი *n.* compact disk, CD

კონსულტანტი *n.* consultant, adviser

კონცერტი *n.* concert

კრ-ავ, (შე-) *v.* (you) tie (1) / შე-კარ-ი *v. aor./imp.*

კუთხე *n.* corner

ლ

ლავაში *n.* flat oven-baked bread

ლამაზი *adj.* beautiful

ლაპარაკ-ობ *v.* (you) speak (3, A)

ლაპარაკი *n.* talk, conversation

ლარი *n.* lari (Georgian currency) / ლარნახევარი lari and a half

ლექსიკონი *n.* dictionary

ლიმონათი *n.* lemonade

ლიმონი *n.* lemon

ლიფტი *n.* elevator

ლობიო *n.* beans

ლოცვა *n.* prayer

ლოცულ-ობ *v.* (you) pray (3, A) / ი-ლოც-ებ *v. fut.*

ლუდი *n.* beer

მ

მაგარი *adj.* strong, hard

მაგიდა *n.* table

მაგრამ *conj.* but

მადლობა *n.* thank

დიდი მადლობა thank you very much

მაკარონი *n.* macaroni

მალ-ავ (და-) *v.* (you) hide (1, A)

მამა *n.* father

მანქანა *n.* car

მართალი *adj.* right, true

მართალი ხარ you are right

მართლა *adv.* really

მართლაც indeed

მარილი *n.* salt

მარილიანი *adj.* salty, with salt

მარცხნივ *adv.* on the left / ხელმარცხნივ *adv.* on the left hand side

მარჯვენივ *adv.* on the right / ხელმარჯვენივ *adv.* on the right hand side

მასწავლებ-ე-ლი *n.* teacher, tutor

მაღაზია *n.* store

მაშინ *adv.* then, in that case

მაწონი *n.* yogurt / მაწვნის *n. gen.*

მგზავრ-ობ *v.* (you) travel (3, A)

მდიდარი *adj.* rich

მთა *n.* mountain

მთიანი *adj.* mountainous

მთავრობა *n.* government

მგონი(ა) it seems like, it seems to me

მეგობ-ა-რი *n.* friend

მეგობრობა *n.* friendship

მეზობ-ე-ლი *n.* neighbor

მეორე სართული second floor

მერე *adv.* afterwards, after

მეტი *adj.* more

მეტრო *n.* subway

მეუღლე *n.* spouse

მეჩეთი *n.* mosque

მზად *adj.* ready

მზარეული *n.* cook

მზე *n.* sun

მზიანი *adj.* sunny

მთავარი *adj.* main

მთვარე *n.* moon

მთვარიანი *adj.* moon-lit

მისამართი *n.* address

მობილური *n./adj.* cell phone

მოედ-ა-ნი *n.* (city) square

მოლარე *n.* cashier

მოლაპარაკება *n.* negotiation(s)

მომავ-ა-ლი *adj.* next, coming; *n./adj.* future

მომეცი *v. opt./imp.* (you) gave me; give me *(request)*

მოსახლეობა *n.* population

მოქალაქე *n.* citizen

მოქალაქეობა *n.* citizenship

მოწმობა *n.* document, ID

მჟავე *adj.* sour

მრავალქამიერი *n.* Georgian festive folksong

მრგვალი *adj.* round

მსახიობი *n.* actor, actress

მსოფლიო *n./adj.* world

მტ-ე-რი *n.* enemy

მტვერი *n.* dust

მუდმივი *adj.* permanent, endless

მუსულმანი *adj.* Muslim

მუშა-ობ *v.* (you) work (3, A)

მღერ-ი *v.* (you) sing (3, B)

მღვდ-ე-ლი *n.* priest

მშვენიერი *adj.* beautiful, charming

მშობ-ე-ლი *n.* parent

მძიმე *adj.* heavy; difficult

მძღოლი *n.* driver

მწერ-ა-ლი *n.* writer

მწვანე *adj.* green

მხატვარი *n.* painter

მხიარული *adj.* merry, joyful

მხოლოდ *adv.* only

ნ

ნათესავი *n.* relative

ნაკლები *adj.* less

ნაგ-ა-ვი *n.* garbage

ნაგვის ყუთი garbage can

ნამდვილი *adj.* true

ნამდვილად *adj.* for sure, for certain

ნამცხვ-ა-რი *n.* pastry

ნარდი *n.* backgammon
ნარკოტიკი *n.* drugs, narcotics
ნარკომანი *n.* drug addict
ნარკომანია *n.* drug addiction
ნაცნობი *n./adj.* acquaintance
ნაჭ-ე-რი *n.* piece
ნახევ-ა-რი *adj.* half
ნელი *adj.* slow
ნელა *adv.* slowly
ნიორი *n.* garlic
ნივრიანი *adj.* with garlic, garlicky
ნომ-ე-რი *n.* number
ნუ don't (*used only in negative requests*)

ო

ოთახი *n.* room
ომი *n.* war
ორგანიზაცია *n.* organization
ორივე both
ოპოზიცია *n.* opposition
ოპოზიციური *adj.* opposition(al) / ოპოზიციური პარტია opposition party
ოქრო *n.* gold
ოჯახი *n.* family

პ

პალტო *n.* overcoat
პამიდორი *n.* tomato / პამიდვრის *gen.*
პატარა *adj.* small
პატიოსანი *adj.* honest
პასუხი *n.* answer
პასუხ-ობ *v.* (you) answer (3)
პირადი *adj.* personal
პირველი first
პირდაპირ *adv.* straight ahead

პიროვნება *n.* person
პლატო *n.* plateau, flat top of a mountain
პოლიცია *n.* police
პოლიტიკა *n.* politics; policy
პოლიტიკური *adj.* political
პოულ-ობ *v.* (you) find (1, F) / ი-პოვ(ნ)ე *aor./imp.* (you) found
პროფესია *n.* profession
პროფესორი *n.* professor
პური *n.* bread

ჟ

ჟეტონი *n.* token (*for entrance to the subway*)
ჟურნალი *n.* magazine

რ

რა *pron.* what, how
რად *pron.* what for
რაიონი *n.* region, district
რამდენი *pron.* how many
რამე *pron.* something, anything
რასაკვირველია of course
რატომ *pron.* why
რბილი *adj.* soft
რეკ-ავ (და-) *v.* (you) ring, phone (1, A)
რელიგია *n.* religion
რელიგიური *adj.* religious
რესტორ-ა-ნი *n.* restaurant
როგორ *pron.* how
როგორი *pron.* what kind
როგორც *pron.* just like, similar to, just as
რომ *conj.* that
რომ-ე-ლი *pron.* which
რძე *n.* milk

რუსი *adj.* Russian *(person)*
რუსული *adj.* Russian *(thing)* /
რუსულად in Russian
რჩევა *n.* advice

ს

საათი *n.* hour; clock, watch
სააგენტო *n.* agency
საბუთი *n.* document, ID
სად *pron.* where
სადილ-ობ *v.* (you) have dinner
(3, A)
საელჩო *n.* embassy
სავარძ-ე-ლი *n.* armchair
საზოგადოება *n.* society
სათვალე *n.* eyeglasses
საინტერესო *adj.* interesting
საკმაოდ *adv.* rather, significantly
საკმარისი *adv.* sufficient,
enough
სალათი *n.* salad
სალარო *n.* cashier's office
სამზარეულო *n.* kitchen /
მზარეული *n.* cook
სამსახური *n.* office, place of
work
სამწუხარო *adj.* unfortunate
სამწუხაროდ *adv.* unfortunately
სამხრეთი *adj.* south, southern
სანდო *adj.* reliable
საპ-ო-ნი *n.* soap
სართული *n.* floor, level /
მეორე სართული second floor
სარკე *n.* mirror
სასადილო *n.* dining room,
diner
სასაცილო *adj.* funny
სასიამოვნო *adj.* pleasant, nice
სასურველი *adj.* desirable

სასტუმრო *n./adj.* hotel
სასტუმრო (ოთახი) guest room
საუზმე *n.* breakfast
საუზმ-ობ *v.* (you) have breakfast
(3, A)
საუკუნე *n.* century
საუკეთესო *adj.* the best,
outstanding
საფრანგეთი France
საქართველო Georgia
საქმე *n.* business, things to be
done
საქორწინო ბეჭედი wedding
ring
საღამო *n.* evening, in the
evening / ამ საღამოს tonight
საშუალო *adj.* medium, middle
საჩუქ-ა-რი gift
საწოლი *n.* bed
საწოლი ოთახი bedroom
საჭირო *adj.* necessary, required
საჭმელი *n.* food
სახელი *n.* name
სახლი *n.* house, home
სვ-ამ (შე-) *v.* (you) drink (1) /
შე-სვ-ი *aor./imp.*
სიამოვნებით with pleasure
სიგარეტი *n.* cigarette
სიდი *n.* CD
სიდი პლეიერი *n.* CD player
სინაგოგა *n.* synagogue
სინჯ-ავ (გა-) *v.* (you) try, have
some (1, A)
სიმღერა *n.* song
სიყვარული *n.* love
სკამი *n.* chair
სკოლა *n.* school *(from
elementary to high school
inclusive)*

სომეხი *adj.* Armenian *(person)*
სომხური *adj.* Armenian *(thing)*
სოფ-*ე*-ლი *n.* village, countryside
სტადიონი *n.* stadium
სტაფილო *n.* carrot
სტიპენდია *n.* scholarship, stipend
სტუდენტი *n.* student
სტუმ-ა-რი *n.* guest
სულ *adv.* completely, entirely
სუნი *n.* smell, aroma
სურვილი *n.* wish, desire
სურსათი *n.* produce
სუსტი *adj.* weak
სუპი *n.* soup
სქელი *adj.* fat *(person)*
სწავლ-ობ *v.* (you) study (1, F)
სწორი *adj.* correct, precise
სწორად *adv.* exactly, precisely
სწრაფი *adj.* quick, fast
სწრაფად *adv.* quickly
სხვადასხვა *n.* variety

ტ
ტანსაცმ-*ე*-ლი *n.* clothes, garments
ტაფა *n.* skillet
ტაქსი *n.* taxi
ტაძ-ა-რი *n.* cathedral
ტელევიზორი *n.* television
ტელეარხი *n.* TV channel
ტელეკომენტატორი *n.* TV commentator
ტელეფონი *n.* telephone
ტეხ-ავ (გა-) *v.* (you) break (1, A)
ტკბილი *adj.* sweet
ტოლერანტობა *n.* tolerance

გრადიცია *n.* tradition
ტრანსპორტი *n.* transportation

უ
უარესი *adj.* worse
უკანონო *adj.* illegal
უკეთესი *adj.* better
უკვე *adv.* already
უ-კრ-ავ (და-) *v.* (you) play (musical instrument) (1, D) / დაუკარი *aor./imp.*
უზარმაზარი *adj.* very large, huge
უ-მატ-ებ (და-) *v.* (you) add (1, A)
უმravლესობა *n.* majority
უმცირესობა *n.* minority
უმცროსი *adj.* younger
უნივერსიტეტი *n.* university
უსათუოდ by all means, for sure, without fail
უფასო *adj.* free (no pay)
უფასოდ *adv.* for free
უფროსი *adj.* older; *n.* boss
უ-ყურ-ებ *v.* (you) watch, will watch (1, A)
უცხო *adj.* foreign, unfamiliar
უცხოური ვალუტა foreign currency

ფ
ფაკულტეტი *n.* (college) department
ფანჯ-ა-რა *n.* window
ფასი *n.* price, worth
ფერი *n.* color
ფესტივალი *n.* festival / კინოფესტივალი film festival

ფეხი *n.* foot / ფეხით on foot
ფეხსაცმ-ე-ლი *n.* shoe, footgear
ფეხბურთი *n.* football
ფილმი *n.* film, movie
ფიქრ-ობ *v.* (you) think (3, A)
ფორთოხ-ა-ლი *n.* orange
ფორმა *n.* form
ფორმალური *adj.* formal
ფრთხილი *adj.* careful
ფრთხილად *adv.* carefully
ფრანგი *adj.* French *(person)*
ფრანგული *adj.* French *(thing)*
ფული *n.* money
ფურც-ე-ლი *n.* sheet of paper
ფქვილი *n.* flour

ქ
ქათ-ა-მი *n.* chicken
ქალი *n.* woman
ქამ-ა-რი *n.* belt
ქართველი *adj.* Georgian *(person)*
ქართული *adj.* Georgian *(thing)* / ქართულად *adv.* in Georgian
ქარი *n.* wind
ქარიანი *adj.* windy
ქაღალდი *n.* paper
ქვით-ა-რი *n.* receipt
ქირა *n.* rent
ქირა-ობ *v.* (you) rent *(apartment, car, etc.)* (3, A)
ქონი *n.* fat, lard
ქორწილი *n.* wedding / საქორწინო ბეჭედი wedding ring
ქრისტიანი *adj./n.* Christian
ქუდი *n.* hat, headgear
ქურქი *n.* fur coat
ქუჩა *n.* street

ღ
ღამე *n./adv.* night
ღვინო *n.* wine
ღია *adj.* open
ღირს *v.* *(3rd.person sing.)* costs / რა ღირს What does it cost?
ღირსება *n.* honor
ღირსეული *adj.* honorable
ღმერთი *n.* God / ღმერთო ჩემო my God!
ღრუბ-ე-ლი *n.* cloud
ღრუბლიანი *adj.* cloudy

ყ
ყავა *n.* coffee
ყავისფერი *adj.* brown
ყვავილი *n.* flower
ყველა *pron.* all, everybody, everyone
ყველაფ-ე-რი *pron.* everything
ყველი *n.* cheese / ყველიანი *adj.* with cheese
ყიდ-ულ-ობ *v.* (you) buy (1, F)
ყლაპ-ავ (გადა-) *v.* (you) swallow (1, A)
ყოველთვის *adv.* always
ყოფილი *adj.* former
ყოფნა *verbal n.* be; being (2, D)
ყურადღება *n.* attention
ყური *n.* ear
ყურძ-ე-ნი *n.* grape

შ
შავი *adj.* black
შარვ-ა-ლი *n.* pants, trousers
შაქ-ა-რი *n.* sugar / შაქრიანი *adj.* with sugar, sweet
შემდეგ *gen./post.; adv.* afterwards, after

შენობა *n.* building
მესანიშნავი *adj.* remarkable
მორის *dat./post.* among
მორი *adj.* distant, far
მორს *adv.* far, far away
მუა *gen. post/adv.* middle
მუაში *adv.* between

ჩ

ჩაი *n.* tea
ჩამო-დი-(ხარ) *v.* (you) arrive (2, C)
ჩანგ-ა-ლი *n.* fork
ჩეკი *n.* a check
ჩემი *pron.* my
ჩერდ-ებ-ი (გა-) *v.* (you) stop (2, A)
ჩვენ *pron.* we
ჩვენი *pron.* our
ჩვეულებრივი *adj.* regular, ordinary
ჩრდილოეთი *adj.* North, Northern
ჩქარ-ობ *v.* (you) are in a hurry (3, A)

ც

ცალი *adj./n.* piece *(usually used after numerals)*
ცარიელი *adj.* empty
ცეკვავ *v.* (you) dance (3, A)
ცენტრი *n.* center
ცეცხლი *n.* fire
ცვლ-ი (გადა–) *v.* (you) exchange (1, D) / გადა-ცვალ-ე *aor./imp*
ცივი *adj.* cold
ცნობილი *adj.* well-known, outstanding

ცოლი *n.* wife
ცოტა *adj./adv.* a little, few
ცოტ-ცოტა little by little, step by step
ცუდი *adj.* bad, poor
ცუდად *adv.* badly, poorly
ცხელი *adj.* hot / საკმაოდ ცხელი rather hot
ცხელა it's hot
ცხვირი *n.* nose
ცხოვრ-ობ *v.* (you) live (3, A)

ძ

ძალიან *adv.* very
ძაღლი *n.* dog
ძვ-ა-ლი *n.* bone
ძველი *adj.* old
ძვირი *adj.* expensive
ძია *n.* uncle *(an informal manner of addressing a stranger older than you)*
ძმა *n.* brother
ძნელი *adj.* difficult

წ

წარმატება *n.* success
წარსული *n./adj.* past
წასვლა *verbal n.* going
წ-ე-ლი *n.* year
წერ (და-) *v.* (you) write (1, A)
წერ (ჩა-ი-) *v.* (you) write down (1, A)
წვენი *n.* juice
წიგნი *n.* book / წიგნების თარო book shelf
წითელი *adj.* red
წინ *gen. post/adv.* in front of, forward, ahead
წიწაკა *n.* pepper

წლისთავი *n.* anniversary
წყალი *n.* water
წყნარი *adj.* quiet
წყნარად *adv.* quietly

ჭ

ჭამ (შე-) *v.* to eat (1, A)
ჭიქა *n.* cup, glass
ჭკვიანი *adj.* intelligent
ჭრი (და-) *v.* (you) cut (bread)
(1, B) / და-ჭერი *aor./imp*
ჭურჭ-ე-ლი *n.* kitchenware
(glasses, plates, etc.)

ხ

ხალხი *n.* people
ხალხური *adj.* folk
ხანი *n.* period, period of time
ხარბი *adj.* greedy
ხარჯ-ავ (და-) *v.* (you) spend
(1, A)
ხატ-ავ (და-) *v.* (you) paint (1, A)
ხდ-ებ-ი (გა-) *v.* (you) become
(2, A)
ხედ-ავ (შე-) *v.* (you) see, look,
have a look (1, A)
ხელმარჯვნივ *adv.* to the right
hand side

ხელმარცხნივ *adv.* to the left
hand side
ხვალ *adv.* tomorrow
ხვდ-ებ-ი (შე-) *v.* (you) meet
(2, B)
ხეხ-ავ (გა-) *v.* (you) grate
(1, A)
ხელო *n.* hand
ხიდი *n.* bridge
ხილი *n.* fruit
ხმა *n.* voice; vote
ხმარ-ობ *v.* (you) use (3, A)
ხორცი *n.* meat
ხუმრ-ობ *v.* (you) joke (3, A)
ხუმრობა *n.* joke
ხურდა *n.* small change
ხშირად *adv.* often

ჯ

ჯარი *n.* army
ჯდ-ებ-ი (და-) *v.* (you) sit down
(2, A) / დაჯექი *aor./imp.*
ჯვ-ა-რი *n.* cross
ჯიხური *n.* booth, stand
ჯერ *adv.* yet, first (of all)
ჯერი *n.* turn / ჩემი ჯერია my
turn
ჯობია *adj.* (it's) better

ENGLISH-GEORGIAN GLOSSARY

Parts of speech are abbreviated and italicized. (See the list of abbreviations on p. 17.) Syncopating vowels of nouns are printed in italics. All verbs, except the verb *be*, are given in the present-tense, 2nd-person singular, followed by the preverb that forms the future tense in parentheses. (The verb *be* is given in its verbal noun form ყოფნა.) Numbers and capital letters in parentheses indicate verb conjugation groups and subgroups. In addition, the aorist form of irregular verbs is given.

Sample entry:

> **make** *v.* ა-კეთ-ებ (გა-) (1, A)

The abbreviation *v.* indicates the word is a verb; the present-tense, 2nd-person singular form is ა-კეთ-ებ meaning *you make*; -ებ is the PFST or present/future stem formant; the addition of (გა-) to the present tense—გააკეთებ—creates the future tense, meaning *you will make*. The verb is of the 1st conjugation group, subgroup A (1, A). (Conjugation charts can be found in Appendix III.)

A

about *prep.* შესახებ, დაახლოვებით
account *n.* ანგარიში
acquaintance *n.* ნაცნობი
across *adv.* გადაღმა, იქითა მხარეს
address *n.* მისამართი
afraid *adj.* (**you are** ~) გე-შინია *v.* (4, B)
after *prep.* შემდეგ *gen./post*
again *adv.* ისევ
ago *adv.* წინ *gen./post.*
all *n.* ყველა
almost *adv.* თითქმის
alone *adv.* მარტო
already *adv.* უკვე

also *adv.* აგრეთვე
although თუმცა
always *adv.* ყოველთვის
ambassador *n.* ელჩი
America *n.* ამერიკა
American *adj.* ამერიკული (*person*); ამერიკული (*thing*)
among *prep.* შორის *dat./post.*
another *adj./pron.* სხვა
answer *n.* პასუხი; *v.* პასუხ-ობ (1, A)
anybody *pron.* ვინმე
anything *pron.* რაიმე
anywhere *adv.* სადმე
apartment *n.* ბინა
apparently *adv.* თურმე
apple *n.* ვაშლი

243

apology *n.* ბოდიში / **I apologize** ბოდიში, ბოდიშს ვიხდი
argue *v.* კამათ-ობ (3, A)
argument *n.* კამათი
around *prep.* გარშემო *adv./ gen. post.*
arrival *n.* ჩამოსვლა *verbal n.*
arrive *v.* ჩამო-დი-(ხარ) (2, C)
art *n.* ხელოვნება
as როგორც
ask *v.* კითხულ-ობ (1, F)
author *n.* ავტორი

B

back *adv.* უკან *adv./gen.post.*
bad *adj.* ცუდი, გაფუჭებული
badly *adv.* ცუდად
bake *v.* ა-ცხ-ობ, (გამო-) (1, C)
balcony *n.* აივ-ა-ნი
ball *n.* ბურთი
bank *n.* ბანკი
bank teller *n.* (ბანკის) ოპერატორი
bar *n.* ბარი
bath *n.* აბაზანა
be *v.* ყოფნა *verbal n.* (2, D)
beans *n.* ლობიო
beautiful *adj.* ლამაზი
become *v.* ხდ-ებ-ი (გა-) (2, A)
bed *n.* საწოლი
bedroom *n.* საწოლი ოთახი
beer *n.* ლუდი
before *adv./prep.* წინათ; *adv.* წინ *gen./post.*
begin *v.* ი-წყ-ებ, (და-) (1, C)
behind *adv./prep.* უკან *adv./ gen.post.*
being ყოფნა *verbal n.* (2, D)
best *adj.* საუკეთესო

better *adj.* უკეთესი
between *prep.* შორის *dat./post.*
bible *n.* ბიბლია
big (large, great) *adj.* დიდი
bill *n.* ანგარიში
birthday *n.* დაბადების დღე
black *adj.* შავი
book *n.* წიგნი
bookstore *n.* წიგნის მაღაზია
both *pron.* ორივე
bottle *n.* ბოთლი
boy *n.* ბიჭი
bread *n.* პური / **cheese bread** ხაჭაპური
break *v.* ტეხ-ავ (გა-) (1, A)
bridge *n.* ხიდი
bright *adj.* ნათელი
Britain *n.* ინგლისი
British *adj./n.* ინგლისელი *(person)*; ინგლისური *(thing)*
brother *n.* ძმა
build *v.* ა-შენ-ებ (ა-) (1, A)
building *n.* შენობა
bus *n.* ავტობუსი
bus stop *n.* (ავტობუსის) გაჩერება
busy *adj.* დაკავებული
but *conj.* მაგრამ
butter *n.* კარაქი
buy *v.* ყიდ-ულ-ობ (1, F)

C

cabbage *n.* კომბოსტო
cafeteria *n.* კაფეტერია
cake *n.* ტორტი, ნამცხვარი
call *v.* რეკ-ავ (და-) *(by phone)* (1, A)
can *v.* შე-გი-ძლ-ია (4, B)
capital (city) *n.* დედაქალაქი

car *n.* მანქანა
card *n.* ბარათი / **ID card** *n.*
პირადობის მოწმობა
careful *adj.* ფრთხილი
carefully *adv.* ფრთხილად
cashier *n.* მოლარე
cashier's office *n.* სალარო
cathedral *n.* ტაძარი
celebrate *v.* აღნიშნ-ავ (1, A)
cell phone *n.* მობილური
center *n.* ცენტრი
century *n.* საუკუნე
certainly *adv.* უსათუოდ, რა
თქმა უნდა
chair *n.* სკამი
change *v.* ცვლ-ი, გა(და-) (1, D)
cheap *adj.* იაფი
check *n.* ჩეკი
cheese *n.* ყველი
cheese bread *n.* ხაჭაპური
chicken *n.* წიწილა; ქათმი
child *n.* ბავშვი, შვილი
Christian *n.* ქრისტიანი
Christmas *n.* შობა
church *n.* ეკლესია
cinema *n.* კინოთეატრი, კინო
citizen *n.* მოქალაქე
citizenship *n.* მოქალაქეობა
city *n.* ქალაქი
clean *adj.* სუფთა
clear *adj.* გასაგები
coat *n.* პალტო
coffee *n.* ყავა
cold *adj.* ცივი / **it's cold** ცივა
come *v.* მოდი-(ხარ) (2, C)
common *adj.* საერთო,
ჩვეულებრივი
complete *v.* ა-მთავრ-ებ (და-)
(1, A)

completely *adv.* სულ
congratulate *v.* გი-ლოც-ავ
(მო-) (**I congratulate you**)
(1, A)
continue *v.* ა-გრძელ-ებ (გა-)
(1, A)
cook *v.* ა-კეთ-ებ (გა-) (1, A);
n. მზარეული
corner *n.* კუთხე
correct *adj.* სწორი; *v.*
ა-სწორ-ებ (გა-) (1, A)
correctly *adv.* სწორედ,
სწორად
cost *v.* ღირ-ს *(3rd person sing.*
v.) / What does it cost? რა
ღირს?
country *n.* ქვეყანა
cucumber *n.* კიტრი
cup (glass) *n.* ჭიქა
currency *n.* ვალუტა
cut *v.* ჭრ-ი (და-) (1, A);
დაჭერი *aor.*

D

dance *v.* ცეკვ-ავ (3, D)
date (day) *n.* თარიღი
daughter *n.* ქალიშვილი
day *n.* დღე / **the day after**
tomorrow ზეგ
debt *n.* ვალი
delicious *adj.* გემრიელი
dentist *n.* კბილის ექიმი
desk *n.* საწერი მაგიდა
dictionary *n.* ლექსიკონი
diet *n.* დიეტა
difficult *adj.* ძნელი
dine *v.* სადილ-ობ (3, A)
dinner *n.* სადილი
dining room *n.* სასადილო

disconnected *adj.* გამორთული
disease *n.* ავადმყოფობა
dish *n.* თეფში, კერძი
dissertation *n.* დისერტაცია
distance *n.* მანძილი;
  დისტანცია
distant *adj.* შორეული, შორი
district *n.* რაიონი, ოლქი
disturb *v.* ა-წუხ-ებ (შე-) (1, A)
do *v.* ა-კეთ-ებ (გა-) (1, A)
doctor *n.* ექიმი
document *n.* მოწმობა,
  დოკუმენტი, საბუთი
dog *n.* ძაღლი
dollar *n.* დოლარი
door *n.* კარი, კარები
double *adj.* ორმაგი
doubt *n.* ეჭვი; *v.* ეჭვ-ობ (3, A)
down *adv.* დაბლა
dream *n.* სიზმ-ა-რი; ოცნება
dress *n.* განსაცმელი
drink *v.* სვ-ამ (შე-) (1, A)
driver *n.* მძღოლი, შოფერი
drug addict *n.* ნარკომანი
drug addiction *n.* ნარკომანია
drugs (narcotics) *n.* ნარკოტიკი
drunk *adj.* მთვრალი
dry *adj.* მშრალი
dust *n.* მტვ-ე-რი
duty *n.* მოვალეობა, ვალი

E

each *pron.* ყოველი
each other *n.* ერთმანეთი
ear *n.* ყური
early *adj.* ადრე
east *n.* აღმოსავლეთი
Easter *n.* აღდგომა
easy *adj.* ადვილი

eat *v.* ჭამ (შე-) (1, A)
education *n.* განათლება
egg *n.* კვერცხი
eggplant *n.* ბადრიჯ-ა-ნი
elevator *n.* ლიფტი
embassy *n.* საელჩო
empty *adj.* ცარიელი
end *n.* ბოლო, დასასრული
enemy *n.* მტ-ე-რი
England *n.* ინგლისი
English *adj.* ინგლისელი
  (person), ინგლისური *(thing)*
enough *adj.* საკმარისი
enter *v.* შე-დ-ი-(ხარ) (2, C)
envelope *n.* კონვერტი
Euro *n.* ევრო
every *adj.* ყოველი
everybody (everyone) *pron.*
  ყველა
everything *pron.* ყველაფ-ე-რი
everywhere *adv.* ყველგან
example *n.* მაგალითი / **for**
  example მაგალითად
exchange *n.* გაცვლა; *v.* ცვლ-ი,
  (გამო-) (1, D), გამოცვალე
  aor. / **currency exchange**
  ვალუტის გაცვლა
excursion *n.* ექსკურსია
excuse me *n.* ბოდიში
exercise *n.* ვარჯიში; *v.*
  ვარჯიშ-ობ (3, A)
expensive *adj.* ძვირი
experience *n.* გამოცდილება
eye *n.* თვალი
eyeglasses *n.* სათვალე

F

face *n.* სახე
fact *n.* ფაქტი; მოვლენა

family *n.* ოჯახი
famous *adj.* ცნობილი,
სახელოვანი
far *adv.* შორს
fare *n.* ბილეთის ფასი
fat *adj.* ქონი, სქელი *(person)*
father *n.* მამა
feast *n.* ლხინი, სუფრა
fee *n.* გასამრჯელო; ფასი
few *adj.* ცოტა / **a few**
რამდენიმე
film (movie) *n.* (კინო)ფილმი
final *adj.* ბოლო, უკანასკნელი
finally *adv.* ბოლოს
find *v.* პოულ-ობ (1, F)
fine *adj.* კარგი, მშვენიერი
finger *n.* თითი
fire *n.* ცეცხლი
firm *n.* ფირმა
first *num.* პირველი
fish *n.* თევზი
flag *n.* დროშა
flat (apartment) *n.* ბინა
floor *n.* იატაკი; სართული /
first (ground) floor პირველი
სართული
flour *n.* ფქვილი
flower *n.* ყვავილი
folk *adj.* ხალხური
food *n.* საჭმელი
fool *n.* სულელი
foot *n.* ფეხი / **on foot** ფეხით
for *prep.* -თვის *gen./post.*
forever *adv.* სამუდამოდ
forget *v.* ი-ვიწყ-ებ (და-) (1, A)
fork *n.* ჩანგალი
form *n.* ფორმა
former *adj.* ყოფილი
France *n.* საფრანგეთი

free (vacant, unoccupied) *adj.*
თავისუფალი
free (no pay) *adj.* უფასო / **for**
free უფასოდ
freedom *n.* თავისუფლება
French *adj.* ფრანგი *(person)*,
ფრანგული *(thing)*
fried *adj.* შემწვარი
friend *n.* მეგობარი
from *prep.* -დან, -გან; *gen./post.*
fruit *n.* ხილი
front *n.* *adj./gen.post* / **in front**
of წინ *gen./post.*
fulfill *v.* ასრულ-ებ (შე-) (1, A)
fun *n.* გართობა
future *n./adj.* მომავ-ა-ლი

G

game *n.* თამაში
garage *n.* გარაჟი
garbage *n.* ნაგ-ა-ვი
garbage can ნაგვის ყუთი
garden *n.* ბაღი
general *adj.* საერთო / **in**
general საერთოდ
genuine *adj.* ნამდვილი
Georgia *n.* საქართველო
Georgian *adj.* ქართველი
(person); ქართული *(thing)*
gift *n.* საჩუქარი
girl *n.* გოგონა, გოგო;
ქალიშვილი
give *v.* მი-სცემ *fut.* / **give me**
მომეცი *imp.*
glad *adj.* მოხარული
glass *n.* ჭიქა
glossary *n.* ლექსიკონი
glove *n.* ხელთათმანი
go *v.* მი-დი-(ხარ) (2, C)

goal *n.* მიზ-ა-ნი
God *n.* ღმერთი
gold *n.* ოქრო
good *adj.* კარგი
good-bye ნახვამდის
government *n.* მთავრობა
grandchild *n.* შვილიშვილი
grandfather (granddad) *n.*
პაპა, ბაბუა
grandmother (grandma) *n.*
ბებია
grape *n.* ყურძ-ე-ნი
grape juice ყურძნის წვენი
grate *v.* ხეხ-ავ (გა-) (1, A)
grated *adj.* გახეხილი
grateful *adj.* მადლობელი
great *adj.* დიდი, დიადი
green *adj.* მწვანე
grey *adj.* ნაცრისფერი
guest *n.* სტუმ-ა-რი
guestroom *n.* სასტუმრო ოთახი

H
habit *n.* ჩვეულება
hair *n.* თმა
hairdresser *n.* პარიკმახერი
half *adj./n.* ნახევარი
hall *n* დარბაზი
ham *n.* შაშხი, ბეკონი
hand *n.* ხელი
handbag *n.* ხელჩანთა
handsome *adj.* ლამაზი
happiness *n.* ბედნიერება
happy *adj.* ბედნიერი
hat *n.* ქუდი
have *v.* გაქვს (4, A)
he *pron.* ის
head *n.* თავი
headache *n.* თავის ტკივილი

health *n.* ჯანმრთელობა
heavy *adj.* მძიმე; ძნელი
her *pron.* მისი
here *adv.* აქ / here is აი
hide *v.* მალ-ავ (და-) (1, A)
high *adj.* მაღალი
hill *n.* ბორცვი, გორა
his *pron.* მისი
history *n.* ისტორია
holiday *n.* დღესასწაული,
დასვენების დღე
home (or house) *n.* სახლი / at
home სახლში
honest *adj.* პატიოსანი
honey *n.* თაფლი
hope *n.* იმედი
hopefully *adv.* იმედია
hot *adj.* ცხელი
hotel *n.* ოტელი, სასტუმრო
hour *n.* საათი / in an hour
ერთ საათში
house *n.* სახლი
how *adv.* როგორ
how many? რამდენი?
how much? რამდენი?
hungry *adj.* მშიერი
hurry *v.* ჩქარ-ობ (3, A)
husband *n.* ქმ-ა-რი

I
ice *n.* ყინული
ID card *n.* პირადობის
მოწმობა
idea *n.* იდეა
if *conj.* თუ
ill *adj.* ავად
illegal *adj.* უკანონო
immediately *adv.* ახლავე
important *adj.* მნიშვნელოვანი

in *prep.* -ში *gen. post.*
indeed *adv.* მართლაც
independence *n.* დამოუკიდებლობა
independent *adj.* დამოუკიდებელი
infection *n.* ინფექცია
inform *v.* ა-ტყობინ-ებ (შე-) (1, A)
information *n.* ცნობა, ინფორმაცია
inside *adv.* შიგნით, შიგ
insomnia *n.* უძილობა
instead *adv.* მაგიგრად *gen. post.*
intelligent *adj.* ჭკვიანი
interesting *adj.* საინტერესო
interpreter *n.* თარჯიმ-ა-ნი
invitation *n.* დაპატიჟება
invite *v.* პატიჟ-ებ (და-) (1, A)

J
jail *n.* ციხე
jam *n.* მურაბა
Jew *n.* ებრაელი *(person)*
Jewish *adj.* ებრაული *(thing)*
job *n.* სამუშაო, საქმე
joke *n.* ხუმრობა; *v.* ხუმრ-ობ (3, A)
journal *n.* ჟურნალი
journey *n.* მგზავრობა; *v.* მგზავრ-ობ (3, A)
judge *n.* მოსამართლე
juice *n.* წვენი
just *adj.* მხოლოდ, სამართლიანი; **just person** სამართლიანი ადამიანი; *adv.* **just a moment!** ერთი წუთით!; **just like** როგორც

K
keep *v.* ი-ნახ-ავ, (შე-) (1, A)
key *n.* გასაღები
kilogram *n.* კილო, კილოგრამი
kind *adj.* კეთილი
king *n.* მეფე
kiosk *n.* კიოსკი
knife *n.* დანა
knock *(at s.th.)* *v.* ა-კაკუნ-ებ (და-) (1, A)
know *v.* იცი (1, E)

L
lake *n.* ტბა
lamp *n.* ლამპა, ნათურა
land *n.* მიწა
language *n.* ენა
large *adj.* დიდი
last *n.* უკანასკნელი; *v.* გრძელდ-ებ-ა (გა-) (2, A)
late *adj.* გვიანი; დაგვიანებული
laugh *n.* სიცილი; *v.* იცინ-ი (3, B)
laundry *n.* სარეცხი / **washing machine** სარეცხი მანქანა
law *n.* კანონი
lawyer *n.* ვექილი, იურისტი
lazy *adj.* ზარმაცი
leave *v.* მიდი-ხარ (2, C)
lecture *n.* ლექცია
lecturer *n.* ლექტორი
left *adj.* მარცხენა / **to the left** მარცხნივ / **on the left hand side** ხელმარცხნივ
leg *n.* ფეხი
legal *adj.* კანონიერი, ლეგალური

lemonade *n.* ლიმონათი
less *adj.* ნაკლები
lesson *n.* გაკვეთილი
letter *n.* ასო; წერილი
level *n.* დონე
lie *n.* ტყუილი
life *n.* სიცოცხლე, ცხოვრება
light *n.* სინათლე, შუქი; *adj.* მსუბუქი
like *v.* მო-გ-წონ-ს (4, A)
listen *v.* უ-სმენ (მო-) (1, D), მოუსმინე *aor.*
little *adj. (a few)* ცოტა / *(small)* პატარა
little by little ცოტ-ცოტა
live *v.* ცხოვრ-ობ (3, A)
living-room *n.* სასტუმრო ოთახი
lock *v.* კეტ-ავ (და-) (1, A)
long *adj.* გრძელი
long ago დიდი ხნის წინათ
lose *v.* კარგ-ავ (და-) (1, A)
love *n.* სიყვარული; *v.* გი-ყვარ-ს (4, A)
lovely *adj.* მშვენიერი, ლამაზი
luck *n.* ბედი, იღბალი
lucky *adj.* ბედნიერი
lunch *n.* ლანჩი, სადილი; *v.* სადილ-ობ (3, A)

M

magazine *n.* ჟურნალი
mail *n.* ფოსტა; *v.* გზავნ-ი (გა-) (1, A)
main *adj.* მთავარი
majority *n.* უმეტესი
make *v.* ა-კეთ-eб (გა-) (1, A)
man *n.* ადამიანი, კაცი
manager *n.* მენეჯერი

manner *n.* მანერა / **in this manner** *(this way)* ასე
many *adj.* მრავალი, ბევრი
map *n.* რუკა
market *n.* ბაზ-არი
married *adj.* ცოლიანი *(male)*, გათხოვილი *(female)*
matches *n.* ასანთი
matter *n.* საქმე, საკითხი
meal *n.* საჭმ-ე-ლი
meat *n.* ხორცი
medicine *n.* წამალი
medium *adj.* საშუალო
meet *v.* ხვდ-ებ-ი (შე-) (2, B)
meet *(be introduced)* *v.* ი-ცნ-ობ (გა-) (1, D), გა-ი-ცან-ი *aor.*
meeting *n* შეხვედრა
member *n.* წევრი
memory *n.* ხსოვნა, მახსოვრობა
merry *adj.* მხიარული
middle *adj.* საშუალო / **in the middle** შუაში
midnight *n.* შუადამე
mile *n.* მილი
milk *n.* რძე
mineral *adj.* მინერალური
mirror *n.* სარკე
mistake *n.* შეცდომა
money *n.* ფული
month *n.* თვე
monthly *adj.* თვიური
moon *n.* მთვარე
moonlit *adj.* მთვარიანი
more *adj.* მეტი; კიდევ
morning *n.* დილა
mosque *n.* მეჩეთი
most *adj.* უმეტესი
mother *n.* დედა

mouth *n.* პირი
movie (movie theater) *n.* კინო
much ბევრი / **how much?**
რამდენი?
must უნდა
my *pron.* ჩემი

N

name *n.* სახელი
narcotics. *See* drugs
nation *n.* ერი; ხალხი
nature *n.* ბუნება
near *adv.* ახლოს
necessary *adj.* საჭირო
need *v.* გ-ჭირდ-ებ-ა (4, B)
neighbor *n.* მეზობელი
neither არც ერთი
neither ... nor არც ... არც
never *adv.* არასოდეს,
არასდროს
new *adj.* ახალი
New Year ახალი წელი
news *n.* ცნობა, ახალი
ამბები
newspaper *n.* გაზეთი
next *adj.* შემდეგი
nice *adj.* სასიამოვნო,
სიმპატიური
night *n.* ღამე
nobody *pron.* არავინ
noise *n.* ხმაური
noon *n.* შუადღე
north *adj.* ჩრდილოეთი
nose *n.* ცხვირი
note *n.* შენიშვნა
nothing *pron.* არაფ-ე-რი
now *adv.* ახლა, ეხლა
nowhere *adv.* არსად
number *n.* რიცხვი, ნომ-ე-რი

numerous *adj.* მრავალი
nurse (medical personnel) *n.*
ძიძა; სანიტარი

O

occupation *n.* ხელობა,
პროფესია
often *adv.* ხშირად
oil *n.* ზეთი
old *adj.* მოხუცი *(person)*;
ძველი *(thing)*
once ერთხელ
only ერთადერთი, მხოლოდ
open *adj.* ღია; *v.* ა-ღ-ებ (გა-)
(1, C)
opinion *n.* აზრი
or *conj.* თუ, ან
ordinary (regular) *adj.*
ჩვეულებრივი
organization *n.* ორგანიზაცია
other *adj.* სხვა
our *pron.* ჩვენი

P

pain *n.* ტკივილი
paint *v.* ხატ-ავ (და-) (1, A)
painter *n.* მხატვ-ა-რი
palace *n.* სასახლე
pan *n.* ტაფა
paper *n.* ქაღალდი
parent *n.* მშობ-ე-ლი
part *n.* ნაწილი
past *n./adj.* წარსული
pastry *n.* ნამცხვა-რი
pay *v.* ი-ხდ-ი (გადა-) (1, D)
payment *n.* გადასახადი
peach *n.* ატ-ა-მი
pen *n.* კალ-ა-მი
pencil *n.* ფანქ-ა-რი

people *n.* ხალხი, ერი
pepper *n.* წიწაკა
period *n.* ხ-ა-ნი
person *n.* პიროვნება, პირი
pharmacy *n.* აფთიაქი
phone *n.* ტელეფონი; *v.* რეკ-ავ
(და-) (I, A)
physician *n.* ექიმი
pick up *v.* ი-ღ-ებ (ა-) (I, C)
picture *n.* სურათი
piece *n.* ნაჭ-ე-რი
pity *n.* სინანული / **What a**
pity! რა სამწუხინია!
place *n.* ადგილი
plan *n.* გეგმა; *v.* გეგმ-ავ (და-)
(1, A)
plate *n.* თეფში
plateau *n.* პლატო
play (game) *n.* თამაში; *v.*
თამაშ-ობ (3, A)
pleasant *adj.* სასიამოვნო
pleasure *n.* სიამოვნება / **with**
pleasure სიამოვნებით
pocket *n.* ჯიბე
police *n.* პოლიცია
polite *adj.* ზრდილობიანი,
თავაზიანი
poor *adj.* ღარიბი; საწყალი
population *n.* მოსახლეობა
post-office *n.* ფოსტა
potato *o.* კარტოფილი
pour *v.* ა-სხ-ამ (და-) (1),
და-ა-სხ-ი *aor.*
precisely (exactly) *adv.* ზუსტად
prefer *v.* გი-რჩევნია (4)
present *n.* საჩუქ-ა-რი
price *n.* ფასი
priest *n.* მღვდელი
private *adj.* კერძო

probably *adv.* ალბათ
produce *n.* სურსათი
proud *n./adj.* ამაყი
put (down) *v.* დ-ებ (და-) (1, C)

Q
queen *n.* დედოფ-ა-ლი
question *n.* საკითხი, კითხვა;
v. კითხულობ (1, F)
quick *adj.* სწრაფი, ჩქარი
quickly *adv.* სწრაფად, ჩქარა
quiet *adj.* წყნარი
quietly *adv.* ჭყნარად
quite *adv.* საკმაოდ

R
rain *n.* წვიმა; **it rains, it's**
raining *(3rd pers. sing.) v.*
წვიმს
rather *adv.* საკმაოდ
raw *adj.* უმი
read *v.* ი-კითხ-ავ (წა-) (1, F)
ready *adj.* მზად
real *adj.* ნამდვილი, რეალური
really *adv.* მართლა
reason *n.* მიზეზი
receipt *n.* ქვით-ა-რი
receive *v.* ი-ღ-ებ (მი-) (1, C)
red *adj.* წითელი
region *n.* რაიონი, ოლქი
regular (ordinary) *adj.*
ჩვეულებრივი
relative *n.* ნათესავი
reliable *adj.* სანდო
religion *n.* რელიგია
religious *adj.* რელიგიური
remarkable *adj.* შესანიშნავი
remember *v.* გა-ხსოვს (4, A)
rent *n.* ქირა; *v.* ქირა-ობ (3, A)

rent out v. ა-ქირავ-ებ (გა-)
(1, A)
request n. თხოვნა
required (necessary) adj.
საჭირო
rice n. ბრინჯი
rich adj. მდიდარი
right n. უფლება; adj.
მარჯვენა / **to the right**
მარჯვნივ / **on the right-hand
side** ხელმარჯვნივ
river n. მდინარე
road n. გზა
room n. ოთახი
round adj. მრგვალი

S
salad n. სალათი
salesperson n. გამყიდველი
salt n. მარილი
salty adj. მარილიანი
same adj. იგივე
school n. სკოლა
seat n. სკამი
see v. ხედ-ავ (შე-) (1, A)
send v. გზავნ-ი (გა-) (1, B)
several pron. რამდენიმე
short adj. მოკლე, დაბალი
sing v. მღერ-ი (3, B)
sister n. და
sit v. ჯდ-ებ-ი, (და-) (2, C),
დაჯექი aor.
skillet n. ტაფა
slow adj. ნელი
slowly adv. ნელა
small adj. პატარა
smell n. სუნი
so adv. ასე / **and so on** და ასე
შემდეგ

soap n. საპ-ო-ნი
soft adj. რბილი
some adj. ზოგი; რამდენიმე
somebody pron. ვიღაცა, ვინმე
something pron. რაღაცა, რამე
sometimes adv. ზოგჯერ
somewhere adv. სადმე
son n. ვაჟიშვილი
song n. სიმღერა
soon adv. ჩქარა, მალე
soup n. სუპი
sour adj. მჟავე
speak v. ლაპარაკ-ობ (1, A)
spend (money) v. ხარჯ-ავ
(და-) (1, A)
spicy adj. ცხარე
spoon n. კოვზი
spouse n. მეუღლე
spring n. გაზაფხული
square n. მოედ-ა-ნი
start (s.th.) v. ი-წყ-ებ (და-)
(1, A)
state n. სახელმწიფო
still adv. ჯერ კიდევ; აქამდე;
მაინც
stop n. გაჩერება / **bus stop**
ავტობუსის გაჩერება
store n. მაღაზია
street n. ქუჩა
strong adj. მაგარი, ძლიერი
study v. სწავლ-ობ (1, F)
subway n. მეტრო
sugar n. შაქ-ა-რი
summer n. ზაფხული
supper n. ვახშ-ა-მი
sure adj. დარწმუნებული;
რასაკვირველია
sweet adj. ტკბილი
synagogue n. სინაგოგა

T

table *n.* მაგიდა
take *v.* ი-ღ-ებ, (ა-) (1, C)
tall *adj.* მაღალი
taste *v.* სინჯ-ავ (გა-) (1, A); *n.* გემო
taxi *n.* ტაქსი
tea *n.* ჩაი
teach *v.* ა-სწავლ-ი (1, B)
teacher *n.* მასწავლებ-ე-ლი
teller *n.* ოპერატორი / bank teller (ბანკის) ოპერატორი
than *conj.* ვიდრე
thank *n.* მადლობა
thank you გმადლობთ
that *pron.* ის; *conj.* რომ, რომელიც
then *adv.* მაშინ
there *adv.* იქ
think *v.* ფიქრ-ობ (3, A)
this *pron.* ეს
till *prep.* -მდე *adv./post.* / **till now** აქამდე
time *n.* დრო, ხანი
toast *n.* სადღეგრძელო
today *adv.* დღეს
together *adv.* ერთად
tolerance *n.* ტოლერანტობა
tomato *n.* პამიდორი; *gen.*: პამიდვრის
tomorrow *adv.* ხვალ
tonight *adv.* სადამოს, ამ სადამოს
too *adv.* მალიან
town *n.* ქალაქი
transportation *n.* ტრანსპორტი
true *adj.* მართალი

U

uncle *n.* ბიძა, მია
under *prep.* ქვეშ *adv./gen. post.*
unoccupied *(vacant) adj.* თავისუფალი
unpleasant *adj.* არასასიამოვნო, უსიამოვნო
until *prep.* -მდე / **till now, till here** აქამდე
use *v.* ხმარ-ობ (3, A)
useful *adj.* საჭირო, სასარგებლო
usually *adv.* ჩვეულებრივ(ად)

V

vacant *(unoccupied) adj.* თავისუფალი
vegetable *n.* ბოსტნეული
vegetarian *n.* ვეგეტარიანელი

W

wait *v.* ი-ცდ-ი (მო-) (1, D), მოიცადე *aor.*
want *v.* გი-ნდა (4, B)
warm *adj.* თბილი
watch *n.* საათი
water *n.* წყ-ა-ლი
weather *n.* ამინდი
well *adv.* კარგად
west *n.* დასავლეთი
what *pron.* რა / **what for?** რისთვის?
when *adv.* როდის
where *adv.* სად / **where to?** საით?
which *pron.* რომ-ე-ლი
white *adj.* თეთრი

who *pron.* ვინ
why *adv.* რატომ
wine *n.* ღვინო
with *prep.* -თან *dat.post.* / **with you, at your place** შენთან *sing.*
without *prep.* გარეშე *gen. post.*
word *n.* სიტყვა
work *n.* სამუშაო; *v.* მუშა-ობ (3, A)
world *n.* მსოფლიო

worse *adj.* უარესი
worst *adj.* ყველაზე ცუდი, ყველაზე უარესი
write *v.* წერ, (და-) (1, A)
write (down) *v.* წერ (ჩაი-) (1, A)

Y

year *n.* წელიწადი, წ-ე-ლი
yes *part.* დიახ; *pol.* კი, ჰო, ხო
yesterday *adv.* გუშინ
yet *adv.* (ჯერ) კიდევ

APPENDIX I: NOUNS, ADJECTIVES, PRONOUNS, AND POSTPOSITIONS

Declension of Nouns

Georgian nouns are declined in seven cases.* Each case is used for a variety of purposes to clarify the function of nouns in a sentence and the relationship between nouns.

1. **Nominative:** nouns in this case designate either the *subject* or *direct object*, depending on the tense of the verb used in the sentence. This is the *basic* form of any noun.

2. **Ergative:** nouns in this case designate the subject in the *aorist* and *optative* tenses.

3. **Dative/Accusative:** nouns in this case designate *direct* or *indirect objects*.

4. **Genitive:** this case designates a *possessive* relationship between nouns. It functions like *'s* in English, e.g.: father's, brother's, friend's, etc.

5. **Instrumental:** as its name suggests, this case often denotes the *instrument* through which an action is carried out.

6. **Adverbial:** this case can transform nouns and adjectives into *adverbs*.

7. **Vocative:** nouns in this case are used when addressing someone or even something. It is almost obsolete, and only a few words still take this case.

*For brief definitions of grammatical terms used here and throughout this book, please see Appendix IV.

Declension types

The declension of Georgian nouns may vary slightly depending on their ending. Nouns may end in any of the five vowels: -ა, -ე, -ი, -ო, -უ. The majority of nouns and almost all words borrowed from European languages end in -ი. This is the largest group of nouns in Georgian. The smallest group is those ending in -უ; there are only five or six words of this type. Personal and place names such as **ნუნუ** *Nunu* or **პერუ** *Peru* also belong to this group. Below is a chart of the various types of declension:

	-ი **woman**	-ა **brother**	-ე **king**	-ო **gold**	-უ **turtle**
nom.	ქალ-ი	ძმ-ა	მეფ-ე	ოქრ-ო	კუ-უ
erg.	ქალ-მა	ძმა-მ	მეფე-მ	ოქრო-მ	კუ-მ
dat./acc.	ქალ-ს	ძმა-ს	მეფე-ს	ოქრო-ს	კუ-ს
gen.	ქალ-ის	ძმ-ის	მეფ-ის	ოქრო-ს(ი)	კუ-ს(ი)
inst.	ქალ-ით	ძმ-ით	მეფ-ით	ოქრო-თ(ი)	კუ-თ(ი)
adv.	ქალ-ად	ძმ-ად	მეფ-ად	ოქრო-დ	კუ-დ
voc.	ქალ-ო	ძმა-ო	მეფე-ო	ოქრო-ჲ	კუ-ჲ

The most frequently used cases are nominative, dative/accusative, and genitive. The rest require either a specific verbal tense or are primarily used in fixed expressions.

Some nouns may lose the vowels -ა-, -ე-, and less frequently -ო before the consonants -ლ-, -მ-, -ნ, and -რ- in the last syllable before the ending -ი. This is called *syncope*. It occurs only in three cases: *genitive*, *instrumental*, and *adverbial*. There is no rule as to when syncopation may occur. Do not worry if you pronounce the nouns without syncopation; their meaning will still be quite clear. You'll gradually get the hang of it.

Note the syncopation in the genitive, instrumental, and adverbial cases of the following examples:

	water	pen	market	soap
nom.	წყალ-ი	კალამ-ი	ბაზარ-ი	საპონ-ი
erg.	წყალ-მა	კალამ-მა	ბაზარ-მა	საპონ-მა
dat./acc.	წყალ-ს	კალამ-ს	ბაზარ-ს	საპონ-ს
gen.	წყლ-ის	კალმ-ის	ბაზრ-ის	საპნ-ის
instr.	წყლ-ით	კალმ-ით	ბაზრ-ით	საპნ-ით
adv.	წყლ-ად	კალმ-ად	ბაზრ-ად	საპნ-ად

Plural form of nouns

The marker of the plural form of nouns is -ებ. Nouns with -ი and -ა endings drop the final vowel. Nouns that have syncopation add -ებ to their syncopated stem.

boy	boys	school	schools
ბიჭ-ი	ბიჭ-ებ-ი	სკოლ-ა	სკოლ-ებ-ი

tree	trees	pen	pens
ხე	ხე-ებ-ი	კალამ-ი	კალმ-ებ-ი

soap	soaps	mushroom	mushrooms
საპონ-ი	საპნ-ებ-ი	სოკო	სოკო-ებ-ი

Nouns in the plural have only one type of declension pattern. They have exactly the same endings as nouns with the final vowel -ი in the singular forms of the nominative case. See the pattern above.

Use and Function of Cases

The explanation of case use below refer to tenses covered in this textbook.

Nominative Case

Nominative case designates:

a. subject of the 1st and 3rd conjugation verbs in present, imperfect and future tenses;

b. subject of 2nd conjugation verbs in all tenses;

c. direct object of 1st and 3rd conjugation verbs in aorist and optative tenses;

d. direct object of the 4th conjugation verbs in present, imperfect and future tenses.

ეს ქალი აქ ცხოვრობს.
This woman lives here.

ჩემი ძმა აქ მუშაობს.
My brother works here.

Ergative Case

Ergative case designates subject of 1st and 2nd conjugation verbs in aorist and optative tenses.

პროფესორმა ლექცია დაიწყო.
(The) professor started his lecture.

მოლარემ ხურდა უნდა დააბრუნოს.
(The) cashier should return the change.

Dative/Accusative Case

Dative case designates:

a. direct and indirect objects of the 1st and some 3rd conjugation verbs in present, imperfect and future tenses;

b. subject of the 4th conjugation verbs in present, imperfect and future tenses.

დედა სადილს აკეთებს.
Mother is making **dinner**.

თინა მეგობარს წერილს წერს.
Tina is writing **a letter to a friend**.

Genitive Case

This case may sometimes be confusing because this kind of posses-sive construction occurs less frequently in English than in Georgian. To understand this case correctly, the English word order should be *reversed* when this case is used in Georgian. Another way of figuring out the relationship between words linked through the genitive case is to use *'s* in English. If this sounds too awkward, you may rearrange the word order after clarifying the meaning of the Georgian phrase.

ბინის ქირა
apartment rent (*lit*.: apartment's rent)

ბანკის დირექტორი
director **of the bank** (*lit*.: bank's director)

დილის მატარებელი
morning train (*lit*.: morning's train)

Reversing word order or using *'s* is particularly useful when a chain of several nouns in the genitive case occurs in a sentence.

თბილისის უნივერსიტეტის სტუდენტი
Tbilisi's University's student
student of the University of Tbilisi

ბანკის დირექტორის ცოლის სახელია
(the) bank's director's wife's name
the name of the wife of the bank director

Instrumental Case

Most frequently, nouns in instrumental case indicate tools or other implements that were used to perform an action. In English these nouns will require use of prepositions *with* or *by*.

ჩიკაგოში **ავტობუს-ით** მივდივარ.
I am going to Chicago **by bus**.

ეს ხალიჩა **ხელ-ით** არის მოქსოვილი.
This rug is handmade (i.e. woven **by hand**).

Adverbial Case

This case is used mostly in fixed phrases and idiomatic expressions. Memorizing individual instances would be the best way to learn how to use it.

ეს კაბა ათ **დოლარ-ად_**ვიყიდე.
I bought this dress **for ten dollars**.

ირაკლი **დირექტორ-ად** დანიშნეს.
(They) appointed Irakli **as the director**.

ეს ფიცარი **მაგიდა-დ** გამოვიყენე.
(I) used this wooden board **as a table**.

Vocative Case

Only a few words still have this case. It is used when addressing a person. Below is a list of the seven most frequently used and useful vocative forms.

1. კაც-ი *nom.*   **კაც-ო** *voc.*   man, human being
The word is used in a similar way to *man* in spoken English, and is too colloquial for a formal, polite conversation. It does not have strict gender identity, and could be used in speaking to both men and woman.

რა გინდა, **კაცო**? თავი დამანებე!
What do you want, **man**? Leave me alone!

2. ქალ-ი *nom.*   **ქალ-ო** *voc.*   woman
This form can be used informally when addressing a woman friend, wife, or even a stranger. Like **კაცო** *man*, it should be avoided in formal, polite conversation.

3. ბატონ-ი *nom.*   **ბატონ-ო** *voc.*   master, Sir, Mister
This form is used most often in two cases: a) before the first name of a person whom you are addressing in formal, polite conversation; b) when responding to both a man and a woman when they call you by name. In the latter case it means: *yes, I am here*; *yes, I am listening to you*, etc.

4. ქალბატონ-ი *nom.*   ქალბატონ-ო *voc.*   lady, Madam
This form is used before the first name of a woman you are
addressing in a formal, polite conversation, or when addressing a
stranger.

5. დედა *nom.*   დედა-ო *voc.*   mother
The Georgian word for mother in the vocative case has very specific
applications. It is used while addressing a nun, or in prayers to the
Virgin Mary.

6. მამა *nom.*   მამა-ო *voc.*   father
The vocative form of this word is used only when addressing a priest.

7. ღმერთ-ი *nom.*   ღმერთ-ო *voc.*   God
Apart from prayers, the most frequently used expression with this
form is ღმერთო ჩემო! *My God!* The word order in this expression
is *always reversed*.

Declension of Adjectives

A. If adjectives are used independently, i.e. when they are *not preceding* a noun, they decline almost exactly in the same manner as
nouns. The final vowel affects their declension type. Only -ო ending
adjectives have a vocative case ending with -ო.

	beautiful	little	short	heartless	ugly
nom.	ლამაზ-ი	პატარა	მოკლე	უგული	უშნო
erg.	ლამაზ-მა	პატარა-მ	მოკლე-მ	უგულო-მ	უშნო-მ
dat./acc.	ლამაზ-ს	პატარა-ს	მოკლე-ს	უგულო-ს	უშნო-ს
gen.	ლამაზ-ის	პატარ-ის	მოკლე-სი	უგულო-სი	უშნო-სი
inst.	ლამაზ-ით	პატარ-ით	მოკლე-თი	უგულო-თი	უშნო-თი
adv.	ლამაზ-ად	პატარა-დ	მოკლე-დ	უგულო-დ	უშნო-დ
voc.	ლამაზ-ო	პატარ-ა(ვ)	მოკლე-(ვ)	უგულო-(ვ)	უშნო-(ვ)

The majority of adjectives in the adverbial case become adverbs. Thus, in the *adverbial* case these adjectives have the meaning:

ლამაზად	beautifully
მოკლედ	in short, briefly
უგულოდ	heartlessly, without proper attention or care
უმნოდ	in an ungainly manner

B. If adjectives precede a noun, all except those ending in -ო remain unchanged. Notice the declension of adjectives with various vowel endings in the example below.

	white dog	little cat	sugarless coffee
nom.	თეთრ-ი ძაღლი	პატარა კატა	უშაქრო ყავა
erg.	თეთრ-მა ძაღლმა	პატარა კატამ	უშაქრო ყავამ
dat./acc.	თეთრ- ძაღლს	პატარა კატას	უშაქრო ყავას
gen.	თეთრ-ი ძაღლის	პატარა კატის	უშაქრო ყავის
instr.	თეთრ-ი ძაღლით	პატარა კატით	უშაქრო ყავით
adv.	თეთრ- ძაღლად	პატარა კატად	უშაქრო ყავად
voc.	თეთრ-ო ძაღლო	პატარა კატავ	--------------------

As shown above, in the ergative and vocative cases adjectives ending with -ო have the same ending as nouns ending with -ო. In the dative/ accusative and adverbial cases they drop the final vowel, and remain unchanged in the nominative, genitive, and instrumental cases. The syncopation rule also applies to adjectives.

Declension of Pronouns

There are several groups of pronouns. Here we will give only some of those most frequently used.

1. Personal pronouns

There are six personal pronouns:

	singular		plural	
1st	მე	*I*	ჩვენ	*we*
2nd	შენ	*you*	თქვენ	*you*
3rd	ის	*he/she*	ისინი	*they*

The 1st and 2nd person pronouns remain unchanged in all cases. Only the 3rd person pronouns have the ergative and dative/accusative case forms. Notice below that plural forms are the same in both cases.

3rd person pronouns

	singular (he/she)	**plural** (they)
nom.	ის	ისინი
erg.	მან	მათ
dat./acc.	მას	მათ

In more colloquial forms ი**მან** *he/she* and ი**მათ** *they* are used.

2. Demonstrative pronouns

The two most important demonstrative pronouns are **ეს** *this* and **ის** *that*. When preceding a noun, they have two basic forms, direct for nominative and indirect for the other cases. These are **ამ** and **იმ** respectively. They are never used in the vocative case.

	this woman	that man
nom.	ეს ქალი	ის კაცი
erg.	ამ ქალმა	იმ კაცმა
dat./acc.	ამ ქალს	იმ კაცს
gen.	ამ ქალის	იმ კაცის
inst.	ამ ქალით	იმ კაცით
adv.	ამ ქალად	იმ კაცად

3. Interrogative pronouns

Interrogative pronouns that may have forms for some cases are the following:

	what	who
nom.	რა	ვინ
erg.	რამ	ვინ
dat./acc.	რას	ვის

Pronouns **როგორი** *what kind*, **რომელი** *which* and **რამდენი** *how many* are declined precisely like adjectives ending with -ი. In

რომელი syncopation would occur, and the vowel -ე will be dropped in the genitive, instrumental, and adverbial.

4. Possessive pronouns

Possessive pronouns decline the same way as adjectives. For practical purposes, the nominative, ergative and dative cases should be learned. In these cases they have similar forms whether or not they precede a noun. Only 1st person pronouns have a vocative case form.

Declination of possessive pronouns not preceding a noun

	my	your (sing.)	his/her	our	your (pl.)	their
nom.	ჩემი	შენი	მისი	ჩვენი	თქვენი	მათი
erg.	ჩემ-მა	შენ-მა	მის-მა	ჩვენ-მა	თქვენ-მა	მათ-მა
dat./acc.	ჩემ-ს	შენ-ს	მის	ჩვენ-ს	თქვენ-ს	მათ
voc.	ჩემ-ო	-------	-------	ჩვენ-ო	----------	--------

Declination of possessive pronouns preceding a noun

	my friend	his/her sister
nom.	ჩემი მეგობარი	მისი და
erg.	ჩემ-მა მეგობარმა	მის-მა დამ
dat./acc.	ჩემ-ს მეგობარს	მის დას
voc.	ჩემ-ო მეგობარო	---------

Postpositions

Postpositions may be added to nouns and personal names, as well as adjectives and pronouns when these do not precede a noun. Each case has its set of postpositions. It should be remembered that the use of Georgian postpositions does not always coincide with English usage. Most often postpositions are added to the stems of nouns, adjectives, or pronouns while the case endings of these words are dropped. A few postpositions are added to full-case forms of words. Below are the most frequently used postpositions.

1. Genitive case postpositions

-თვის for *(added to full-case forms)*

nom.	gen.	gen. + -თვის	
სადილ-ი	სადილ-ის	სადილ-ის-თვის	for dinner
მანქან-ა	მანქან-ის	მანქან-ის-თვის	for (a) car
სარკ-ე	სარკ-ის	სარკ-ის-თვის	for (a) mirror
თარო-ო	თარო-ოს	თარო-ოს-თვის	for (a) shelf

-გან out of, from someone *(added to full-case forms)*

nom.	gen.	gen. + -გან	
მეგობარ-ი	მეგობრ-ის	მეგობრ-ის-გან	for a friend
ქალ-ი	ქალ-ის	ქალ-ის-გან	from (a) woman
თინ-ა	თინ-ა-ს	თინ-ა-ს-გან	from Tina
ნინ-ო	ნინ-ო-ს	ნინ-ო-ს-გან	from Nino

2. Dative/Accusative case postpositions

-ში in, to, at

nom.	dat./acc.	dat./acc. + -ში	
სახლ-ი	სახლ-ს	სახლ-ში	to or at home, in the house
ფოსტა	ფოსტა-ს	ფოსტა-ში	to or at the post office
სასადილო	სასადილო-ს	სასადილო-ში	to or in the dining room

-ზე on, to, at, about

nom.	dat./acc.	dat./acc. + -ზე	
აივან-ი	აივან-ს	აივან-ზე	on the balcony
კონცერტი	კონცერტ-ს	კონცერტ-ზე	to or at the concert

-თან with, together with (nouns ending with vowels other than **-ი** will retain the case ending).

nom.	dat./acc.	dat./acc. + -თან	
მეგობარ-ი	მეგობარ-ს	მეგობარ-თან	with (to) a friend
ძმა	ძმა-ს	ძმა-ს-თან	with (to) brother
ნუნუ	ნუნუ-ს	ნუნუ-ს-თან	with (to) Nunu *(personal name)*

3. Independent postpositions

Some adverbs (behind, ahead, after, etc.) may function as postpositions. The majority of them follow nouns in the genitive case. Below are a few examples:

სახლის **უკან**	**behind** the house
ლექციის **შემდეგ**	**after** the lecture
ორი დღის **წინ**	two days **ago**
ავადმყოფობის **გამო**	**because of** illness

APPENDIX II: GEORGIAN VERBS

The verbal system is the most challenging part of Georgian grammar. Without understanding the structure of the verb it is impossible to understand either written or spoken Georgian. One of the problems in identifying and learning Georgian verbs is the absence of infinitive forms. **There is no infinitive in Georgian.** Verbs should therefore be memorized in one of the active forms. In this book, verbs will be listed in the 2nd-person singular form of the present/future tense (in Georgian, present tense becomes future simply by adding a *preverb*).

Tenses of Verbs

There are ten tenses in Georgian. In this book, only five of them are discussed in detail. These are the most frequently used forms in spoken Georgian.

Below is a brief outline of these five tenses:

1. **Present**: conveys a habitual, frequent, or usual action, or one that takes place here and now. თინა წერილს წერს is the equivalent of English: a. *Tina **writes** a letter* (i.e. frequently); b. *Tina **is writing** a letter* (right now).

2. **Imperfect**: conveys an action that was habitual, frequent or usual in the past, or was in progress but not necessarily completed. თინა წერილს წერდა is the equivalent of English: a. *Tina **wrote** a letter* (i.e. often); b. *Tina **was writing** a letter* (in the morning).

3. **Future**: conveys an action that will take place in the future and will be completed. თინა წერილს დაწერს is the equivalent of English: *Tina **will write** a letter*.

4. **Aorist**: conveys an action that was completed in the past; its goal has been achieved. თინამ წერილი დაწერა *Tina **wrote** a letter* (i.e. the letter is finished and ready to be sent).

269

5. Optative: this is a very versatile tense and is used for many different purposes. Basically, it conveys a modality of action, intention, necessity, possibility, desirability, etc. of doing something. თინამ წერილი დაწეროს can be translated as: *Let Tina **write** a letter* (she should do it). The optative form is often preceded by other verbs or auxiliary words. If the optative is used, the case of the third person subject (in the examples below, თინა *Tina*) will be determined by these verbs, not by the optative (here დაწეროს optative form of *write*). In the sentences below, the subject (*Tina*) is in three different cases (nominative, dative, and ergative respectively) because the verbs immediately following the subject require these cases.

თინა აპირებს წერილი დაწეროს.
Tina intends to write a letter.
(აპირებს *intends* is regular 1st conjugation verb in the present tense.)

თინას შეუძლია წერილი დაწეროს.
Tina can write a letter.
(შეუძლია *can* is a 4th conjugation verb in present tense.)

თინამ უნდა წერილი დაწეროს.
Tina should write a letter.
(უნდა is a modal auxiliary meaning *should, must, has to*.)

Structure of Verbs

The structure of Georgian verbs includes a variety of particles (suffixes, prefixes, etc.) which modify the meaning of the verb or mark the grammatical tense (present, future, optative, etc.). One should be able to recognize them and learn their functions in order to understand the written or spoken language. In the example below, we use the verb გააკეთებს *to do, to make* in its 3rd person, future tense form and break down the prefixes, basic root, and suffixes (which, in this case, are five) that make up this verb:

გააკეთებს (he/she will do)

preverb vowel	preradical	root	PFSF	person marker
1	2	3	4	5
გა	-ა	-კეთ	-ებ	- ს

1. გა- is a **preverb** (verbal prefix); it appears in the future, aorist, and optative tenses, defines the verb's dominant meaning, and specifies the direction of the action in time or space.

There are about eight different preverbs plus a few combinations formed by these eight basic preverbs (see section on **Verbs of Motion** below). Each verb must be memorized together with its preverb. Thus, if instead of გა- we use the preverb შე-, the verb შე-ა-კეთ-ებ-ს would mean *s/he will repair* instead of *s/he will do*.

2. -ა is a **preradical vowel**. In various tenses it may be dropped or replaced by other vowels or syllables. It may specify the purpose of the action or even indicate for whom the action is carried out. In this book the use and function of various preradical vowels are not discussed. However, here are some examples that provide some general idea about them:

რუსიკო ჩაის გა-ა-კეთებ-ს.
Rusiko will make tea.

რუსიკო ჩაის გა-ი-კეთ-ებ-ს.
Rusiko will make tea **for herself**.

რუსიკო ჩაის გა-გი-კეთებ-ს.
Rusiko will make tea **for you**.

3. -კეთ- is the basic **root** of the verb to which preradical vowels and preverbs are added.

4. -ებ is the **present/future stem formant** (further identified as **PFSF**). As the term indicates, this ending marks the verb's present and future tenses. Verbs may have different present/future stem formants.

5. -ს is the **person marker**, here **3rd person singular**.

Conjugations

Georgian verbs are divided into four groups or conjugation types. Each group has a distinct conjugation pattern, and memorizing the individual patterns is the best way to learn them.

1st Conjugation

The majority of Georgian verbs belong to this conjugation.

- Verbs of this group are mostly *transitive verbs*, i.e. they have a direct object (further identified as *d.o.*), i.e. something or someone to which action is directed.

- თინა **წერილს** წერს.
  Tina is writing **a letter**.
  (In this sentence **წერილს** *a letter* is the direct object.)

- These verbs may have two kinds of *preradical vowels*, -ა- or -ი-, or no preradical vowel:

  გა-ა-კეთ-ებ   მი-ი-ღ-ებ   და-ხარჯ-ავ
  do, make   receive   spend

- They may have a variety of preverbs: მი-, მო-, და-, შე-, გა-, გადა-, etc. Various preverbs and their functions are discussed in the section on verbs of motion. (See Appendix III for further discussion of preverbs.)

- The **PFSF** (present/future stem formant) of these verbs can be: -ებ, -ობ, -ავ, -ამ, -ი or none at all:

  და-ი-წყ-ებ   გა-ა-თბ-ობ   და-ხაც-ავ
  start   heat up something   paint
  და-ა-სხ-ამ   გადა-თარგმნ-ი   და-წერ
  pour   translate   write

- In the aorist and optative tenses the subject of these verbs must be changed from *nominative* to *ergative* case, while the direct object changes from *dative* to *nominative* case:

pres.:	**ნანა** *(nom.)* **სადილს** *(dat.)* **აკეთებს.**
	Nana *(subj.)* is making **dinner** *(d.o.)*.
aor.:	**ნანამ** *(erg.)* **სადილი** *(nom.)* **გააკეთა.**
	Nana *(subj.)* made **dinner** *(d.o.)*.
opt.:	**ნანამ** *(erg.)* **სადილი** *(nom.)* **გააკეთოს.**
	Nana *(subj.)* should make **dinner** *(d.o.)*.

2nd Conjugation

In this textbook only a few verbs of this group are used. The emphasis is put on *verbs of motion* that belong to this group.

- The verbs of this group are *intransitive*, i.e. they do not have direct objects. The majority of these verbs correspond to English passive forms; they denote change, transformations of some kind that the subject undergoes.

- The *subject* of these verbs remains in the *nominative* case **in all tenses.**

pres.:	**სახლი შენდება.**
	A house is being built.
aor.:	**სახლი აშენდა.**
	A house was built.
opt.:	**სახლი უნდა აშენდეს.**
	A house should be built.

- All verbs of this conjugation have PFSF **-ებ**. These verbs are divided into two subgroups:

1. Verbs with **-ი-** preradical vowel, called *iniani* (**ინიანი**) *forms*

და-ი-წყ-ებ-ა	და-ი-კარგ-ებ-ა	გა-ი-ღ-ებ-ა,
will get started	will be lost	will be open

2. Verbs with -ლ- preceding the PFSF -ებ, called *doniani*
(დონიანი) *forms*

და-მთავრ-**ლ**-ებ-ა	გა-გრძელ-**ლ**-ებ-ა	და-ბერ-**ლ**-ებ-ა
will be completed	will be continued	will get old

The verb *be*

The verb *be* is placed in a subsection of the 2nd conjugation group.
See Appendix III for further details.

Verbs of motion

These verbs are placed in a subsection of the 2nd conjugation group.
(See Appendix III for further details.)

3rd Conjugation

Most verbs of this group denote motion, emission of light and noise,
and the phenomena of weather. Many of them are formed from a
noun.

- This group includes mostly *intransitive* (i.e. those which do not
  have a direct object) and a few *transitive* verbs:

Intransitive	Transitive
მუშაობ work	თამაშობ play
ლაპარაკობ speak	ქირაობ rent

- The majority of these verbs have *no preradical vowel* of any kind.
  There are a few exceptions, such as: ი-ცინ-ის *(s/he) is laughing.*

- The majority of these verbs have *no preverb* in the present and
  imperfect tenses.

- The majority of these verbs have the PFSF -ობ or -ავ; a few of
  them have -ი, -ებ, or none at all:

ქირა-ობ	ცეკვ-ავ	ტირ-ი	კლუკუნ-ებ	ყეფ
rent	dance	cry	chirp	bark

- Like verbs of the 1st conjugation, all verbs of the 3rd conjugation, both transitive and intransitive, require that the subject is changed from *nominative* to *ergative* case in the *aorist* and *optative* tenses.

Pres.: ლალი კარგად ცეკვავს.   **Lali** dances well.
Aor.: ლალიმ კარგად იცეკვა.   **Lali** danced well.
Opt.: ლალიმ კარგად იცეკვოს.   **Lali** should dance well.

- There are a few verbs that denote weather conditions, and they are used only in the 3rd person singular form. A practical way of learning them would be to memorize them in present and imperfect tenses:

Present   **Imperfect**
წვიმ-ს it is raining   წვიმ-და it was raining
თოვ-ს it is snowing   თოვ-და it was snowing

4th Conjugation

This is the most challenging conjugation. Since these verbs are irregular in all tenses, the most practical thing will be to memorize only a dozen most frequently used verbs in the present and imperfect, the tenses in which these verbs are most commonly used.

- The "strangest" aspect of these verbs is the reversed order of subject-object relations. *The subject is in the dative case and the object is in the nominative.*

- It is helpful to remember a similar verb form in old English: **methinks**. there are similar forms in modern German; for example, **es freut mich** *I am glad, I am looking forward to*, or Russian **мне кажется** *it seems to me*.

See conjugation charts in Appendix III.

APPENDIX III: VERB CONJUGATION CHARTS

1st Conjugation Charts

- All verbs of this conjugation have the subject in the ergative case when they are in the aorist and optative forms.

- While the pronouns of the 1st and 2nd persons (მე *I*, შენ *you*, ჩვენ *we*, თქვენ *you pl.*) do not have ergative case endings and remain unchanged, the 3rd person pronouns should be changed in accordance with the rules: ის *he/she* becomes მან, and ისინი *they* will be მათ.

- This rule also applies to nouns and personal names; they too will be in the ergative case in the aorist and optative tenses.

- The conjugation pattern of Group A is the most regular. Some verbs, as shown below, deviate slightly from this pattern.

1st Conjugation, Group A (1, A)

The majority of 1st Conjugation verbs belong to this group.

ა-კეთ-ებ, (გა-) (you) do, make, prepare

Sing.	Present	Imperfect	Future	Aorist	Optative
1st	ვ-ა-კეთ-ებ	ვ-ა-კეთ-ებ-დი	გა-ვ-ა-კეთ-ებ	გა-ვ-ა-კეთ-ე	გა-ვ-ა-კეთ-ო
2nd	ა-კეთ-ებ	ა-კეთ-ებ-დი	გა - ა-კეთ-ებ	გა ა-კეთ-ე	გა - ა-კეთ-ო
3rd	ა-კეთ-ებ-ს	ა-კეთ-ებ-და	გა- ა-კეთ-ებ-ს	გა - ა-კეთ-ა	გა - ა-კეთ-ოს
Pl.					
1st	ვ-ა-კეთებ-თ	ვ-ა-კეთებ-დი-თ	გა-ვ-ა-კეთ-ებ-თ	გა-ვ-ა-კეთ-ე-თ	გა-ვ-ა-კეთ-ო-თ
2nd	ა-კეთებ-თ	ა-კეთებ-დი-თ	გა-ა-კეთ-ებ-თ	გა- ა-კეთ-ე-თ	გა- ა-კეთ-ო-თ
3rd	ა-კეთებ-ენ	ა-კეთებ-დნენ	გა-ა-კეთ-ებ-ენ	გა ა-კეთ-ეს	გა- ა-კეთ-ონ

1st Conjugation, Group B (1, B)

All 1st Conjugation verbs with the present/future stem formant (PFSF) -ი belong to this group. Their conjugation pattern differs from that of Group A only in two forms: *third person plural in the present and future tenses.* In all other forms they follow the pattern of Group A.

Pres.: ისინი გზავნ-იან   they send (are sending)
Fut.: ისინი გა-გზავნ-იან   they will send

1st Conjugation, Group C (1, C)

Some verbs with no vowel in their root belong to this group. They differ from the verbs in Group A only in the *3rd-person singular form of the aorist.* All other forms follow the pattern of Group A.

Pres.: ა-ღ-ებ-ს   (s/he) opens (is opening)
Aor.: გა-ა-ღ-ო   (s/he) opened

1st Conjugation, Group D (1, D)

A small number of 1st Conjugation verbs produce the vowel -ა- in their root in the *aorist* and *optative tenses* in both the singular and plural. In all other ways their conjugation pattern is similar to the verbs in Group A.

Pres./Fut.: (გადა-) ი-ხდ-ი   (you) pay (bill, rent)
Aor.: გადა-ი-ხად-ე
Opt.: გადა-ი-ხად-ო

1st Conjugation, Group E (1, E)

იცი (you) know

This is a unique verb in that the subject must be in the *ergative case* in both the present and the imperfect. For practical purposes, its conjugation should be memorized in these two tenses.

იცი (you) know

Sing.	Present	Imperfect
1st	მე ვ-იცი	მე ვ-იც-ოდი
2nd	შენ იცი	შენ იც-ოდი
3rd	მან იცი-ს	მან იც-ოდა
Pl.		
1st	ჩვენ ვ- იცი-თ	ჩვენ ვ-იც-ოდი-თ
2nd	თქვენ იცი-თ	თქვენ იც-ოდი-თ
3rd	მათ იცი-ან	მათ იც-ოდ-ნენ

ამ კაცმა არ იცის.
This man does not know.

მანანამ არ იცის.
Manana does not know.

Some verbs of the 1st Conjugation are irregular and should be memorized individually. Most of them change their roots in the *future tense*, which is the base for the formation of the *aorist* and *optative*, following the pattern of Group A.

Present	Future	Aorist	Optative	
სწავლ-ობ	ი-სწავლ-ი	ი-სწავლ-ე	ი-სწავლ-ო	study
ყიდულ-ობ	ი-ყიდ-ი	ი-ყიდ-ე	ი-ყიდ-ო	buy
კითხულ-ობ	ი-კითხ-ავ	ი-კითხ-ე	ი-კითხ-ო	read; ask
პოულ-ობ	ი-პოვნ-ი	ი-პოვნ-ე	ი-პოვნ-ო	find

2nd Conjugation Charts

Verbs of this conjugation are *intransitive*, i.e. they do not have a direct object.

- They do not require the ergative case in any of the tenses.

- They often correspond to English passive forms (*was built, was started, was sold*, etc.) denoting a change of state.

- There are two basic conjugation patterns of these verbs; one for *doniani* verbs (Group A), i.e. those which have -დ- inserted just before their PFSF, and the other for *iniani* verbs (Group B), i.e. those that have preradical vowel **-o-**.

- Verbs of motion (Group C) and the verb to be (Group D) are also listed as subgroups of the 2nd conjugation.

2nd Conjugation, Group A (2, A) *doniani* verbs

ჩერ-დ-ებ-ი (გა-) (you) stop

Sing.	Present	Imperfect	Future	Aorist	Optative
1st	ვ-ჩერ-დ-ებ-ი	ვჩერ-დები-ოდი	გა-ვჩერდები	გა-ვ-ჩერ-დი	გა-ვ-ჩერ-დე
2nd	ჩერ-დ-ებ-ი	ჩერ-დები-ოდი	გა-ჩერდები	გა-ჩერ-დი	გა-ჩერ-დე
3rd	ჩერ-დ-ებ-ა	ჩერდებოდღნ6	გა-ჩერდება	გა-ჩერ-და	გა-ჩერ-დეს
Pl.					
1st	ვ-ჩერ-დ-ებ-ით	ვჩერ-დებოდი	გა-ვჩერ-დებიით	გა-ვჩერ-დით	გა-ვ-ჩერ-დეთ
2nd	ჩერ-დ-ებ-ით	ჩერ-დებოდი	გაჩერ-დებიით	გა-ჩერ-დიით	გა-ჩერ-დეთ
3rd	ჩერ-დ-ებ-იან	ჩერ-დებოდღნ6	გა-ჩერ-დებიან	გა-ჩერ-დღნ6	გა-ჩერ-დღნ6

- For practical purposes, some of these verbs should be memorized only in the 3rd person singular form.

Present	Imperfect	Future	Aorist	
მეორ-დ-ებ-ა	მეორ-დ-ებ-ოდა	გა-მეორ-დ-ება	გა-მეორ-დ-ა	is repeated
ტარ-დ-ებ-ა	ტარ-დ-ებ-ოდა	ჩა-ტარ-დ-ებ-ა	ჩა-ტარ-და	is taking place
ლამ-დ-ებ-ა	ლამ-დ-ებ-ოდა	და-ლამ-დ-ებ-ა	და-ლამ-და	is getting dark
შენ-დ-ებ-ა	შენ-დ-ებ-ოდა	ა-შენ-დ-ებ-ა	ა-შენ-და	is built

2nd Conjugation, Group B (2, B) *iniani* verbs

Verbs of this group have the **o-** preradical vowel in all tenses, but follow the conjugation pattern of Group A. A significant majority of these verbs are not used when referring to a person. Below are the 3rd person singular forms of some of the verbs of this group.

Present	Imperfect	Future	Aorist	
ი-ღ-ებ-ა	ი-ღ-ებ-ოდა	გა-ი-ღ-ებ-ა	გა-ი-ღ-ო	is (gets) open
ი-წყ-ებ-ა	ი-წყ-ებ-ოდა	და-ი-წყ-ებ-ა	და-ი-წყ-ო	starts, gets started
ი-ყიდ-ებ-ა	ი-ყიდ-ებ-ოდა	გა-ი-ყიდ-ებ-ა	გა-ი-ყიდ-ა	is on sale, sells
ი-წერ-ებ-ა	ი-წერ-ებ-ოდა	და-ი-წერ-ებ-ა	და-ი-წერ-ა	is written, spelled

Some verbs of this group can also be used when referring to persons:

მე **დავიბადე** თბილისში.
I was born in Tbilisi.

რუსიკო სოფელში **იზრდებოდა**.
Rusiko **was growing up** in a village.

ოთარი საუკეთესო სტუდენტად **ითვლება** ჩვენს კლასში.
Otari **is considered** as the best student in our class.

2nd Conjugation, Group C (2, C)

Verbs of motion

- All verbs of this group have one common stem: **-დი-** in the present and imperfect tenses, to which various preverbs are added.
- Preverbs indicate the direction of movement.
- There are seven basic preverbs, roughly corresponding to the English *to, in, up, down, over,* etc. One of the most frequently used prefixes is **მი-** denoting *going away.*

მი- go (away)

Sing.	Present	Imperfect	Future	Aorist	Optative
1st	მი-ვ-დი-ვარ	მი-ვ-დი-ოდი	მი-ვალ	მი-ვედი	მი-ვიდ-ე
2nd	მი-დი-ხარ	მი- დი-ოდი	მი-ხ-ვალ	მი-ხ-ვედი	მი-ხ-ვიდ-ე
3rd	მი-დი-ს	მი- დი-ოდა	მი-ვა	მი-ვიდა	მი-ვიდ-ეს
Pl.					
1st	მი-ვ-დი-ვარ-თ	მი-ვ-დი-ოდი-თ	მი-ვალ-თ	მი-ვედი-თ	მი-ვიდ-ე-თ
2nd	მი-დი-ხარ-თ	მი-დი-ოდი-თ	მი-ხ-ვალ-თ	მი-ხ-ვედი-თ	მი-ხ-ვიდ-ე-თ
3rd	მი-დი-ან	მი-დი-ოდნენ	მი-ვლ-ენ	მი-ვიდნენ	მი-ვიდ-ნენ

281

Other preverbs denote movement *away* (from the speaker):

ა-	going up	ავდივარ(თ), ადიხარ(თ), ადის, ადიან
ჩა-	going down	ჩავდივარ(თ), ჩადიხარ(თ), ჩადის, ჩადიან
შე-	going in(to)	შევდივარ(თ), შედიხარ(თ), შედის, შედიან
გა-	going out	გავდივარ(თ), გადიხარ(თ), გადის, გადიან
გადა-	going over	გადავდივარ(თ), გადადიხარ(თ), გადადის, გადადიან
და-	going (often)	დავდივარ(თ), დადიხარ(თ), დადის, დადიან

The preverb შო- indicates *to come here* (movement towards the speaker), and could be combined with each of the preverbs listed above: აშო-, ჩაშო-, გადშო-, etc.

2nd Conjugation, Group D (2, D)

The verb *be*

The verb *be* is highly irregular with a different root in all tenses. Here and in the glossaries, the verb is listed in its *verbal noun* form ყოფნა *be; being*.

ყოფნა be

Sing.	Present	Imperfect/Aorist	Future	Optative
1st	ვარ	ვ-იყავ-ი	ვ-იქნებ-ი	ვ-იყ-ო
2nd	ხარ	იყავ-ი	იქნებ-ი	იყ-ო
3rd	არი-ს	იყ-ო	იქნებ-ა	იყ-ოს
Pl.				
1st	ვარ-თ	ვ-იყავ-ი-თ	ვ-იქნებ-ი-თ	ვ-იყ-ო-თ
2nd	ხარ-თ	იყავ-ი-თ	იქნებ-ი-თ	იყ-ო-თ
3rd	არი-ან	იყვ-ნენ	იქნებ-იან	ი-ყვ-ნენ

3rd Conjugation Charts

With a few exceptions, the verbs of this conjugation do not have preverbs. There are only two conjugation types, verbs that have an -ი Present/Future stem formant (PFSF), and the majority that have -ობ PFSF. Their conjugation patterns are similar; they form the future tense by dropping the ending of the present tense and adding an ი-preverb and -ებ PFSF.

3rd Conjugation, Group A (3, A)

The majority of 3rd Conjugation verbs belong to this group.

ცხოვრ-ობ (you) live

Sing.	Present	Imperfect	Future	Aorist	Optative
1st	ვ-ცხოვრ-ობ	ვ-ცხოვრ-ობ-დი	ვ-ი-ცხოვრ-ებ	ვ-ი-ცხოვრ-ე	ვ-ი-ცხოვრ-ო
2nd	ცხოვრ-ობ	ცხოვრ-ობ-დი	ი-ცხოვრ-ებ	ი-ცხოვრ-ე	ი-ცხოვრ-ო
3rd	ცხოვრ-ობ-ს	ცხოვრ-ობ-და	ი-ცხოვრ-ებ-ს	ი-ცხოვრ-ა	ი-ცხოვრ-ოს
Pl.					
1st	ვ-ცხოვრ-ობ-თ	ვცხოვრობ-დით	ვ-იცხოვრებით	ვ-ი-ცხოვრ-ეთ	ვ-იცხოვროთ
2nd	ცხოვრ-ობ-თ	ცხოვრ-ობ-დით	ი-ცხოვრ-ებთ	ი-ცხოვრ-ეთ	ი-ცხოვრ-ოთ
3rd	ცხოვრ-ობ-ენ	ცხოვრ-ობ-დნენ	იცხოვრებ-ენ	ი-ცხოვრ-ეს	ი-ცხოვრ-ონ

3rd Conjugation, Group B (3, B)

All verbs ending with -ი have this conjugation pattern. The suffix forming the imperfect of these verbs is not -დი but -ოდი. The conjugation patterns in future, aorist, and optative tenses are exactly the same as in Group A.

მღერ-ი (you) sing

Sing.	Present	Imperfect	Future	Aorist	Optative
1st	ვ-მღერ-ი	ვ-მღერ-ოდი	ვ-ი-მღერ-ებ	ვ-ი-მღერ-ე	ვ-ი-მღერ-ო
2nd	მღერ-ი	მღერ-ოდი	ი-მღერ-ებ	ი-მღერ-ე	ი-მღერ-ო
3rd	მღერ-ი-ს	მღერ-ოდა	ი-მღერ-ებ-ს	ი-მღერ-ა	ი-მღერ-ოს
Pl.					
1st	ვ-მღერ-ით	ვ-მღერ-ოდით	ვ-ი-მღერ-ებით	ვ-ი-მღერ-ეთ	ვ-ი-მღერ-ოთ
2nd	მღერ-ით	მღერ-ოდით	ი-მღერ-ებთ	ი-მღერ-ეთ	ი-მღერ-ოთ
3rd	მღერ-იან	მღერ-ოდნენ	ი-მღერ-ებ-ენ	ი-მღერ-ეს	ი-მღერ-ონ

4th Conjugation Charts

Subjects of these verbs are in the dative/accusative, while direct objects are in the nominative. There are about three dozen verbs of this conjugation. At this point familiarity with just a few verbs of this type in the present and imperfect tenses is sufficient. The third person markers in parentheses, (ქ) and (ს), are usually dropped in the spoken forms. The division into groups offered below is for the convenience of memorizing the conjugation patterns and does not correspond to a strict scholarly classification of these verbs.

4th Conjugation, Group A (4, A)

1. to have *(inanimate object)*

Present

მე მ-აქვ-ს	ჩვენ გვ-აქვ-ს
შენ გ-აქვ-ს	თქვენ გ-აქვ-თ
მას აქვ-ს	მათ აქვ-თ

Imperfect

მე მ-ქონ-და	ჩვენ გვ-ქონ-და
შენ გ-ქონ-და	თქვენ გ-ქონ-და-თ
მას (ქ)-ქონ-და	მათ (ქ)-ქონ-და-თ

მას შენი მისამართი არა აქვს.
He (she) does not have your address.

მანანას დრო არ ჰქონდა.
Manana didn't have time.

ჩემს მეზობლებს დიდი ბინა აქვთ.
My neighbors have a big apartment.

2. to have *(animate object)*

Present

მე მ-ყავ-ს	ჩვენ გვ-ყავ-ს
შენ გ-ყავ-ს	თქვენ გ-ყავ-თ
მას (ჰ)-ყავ-ს	მათ (ჰ)-ყავ-თ

Imperfect

მე მ-ყავ-და	ჩვენ გვ-ყავ-და
შენ გ-ყავ-და	თქვენ გ-ყავ-და-თ
მას (ჰ)-ყავ-და	მათ (ჰ)-ყავ-და-თ

მათ ლამაზი პატარა ძაღლი ჰყავთ.
They have a cute little dog.

გიას ორი და და სამი ძმა ჰყავს.
Gia has two sisters and three brothers.

ამ ბავშვებს მშობლები არა ჰყავთ.
These children don't have parents.

3. to like, love

Present

მე მი-ყვარ-ს	ჩვენ გვი-ყვარ-ს
შენ გი-ყვარ-ს	თქვენ გი-ყვარ-თ
მას უ-ყვარ-ს	მათ უ-ყვარ-თ

Imperfect

მე მი-ყვარ-და	ჩვენ გვი-ყვარ-და
შენ გი-ყვარ-და	თქვენ გი-ყვარ-და-თ
მას უ-ყვარ-და	მათ უ-ყვარ-და-თ

მე ძალიან მიყვარს ეს ქალაქი.
I love this city very much.

მას უყვარს ხალხური სიმღერები.
She (he) likes folk songs.

ამ გოგონებს უყვართ ეს მსახიობი.
These girls love this actor.

4th Conjugation, Group B (4, B)

1. to want

Present

მე მი-ნდ-ა	ჩვენ გვი-ნდ-ა
შენ გი-ნდ-ა	თქვენ გი-ნდ-ა-თ
მას უ-ნდ-ა	მათ უ-ნდ-ა-თ

Imperfect

მე მი-ნდ-ოდა	ჩვენ გვ-ინდ-ოდა
შენ გი-ნდ-ოდა	თქვენ გი-ნდ-ოდა-თ
მას უ-ნდ-ოდა	მათ უ-ნდ-ოდა-თ

არ გინდა ეს წიგნი?
Don't you want this book?

მათ უნდათ შენი ტელეფონის ნომერი.
They want your phone number.

თამაზის უნდა ლონდონში წავიდეს.
Tamazi wants to go to London.

2. to have pain, to be aching

Present

მე მ-ტკივ-ა	ჩვენ გვ-ტკივ-ა
შენ გ-ტკივ-ა	თქვენ გ-ტკივ-ა-თ
მას (ს)-ტკივ-ა	მათ (ს)-ტკივ-ა-თ

Imperfect

მე მ-ტკი-ოდა	ჩვენ გვ-ტკი-ოდა
შენ გ-ტკი-ოდა	თქვენ გ-ტკი-ოდა-თ
მას (ს)-ტკი-ოდა	მათ (ს)-ტკი-ოდა-თ

გოგის თავი სტკივა.
Gogi has a headache.

რა გტკივათ?
What hurts you?

თინას და ნანას კუჭი სტკიოდათ.
Tina and Nana had a stomachache.

3. to be hungry *(this verb has no d.o.)*

Present

მე მ-ში-ა	ჩვენ გვ-ში-ა
შენ გ-ში-ა	თქვენ გ-ში-ათ
მას ში-ა	მათ ში-ათ

Imperfect

მე მ-ში-ოდა	ჩვენ გვ-ში-ოდა
შენ გ-ში-ოდა	თქვენ გ-ში-ოდა-თ
მას ში-ოდა	მათ ში-ოდა-თ

არ გშია?
Aren't you hungry?

ლალის არ შიოდა.
Lali wasn't hungry.

ბავშვებს ძალიან შიათ.
The children are very hungry.

4th Conjugation, Group C (4, C)

1. to be in a hurry

Present

მე მე-ჩქარ-ებ-ა	ჩვენ გვე-ჩქარ-ებ-ა
შენ გე-ჩქარ-ებ-ა	თქვენ გე-ჩქარ-ებ-ათ
მას ე-ჩქარ-ებ-ა	მათ ე-ჩქარ-ებ-ათ

Imperfect

მე მეჩქარებ-ოდა	ჩვენ გვეჩქარებ-ოდა
შენ გეჩქარებ-ოდა	თქვენ გეჩქარებოდათ
მას ეჩქარებ-ოდა	მათ ე-ჩქარებ-ოდათ

ირაკლის არ ეჩქარება.
Irakli isn't in a hurry.

ჩვენს სტუმრებს ეჩქარებათ.
Our guests are in a hurry.

(თქვენ) გეჩქარებათ?
Are you in a hurry?

APPENDIX IV: GRAMMATICAL GLOSSARY

This glossary contains short definitions of grammatical terms used throughout this book. These explanations and examples are intended to be helpful to those unfamiliar with the terms, and not as formal linguistic definitions.

adjective: a word that precedes a noun, describing and specifying it *(beautiful, cold*, etc.). An adjective answers the question *what kind?*

aspirated: a sound followed by a small puff of air, e.g., *t* in English.

case: the form that a noun, pronoun, or adjective acquires when it is declined, e.g., nominative, genitive, etc. See Appendix 1 for further details.

decline: to change the form, usually the ending, of a noun, pronoun, or adjective depending on its function in the sentence, e.g., *He is a boy*; *I see him*.

demonstrative: pronouns that point out the one referred to, such as *this, that, those*.

enclitic: a word that is attached to another, and becomes part of that word; in Georgian it is the vowel ა, equivalent of the verb *is* (არის.): საინტერესოა *It's interesting*.

gender: refers to groups of nouns that are marked as masculine or feminine. In Georgian, as in English, nouns are not marked for gender.

inanimate: something not alive, e.g., *chair, school*, etc.

interrogative: a question or question word (pronoun), e.g., *who?, what?, why?* etc.

inversion: a change in standard word order, e.g., *You are right* → *Right you are*.

noun: a person, place, thing, or idea. Nouns function as both subjects and objects.

numeral: a word that precedes a noun, answering the question *how many?*

object: a (qualified) noun or pronoun that is affected by the action of a verb, e.g., *John sees a big dog*.

plural: the form of a noun referring to more than one thing, e.g., *books, dogs*.

possessive: pronoun answering the question *whose?* (*my, yours, his, ours, etc.*).

postposition: in Georgian, a suffix that is added to a noun, e.g., სახლ-**ში** *in* the house; მაგიდა-**ზე** *on the table*.

predicate: the part of the sentence (containing a verb) that makes the assertion about the subject and the object, e.g., *John sees the big dog*.

preposition: a word that precedes a noun and answers questions such as *where?* or *when?* e.g., *under, after, with, to*, etc.

preverb: verbal prefix added to verbs in various tenses: **გა**-აკეთებ, **მი**-ხვალ, **წა**-იღებ.

pronoun: a word that replaces a noun; e.g., *I, you, she, him, who, whose*, etc.

qualifier: any of several types of words (pronoun, adjective, numeral) that precede a noun.

singular: the form of a noun referring to a single thing, e.g., *book, dog*.

subject: one who carries out the action of a sentence—either a noun (i.e. person, place, or thing), pronoun (*he, they, this, who*), or noun phrase (*The black dog chases a rabbit.*)—or undergoes a change (*He became a minister.*).

syncopation: omission of a vowel in some nouns.

syllable: a sound-unit that is equivalent to a 'beat', e.g., *In·di·a·na* (4 beats), დი-ლე-დ-ა.

tense: inflection in a verb that indicates whether past, present, or future time is intended.

unaspirated: a sound not followed by a small puff of air; e. g. *m* in English.

unit: any group of words that are naturally grouped together in a sentence; to keep the meaning clear, the units should not be separated: [*The man*] [*was petting*] [*my dog*].

AUDIO TRACK LIST

 Audio files available at:
http://www.hippocrenebooks.com/beginners-online-audio.html

Folder 1
1. Title
2. Pronunciation—the Georgian Alphabet
3. Vowels
4. Consonants Part 1
5. Consonants Part 2
6. Consonants Part 3
7. Borrowed words
8. Georgian last names
9. Georgian first names
10. How to address people
11. Numerals
12. How to tell time
13. Days of the week
14. Parts of the day
15. Names of the months
16. Dates
17. Family members
18. Tongue Twisters
19. Les. 1 Dialogue
20. Les. 1 Dialogue for repetition
21. Les. 1 Vocabulary
22. Les. 1 Idiomatic Expressions
23. Les. 2 Dialogue
24. Les. 2 Dialogue for repetition
25. Les. 2 Vocabulary
26. Les. 2 Idiomatic Expressions
27. Les. 3 Dialogue
28. Les. 3 Dialogue for repetition
29. Les. 3 Vocabulary
30. Les. 3 Idiomatic Expressions
31. Les. 4 Dialogue
32. Les. 4 Dialogue for repetition
33. Les. 4 Vocabulary
34. Les. 4 Idiomatic Expressions
35. Les. 5 Dialogue
36. Les. 5 Dialogue for repetition
37. Les. 5 Vocabulary
38. Les. 5 Idiomatic Expressions
39. Les. 6 Dialogue
40. Les. 6 Dialogue for repetition
41. Les. 6 Vocabulary
42. Les. 6 Idiomatic Expressions

Folder 2
1. Les. 7 Dialogue
2. Les. 7 Dialogue for repetition
3. Les. 7 Vocabulary
4. Les. 7 Idiomatic Expressions
5. Les. 8 Dialogue
6. Les. 8 Dialogue for repetition
7. Les. 8 Vocabulary
8. Les. 8 Idiomatic Expressions
9. Les. 9 Dialogue
10. Les. 9 Dialogue for repetition
11. Les. 9 Vocabulary
12. Les. 9 Idiomatic Expressions
13. Les. 10 Dialogue
14. Les. 10 Dialogue for repetition
15. Les. 10 Vocabulary
16. Les. 10 Idiomatic Expressions
17. Les. 11 Dialogue
18. Les. 11 Dialogue for repetition
19. Les. 11 Vocabulary
20. Les. 11 Idiomatic Expressions
21. Les. 12 Dialogue
22. Les. 12 Dialogue for repetition
23. Les. 12 Vocabulary
24. Les. 12 Idiomatic Expressions
25. Les. 13 Dialogue
26. Les. 13 Dialogue for repetition
27. Les. 13 Vocabulary
28. Les. 13 Idiomatic Expressions

CPSIA information can be obtained
at www.ICGtesting.com
Printed in the USA
JSHW030408210922
30743JS00001B/1

9 780781 814195